CONTENTS

Helion & Company Limited
Unit 8 Amherst Business Centre
Budbrooke Road
Warwick
CV34 5WE
England
Tel. 01926 499 619
Email: info@helion.co.uk
Website: www.helion.co.uk
Twitter: @helionbooks
Visit our blog http://blog.helion.co.uk/

Designed and typeset by Farr out Publications, Wokingham, Berkshire
Cover design Paul Hewitt, Battlefield Design (www.battlefield-design.co.uk)

ISBN 978-1-915070-65-4

British Library Cataloguing-in-Publication Data
A catalogue record for this book is available from the British Library

We always welcome receiving book proposals from prospective authors.

MAP OF EUROPE SINCE 1992

Note: In order to simplify the use of this book, all names, locations and geographic designations are as provided in *The Times World Atlas*, or other traditionally accepted major sources of reference, as of the time of described events.

ACKNOWLEDGEMENTS

The authors wish to thank the following:

The personnel of the 250th Missile Brigade, 230th, 240th and 310th Self-propelled Missile Regiments of the Air Defence, 83rd and 204th Fighter Regiment, 98th Fighter-bomber Regiment, 252nd Fighter-bomber Squadron, 1st Detachment of the 353rd Recce Squadron, 177th Air Base, Aviation Test Centre and Yugoslav Air Force Museum – all of the Yugoslav/Serbian armed forces – who helped us in our research.

The members of the Department of Defense, US Embassy in Belgrade, USAFE HQ and its A-5 Department, 86th Airlift Wing and 37th Airlift Squadron at Ramstein Air Base, and the 31st Fighter Wing (510th FS, 555th FS and 603rd Squadron) at Aviano Air Base.

Also, those who provided us with other valuable information, photos or documents: Lieutenant General Zdravko Ponoš CHOD, Brigadier General Stanko Vasiljevic, Lieutenant General Luka Kastratović and Lieutenant General Sladjan Djordjević. Colonels Rajica Bosković, Dragan Stanković, Milan Milinković, Dragan Pauljevic, Gvozden Urošević and Sladjan Ristić, Lieutenant Colonel Saša Olulić and Nikola Ramljak, Major Miroslav Čeman, and finally NCOs Miroslav Špica and Slobodan Mihajlović of the Serbian Armed Forces. Also Lieutenant Colonels Alexander Milutinović (US Army), Samuel Shult and John Capello (USAF). To old friends Milan Micevski and Bojan Ristić as well. Also to Rebeccah A. Woodrow, TSgt, Public Affairs, 31st Fighter Wing USAF, who provided us with guidance on USAF photo materials.

The authors wish to thank all of the listed people, and finally our editor Tom Cooper and kind members of the Helion staff: Andy Miles, Vicky Powell and of course Duncan Rogers, for their confidence and mutual work.

ABBREVIATIONS

AA	anti-aircraft (artillery)
ABCCC	Airborne Battlefield Command and Control Center
AGM	Air Guided Missile
AEW	Airborne Early Warning
A-FAC	Airborne Forward Air Controller
AFRES	Air Force Reserve
AFSOUTH	Allied Forces in South Europe
AIRSOUTH	Allied Air Force Commander in South Europe
ALAT	*Aviation légère de l'armée de Terre* (French Army light aviation)
AMI	*Aeronatuica Militare Italiana* (Italian Air Force)
AMRAAM	Advanced Medium-Range Air-to-Air Missiles
ANG	Air National Guard
AS	Airlift Squadron
ATAF	Allied Tactical Air Force
ARS	Air Refuelling Squadron
ARW	Air Refuelling Wing
AW	Airlift Wing
AWACS	Airborne Warning and Control System
BAI	Battlefield Air Interdiction
BDA	Bomb Damage Assessment
BS	Bomber Squadron
BW	Bomber Wing
C-ALCM	Conventional Air Launched Cruise Missile
CAG	Carrier Air Group
CAOC	Combined Air Operations Center
CAW	Carrier Air Wing
CAP	Combat Air Patrol
CAS	Close Air Support
CINCSOUTH	Commander-in-Chief, Allied Forces Southern Europe
CONUS	Continental United States
CSAR	Combat Search and Rescue
DoD	Department of Defense
ECR	Electronic Combat and Reconnaissance
ECM	Electronic Countermeasures
EFS	Expeditionary Fighter Squadron
ELINT	electronic intelligence
FAC	Forward Air Controller
FRY	Federal Republic of Yugoslavia
FS	Fighter Squadron
FW	Fighter Wing
HARM	High Speed Anti-Radiation
HAS	Hardened Aircraft Shelter
HTS	HARM Targeting System
J-STARS	Joint Surveillance Target Attack Radar System
LANTIRN	Low Altitude Navigation and Targeting Infrared for Night
LGB	Laser-Guided Bomb
MANPADS	Man-portable air defence system
MEDEVAC	Medical Evacuation
MUP Srbije	Serb Ministry of Interior
NAC	North Atlantic Council
NAC/DoD	National Archives Catalogue/US Department of Defense
NATO	North Atlantic Treaty Organisation
PGM	Precision Guided Missiles
PVO	*protivvazdušna odbrana* (air defence)
RAF	Royal Air Force
Recce	Reconnaissance
ROE	Rules of Engagement
RNLAF	Royal Netherlands Air Force
R-StON	*radarska stanica za osmatranje i navođenje* (Kub-M or SA-6 battery radar)
RS	Reconnaissance squadron
RV i PVO	*Ratno vazduhoplovstvo i protivvazdušna odbrana* (Air Force and Air Defence)
RW	Reconnaissance Wing
SACEUR	Supreme Allied Commander Europe
SEAD	Suppression of Enemy Air Defence
SHAPE	Supreme Headquarters Allied Powers Europe

SIGINT	Signals Intelligence
SLAM	Standoff Land Attack Missile
TLCM	Tomahawk Land-attack Cruise Missile
VJ	*Vojska Jugoslavije* (Yugoslav Army)
UAV	Unmanned Aerial Vehicle
UCK	*Ushtria Clirimtare e Kosoves* (Kosovo Liberation Army, KLA)
UN	United Nations
USAF	United States Air Force
USAFE	United States Air Force in Europe
USMC	United States Marine Corps
USN	United States Navy

INTRODUCTION

If one looks at the film industry, it is always difficult to match the original film with the sequel to it. But in the case of *Operation Allied Force*, the second part is a continuation of the previous volume, which was a chronological survey of the air campaign against Serbia in 1999. The authors' intention is to provide the readers with a conclusion to this air operation, including the experiences of both the engaged sides: NATO and Serbia/Yugoslavia.

In this volume of *Operation Allied Force*, the story will be continued by outlining the experiences of both sides during the campaign. Several other titles with a similar subject were published in the first few years after the campaign. However, nearly all of them focused only on US and NATO experiences, stressing the success of their air power and lack of casualties on the US/NATO side. Until now, there has not been a single title in English on Serbian/Yugoslav military experiences in the air war of 1999.

The main novelty of this volume is that the combat experiences of those who fought on the Serbian/Yugoslav side are coupled with NATO/US recollections. The authors put in great efforts to assemble the facts and figures of the operation, based on first-hand experiences and original documents.

As 22 years have elapsed since the conflict and several titles have already debated many aspects surrounding the air campaign, the authors did not want to enter into debates about the rights and wrongs of Operation Allied Force or repeat the scores of questions and different opinions about the campaign. They instead focus on the documented facts from both sides, particularly trying to outline the previously unknown experiences of the Serbian/Yugoslav side in the campaign.

The fact that most of this air war had a 'virtual' character that was conducted in the media and on the internet led to the exaggeration of successes on both sides. This practice continued for some time after the campaign and does so in Serbia almost to this day. Democratic changes in Serbia in October 2000 and the terrorist attacks of 9/11 in the United States in 2001 shifted the scope to other issues on both sides. This meant that a true estimation of the military effort in the NATO-Serb war somehow remains missing on both sides. Wars in other places also overshadowed Operation Allied Force, apart from its political outcome regarding Kosovan independence and relations with Serbia.

It is still fascinating, at least for authors who commented on the efforts of the NATO and American side in the campaign, that there is no proper knowledge of the VJ/MUP Srbije strength, deployment, types of armament and other relevant issues. While it is naturally difficult to provide exact figures on damaged or destroyed systems and weapons during the operation, the lack of information about the initial strength of the Jugoslav Army, and the RV i PVO (Air Force and Air Defence) in particular, is hardly understandable. There have been constant repetitions mentioning obsolete SAM systems such as SA-2 (Dvina), incorrect numbers of the types of aircrafts in RV i PVO service or the listing of types that were phased out from service many years before, as well as mentioning Russian advisors and/or military presence or using the wrong names, such as 'Obrva' for Ladjevci Air Base. If these were mistakes made by non-military commentators, it would not be a huge problem. But it is quite fascinating that these mistakes were noted in addresses by senior USAF/NATO commanders in several press conferences during the campaign.

The authors have chosen several aspects of the campaign which they consider are worth describing to the broader public around the world more than 20 years after the event: from the command of the operation to mutual experiences in combat, casualties and the final outcome in a military and political sense. The reader will find that the authors extensively use Yugoslav Air Force sources that are still out of reach for wider research. But thanks to their high position in the Serbian defence system and their privilege in exchanging views with their American counterparts, they managed to combine the experiences of both sides. The main intention of this volume is to explain the complex issues surrounding Operation Allied Force in a balanced manner. The authors hope that the reading public with a preference for contemporary military history will welcome this volume. If some military officials also find it useful, then it will be another step in outlining the experiences of the last war in Europe in the twentieth century. Once again, as was the case with Volume 1 of *Operation Allied Force*, this second volume was written without the intention of portraying either side in a positive or negative light, no matter what the personal experience of the authors from those days.

1
COMMANDING OPERATION ALLIED FORCE

Planned Phases of the Operation

In the Western media, Operation Allied Force (OAF) was afterwards described as an 'air operation', 'air campaign' or 'intervention', and sometimes as a 'bombardment'. In the Serbian media, however, it is still known as an 'aggression'.

OAF started off as combination of two plans for airstrikes. According to General Wesley Clark, Supreme Allied Commander Europe (SACEUR), these were titled a 'Phased Air Operation' and a 'Limited Air Operation'. Both were approved in NATO's highest circles. Clark explained that the intention was to carry out both plans simultaneously, but an unpredicted course of events on the ground merged those plans into a single air operation.

The proclaimed aims of the operation, that were announced by US President Bill Clinton on 24 March 1999, were modified and expanded during its course.

As described by many authors, the air campaign had five phases, besides the preparatory phase. The first phase featured airstrikes on military targets, particularly the air defence system throughout the Federal Republic of Yugoslavia (FRY). This initial phase was expected to bring the Serbian side back into the negotiation process. The second phase included attacks on Serbian/Yugoslav security forces in Kosovo, as well on their reinforcements. This stage was approved on 27 March 1999. The third phase anticipated a widening of the airstrikes against other important targets all over the FRY. As this phase did not fulfil its expectations, NATO, upon the insistence of the US senior leadership, then expanded Operation Allied Force without specific authorisation of the third phase.[1]

At the April 1999 summit of NATO leaders, General Clark was allowed the flexibility to use airstrikes against other targets that were felt necessary to increase the pressure on the Serbians. The selection of targets had been made earlier and were then grouped according to the phases. The fourth and fifth phases of the campaign involved air cover and the support of ground forces that were deployed in Kosovo in mid-June, once a political agreement was reached.[2]

After Operation Allied Force started, the political pressure obviously became tremendous. Such pressure meant that the operation started to suffer delays in its tempo, due to the application of the phases mentioned above and the limitation of the use of airstrikes. This pressure only grew during the campaign, with various different limitations on the carrying out of aerial attacks,

Two USAF F-16 Fighting Falcons are framed by the boom operator's window as they move into position to take on fuel behind a KC-135 Stratotanker over the Mediterranean on 26 February 1999. (National Archives Catalogue)

A Stealth F-117A from the 49th Fighter Wing, Holloman AFB, arrives at Aviano Air Base in Italy on 21 February 1999. (DoD)

An F-16CG belonging to the 510th Fighter Squadron, 31st Fighter Wing, takes off from its home base at Aviano, prior to the launch of Operation Allied Force. F-16 (Viper) units engaged in OAF were: the 31st FW, equipped with 43 F-16C/Ds (510th and 555th FS), the 52nd FW at Spangdahlem (22nd and 23rd FS), fielding up to 42 F-16 Block 50 CJs, and (deployed later to Aviano) the 78th EFS, which consisted of 20 Block 52 F-16CJs of different squadrons of the 20th FW from Shaw AFB, South Carolina. (DoD)

A crewmember of a KC-135R Stratotanker of 351st Air Refuelling Squadron, 100th Air Expeditionary Wing, observes an F-16CJ approaching for refuelling on 31 March 1999. (NAC)

including restricted altitudes, limitations to night strikes and different procedures prior to attack. Moreover, NATO's lengthy preparations and deployment had eliminated the factor of surprise that was necessary for an effective outcome. Bad weather over the Balkans in the earliest days of the campaign only increased the constraints on the operation, adding more frustration for the NATO military planners. Such restrictions meant that there would be no massive airstrike which could knock out the Milošević regime, as had been expected by many of the USAF senior leadership.

Combined Air Operations Center at Vicenza

Operation Allied Force had a chain of command that had been established and proved in earlier engagements over the Balkans. The Supreme Allied Commander in Europe (SACEUR), with a HQ in Mons, Belgium, delegated the responsibility for the conducting of the operation to the Commander-in-Chief of the Allied Force in South Europe, and he to the Commander of the Allied Air Force in South Europe,[3] both of whom had their respective HQs in Naples, Italy. Commanding the operation on a daily basis was the 5th ATAF commander based in Vicenza, Italy.[4]

The main command and coordination body of the air operations was the CAOC (Combined Air Operations Center), located with the 5th ATAF HQ in Vicenza. The CAOC, commanded by General Michael 'Mike' Short, had coordinated NATO air operations over the Balkans since the time of the Bosnian crisis, from 1993–1996. It was a large command cell, with some 400 regular personnel, whose number increased to between 1,300 and 1,400 during OAF.[5]

The CAOC coordinated and approved air attacks by communicating with the crews over the theatre. A C-5 detachment named Master Air Attack Plan (MAAP) planned the air attacks. Selection and preparation of the targets for the operation took a huge amount of work and analysis of the facts received from many different aircraft and platforms, ranging from satellites to AWACS, J-STARS and Rivet Joint electronic surveillance aircraft and UAVs.

During Operation Allied Force, the CAOC had many problems with the approval of targets that were identified by the air crews over the battlefield. Restrictions and the fear of collateral damage became a serious problem. Even more so, later in the operation, political approval was needed for targets around Belgrade or in Montenegro. Such a practice was possible since the CAOC Intelligence Cell was under US control. This was especially the case with B-2 Spirt stealth bomber sorties, which arrived in the theatre directly from the CONUS.[6]

Joint Staff Vice Director for Strategic Plans and Policy, Major General Charles F. Wald, USAF, briefs reporters in the Pentagon on NATO's Operation Allied Force on 29 April 1999. (NAC)

General John Jumper, commander of US Air Forces Europe, during the briefing on 14 May 1999. (NAC)

Several case studies after the war concluded that the CAOC did not manage to produce accurate daily Air Tasking Orders (ATOs). The main reason for this was daily planning subsequent to changes and interventions from upper levels of command. The USAF representatives complained that such a practice was contrary to their doctrinal approach. Later practice for the usage of strike aviation extended the planning from 24 hours – as was the case at the beginning of the operation – to 72 hours.

During the operation, on a daily basis at 1700 hours, the CAOC planners briefed General Short and representatives of the NATO air forces on the ATO for the following day. Short and NATO representatives usually commented on the selection of targets. On several occasions, European allies vetoed certain important targets, mostly because of political directions from their governments. Two RNLAF (Royal Netherlands Air Force) members of the CAOC criticised the fact that at the beginning of the operation there were only 51 targets, but that their number had increased to 1,021 by its last phase. They commented that the North Atlantic Council (NAC) of NATO did not approve some 400–500 targets. Changes to the ROE (Rules of Engagement) also produced problems and constrains for the CAOC, as well as for the crews who flew the missions. Collateral damage and other risks had to be taken into consideration. Such practice led to numerous sorties attacking targets that had already been attacked, or to missions being cancelled. One of the Dutch officers said that working in the CAOC was "eye-opening" for him: "The CAOC was just not prepared for long-term operations." They both confirmed: "We, as the first non–Americans [involved], felt initially like odd men out. Many of them had flown in straight from the United States for this operation and were not well informed about NATO."[7]

The complexity of Operation Allied Force would soon show that this chain of command was too complicated and was inadequate to follow the situation on the ground. Many contemporaries testified that in numerous ways, the US and NATO chains of command remained separate through the operation.

Former RAF Wing Commander Andrew Brookes criticised this practice, pointing out that the CAOC which was established in Ramstein to conduct such joint combat operations was not activated to run Allied Force: "Come 24 March and all the hitherto hard-won expertise went out of the window. As the Americans were leading the show, they flew in a whole new bunch of folk from the US to start from the scratch." General Short himself admitted: "NATO did not fight the way it trained. The US joint task force took over everything and left other nations watching from the sidelines. This was a major source of friction throughout the air campaign." In the beginning, all operations north of the 44th parallel were allocated to high-value US assets such as the B-2s. Far from being on the NATO Air Tasking Order – the White ATO – operations against Belgrade or Novi Sad "were for US eyes-only – Black ATO".[8]

As Jim Hedge pointed out in *AFM* magazine:

> The Pentagon was only prepared to say that 'some of the F-117 and B-2 missions were used as "national assets" and therefore did not pass through NATO command structures,' despite the requirement under the NATO charter to clear all missions carried out under NATO auspices with [the] NATO general council… Technically this means that the US waged a unilateral, undeclared war in addition to the NATO air campaign.[9]

General John Jumper, commander of USAFE during the operation, stated in 2018 that the US chain of command was "goofy" and "not one that we wanted to repeat". Jumper regarded that General Short as head of the CAOC had an "impossible task" to try and integrate this diverse set of interests but nevertheless did a "brilliant job". Jumper said that the CAOC was the operation's "center of gravity".[10]

Operational Problems During the Campaign

During Operation Allied Force, NATO air operations were planned at several levels (at CAOC, 31st Expeditionary Wing 1 – in the cell named 'Wingtip' – and in the individual units). Horizontal

The cruiser USS *Philippine Sea* steams alongside as an F/A-18C Hornet launches from the flight deck of the aircraft carrier USS *Enterprise* in the Adriatic Sea on 25 February 1999. (DoD)

An F-14 Tomcat launches from the waist catapult as four F/A-18 Hornets wait to launch from the bow catapults of the aircraft carrier USS *Enterprise* in the Adriatic Sea on 23 February 1999. (DoD)

coordination at the unit level was good among the units based at Aviano. Later, when some of these units deployed to other Italian air bases, horizontal coordination proved more difficult among the different types of aviation that joined together in strike packages. There was then no possibility to exchange and compare facts or experience gathered during the missions. Even the CAOC did not distribute frequently the satellite footage of the target location or other similar facts and figures. Neither was UAV footage from their missions distributed among the units. On the other hand, some new means of mutual cooperation and coordination were developed, such as between the USAF A-10 unit and RAF Harrier unit at Gioia del Colle.

During OAF, some of the USAF units were redeployed to other air bases because the main hub at Aviano became overcrowded. It was a similar case with several RAF units, which were landing at air bases which were not initially planned to be used in the operation.

A B-2A Spirit stealth bomber refuels from a KC-135 Stratotanker during its long sortie to Serbia on 6 April 1999. (NAC)

A pair of A-10As belonging to the 81st Fighter Squadron, 52nd Fighter Wing, at Spangdahlem Air Base in Germany, during one of the Operation Allied Force combat missions. The squadron operated from Aviano and later from Gioia del Colle Air Base, (DoD)

Despite them all being part of NATO, the different countries issued different limitations or procedures. Redeployment also brought logistical problems, caused by the distance from home bases. There were other problems too, involving matters such as the presence of local media, accommodation, food supplies, usage of private cars, telephone calls and bank accounts. Even the meteorological data was different in its estimation of weather conditions, visibility and operational ceiling.[11] Those airmen who were deployed to Rinas Airport in Albania operated in totally unprepared and rugged conditions. Finally, in the latest stages of OAF, some of the units were ordered to deploy to Turkey, to air bases that were not intended to be used in Allied Force.

Many of the engaged pilots (mainly USAF, but other NATO air forces as well) did not have any combat experience prior to the start of the campaign. For example, at Gioia del Cole, the 40th EOG commander and both A-10 squadron commanders did not have any combat experience.[12] At the 8th EFS, equipped with F-117As, among the pilots who launched missions on 24 March, only three of them had previous combat experience from Iraq. A significant portion of SEAD (Suppression of Enemy Air Defence) pilots from the 23rd EFS at Spangdahlem did not have any combat experience. It was no wonder that many of them were unpleasantly surprised when they came under fire from the ground.

Stress became a constant issue with the NATO pilots who carried out the air operations. A usual mission comprised flying over the Adriatic Sea, through some of the allied countries' air spaces with air refuelling, before entering into hostile FRY/Serbian air space, carrying out the mission under AA missile or artillery fire, and finally – after many hours – returning to home base. Such missions could last up to seven or eight hours, initially during the hours of darkness but later by day. The pilots had multiple roles, including taking part in strike packages as well as CSAR or CAP missions.

Detailed study of A-10 missions that were flown by the 40th EOG from Aviano and Gioia del Colle speak of the heavy burden taken on by USAF (and other NATO member) combat aviation during OAF. During the peak of the campaign, the group operated 25 airframes and some 700 servicemen. There were always around 22 A-10s available at Gioia, while between two and four were undergoing different checks and overhauls at the home base of Spangdahlem. Those 22 airframes usually logged around 30 combat missions per day, operating between 0600 and 1830 hours, while six aircraft remained

An RAF Harrier GR.7 armed with BL755 cluster bombs, seen prior to take off from Gioia del Colle. (RAF/MoD)

A maintenance crew of the 23rd Expeditionary Fighter Squadron of the 52nd Fighter Wing position an engine for installation in a F-16CG at Aviano Air Base on 7 April 1999. (NAC)

on alert between 1830 and 0600 hours for any CSAR missions. This was a burden for the ground crew as well as for the pilots, operating around the clock, 24 hours a day. Redeployment to Gioia was an extra challenge for the technicians, who had to reorganise their work in the completely different environment of the Italian Air Force base. Problems they routinely encountered ranged from delivery of spare parts to accommodation, and lack of food and drinkable water to hygiene issues. Such matters could highlight the differences between the US and its European allies. At the same Italian base was an RAF unit that maintained an aggressive tempo of up to 10 missions per day with only 12 available Harriers. The Italians, however, who had 24 Tornados available at Gioia, carried out only up to six missions per day. The French Air Force, which deployed a contingent of 15 Mirage 2000D fighter-bombers, operated six days per week and rotated its personnel every three to six weeks. Meanwhile, the USAFE 40th EOG operated throughout Allied Force without any replacements, with only one day free: May Day. Even on that day, they maintained six A-10s on alert for CSAR missions.[13]

The most serious political implications were caused by cases of collateral damage, which severely limited air operations from mid-April. In the first volume of this work, we noted the cases of collateral damage that caused loss of life among Serb and Kosovar Albanian civilians. The most serious case was the targeting of the Chinese Embassy in Belgrade on the night 7/8 May, which caused three deaths and left nearly two dozen wounded and injured Chinese journalists and diplomats. As journalist Adam J. Hebert has pointed out, "The drop was a perfect strike, but an intelligence disaster", stressing "a series of Intelligence Community errors".[14] Cases of collateral damage were exploited by the Serbian media, which broadcast the dramatic scenes of air attacks that caused the loss of civilian life. Such powerful footage was a strong weapon to use against the NATO strikes. In regular daily press conferences by NATO or the Pentagon, journalists often raised questions about the loss of civilian lives. The international human rights organisation Amnesty International also raised its voice in the media, accusing NATO of not having verified targets and claiming the operation had violated human rights.[15]

Such media pressure grew into political pressure and created dilemmas for some European allies, which caused many problems over whether or not to attack certain targets, fearing the inevitable loss of civilian lives. General Clark later lamented that public pressure had managed what the Serbian air defences could not: to limit the NATO airstrikes.[16]

Fear of collateral damage made the strike missions more complex, with many more new ROEs and checks within the command chain. If it was evident that an attack would bring about collateral damage, it had to be stopped. Many of the USAF pilots had flown over Bosnia and Herzegovina (BiH) earlier in peace-enforcing missions. They worked under different restrictions and ROEs, mainly concerning their altitude. Now their new orders frustrated the combat pilots, who in many cases orbited over their targets, waiting for approval

Ground crew personnel prepare an F-16CG HARM fighter of the 52nd Fighter Wing at Aviano Air Base, in readiness for a night mission over Serbia. The usual F-16 SEAD payload included two AGM-88 HARM missiles, an HTS-213 targeting pod and AN/ALQ-131 ECM pod. (NAC)

to launch a strike. Meanwhile, there were also differences in the ROEs imposed by NATO and individual air forces. Many countries' ROEs were much more strict than those imposed by NATO. On the other hand, many of NATO's highest institutions (NAC, SACEUR, AFSOUTH, AIRSOUTH, CAOC, etc.) debated, imposed or changed the ROEs during the course of Operation Allied Force.

Nevertheless, collateral damage became significant as the war proceeded, and the globalisation of communications and the near real-time ability to report on unintended injuries created public images that made each case of collateral damage steadily more politically sensitive. As a result, collateral damage became a political weapon that Serbia could exploit against the US and its allies.[17]

The effects of collateral damage, in combination with the 'CNN-factor' – public opinion created by the media, and the influence of this on NATO in Brussels – had an enormous effect on the planners of the air campaign, who stated: "We know that if there had been a severe collateral damage incident, tighter rules for the ATO had to be applied two days later."[18]

Some of the altitude limitations over Kosovo were changed during the operation. From 30 March it was 15,000ft, but on 6 April it changed to 10,000ft. After a case of collateral damage when a refugee convoy of Kosovar Albanians was attacked in the Djakovica area by a pair of F-16Cs from the 31st Wing, it was decided that strike aviation could fly low as 8,000ft, and A-FAC (Airborne Forward Air Controller) crews even down to 5,000ft. When this practice showed that these aircraft then became targets for the Serbian air defence, the limit for the A-10 was set back at 10,000ft. A further restriction was a 10 nautical mile zone alongside the FRY/Serbian (Kosovo and Metohija) border with Macedonia to prevent the spread of the conflict into this country with the Albanian minority that lived in the border area. There was also the introduction of prohibited areas in which UCK (Kosovo Liberation Army) forces or concentrations of refugees were noted. The KEZ (Kosovo Exclusion Zone) extended 10–15 miles into Serbia, and when fighter-bombers could not attack in Kosovo because of bad weather or for other reasons, they could go after back-up targets in this area.[19]

The pilots started to complain that when flying at such altitudes, they could not correctly identify their targets: "[W]e were faced with small groups, of, say, a dozen vehicles or more frequently individual vehicles. This posed entirely new problems of location, verification and attack, especially when [the] attack often needed to be carried out within a matter of minutes, coupled with the problem that Serbian forces were frequently using refugees and their buildings as natural cover."[20] Moreover, some of the ROEs were changed on a daily basis (altitude, prohibited zones, different attacking procedures, etc.). In many cases, the decision to attack a certain target was transferred from the pilot or leader of the strike package to someone almost 1,000km away "at the desk in CAOC in Vicenza". Such operations reflected much more political issues than the military logic of air attacks. To receive approval to attack a certain target on the ground involved 15–20 minutes of waiting/orbiting over the combat theatre. Once the pilot spotted the target (be it a tank, artillery or certain grouping of infantry), he reported to the ABCCC (Airborne Battlefield Command and Control Center), which orbited in the air and passed the information to the CAOC, whereupon the attack would be either granted or not. Meanwhile, combat pilots were left in the air, exposed to hostile AAA fire from the ground. As Air Chief Marshal Sir John Day, Deputy Chief of the British Defence Staff, pointed out on 7 March 2000: "NATO aircraft operated mainly at medium level altitude."[21]

French pilots complied to their own ROEs. They were ordered to fly above 16,000ft, and at such altitudes, and above the clouds or with strong wind, the usage of LGBs (Laser-Guided Bombs) was difficult and inaccurate. The strikes were occasionally cancelled due to difficulties with identification of the targets. The ALA (Armée de l'Air, the French air force) cancelled 420 out of 851 started strike missions, while their naval counterparts cancelled 88 out of 412 such missions. In the case of the French Navy, the pilots were obliged to jettison the ordnance into the sea, since it was forbidden to land with underwing weaponry. It was found that some 18 percent (or 49 out of 268) of GBU-12 bombs used by Super Étandard crews from the carrier *Foch* were lost in this way. Their value was estimated at US$2.2 million. After OAF, the French Navy changed the ROEs and enabled the aircraft to return to the carrier with 'live' ordnance under their wings. General Short explicitly criticised France for removing particular groups of targets from the list to be attacked. Short was from the beginning of Allied Force in favour of heavy airstrikes, later explaining: "I'd have gone for the head of [the] snake on the first night. I'd have turned the lights out [in Belgrade] the first night. This would have gotten Milošević's attention."[22]

Structure of the Airstrikes

FRY territory was divided into two main zones, with the 44th parallel as the demarcation point. The northern part had Belgrade as the main centre with most of the important targets, while the southern portion had Kosovo province as the pivotal area for airstrikes.

Two EA-6B Prowlers take off from Aviano Air Base. In the foreground, an RCAF CF-18 Hornet, armed and ready, waits for its turn. The RCAF's deployment for Allied Force was named Operation Echo. (NAC)

There were three main routes of entry into Serbian air space: a southern one from Albania and Macedonia, a western one from Bosnia and Herzegovina and a northern one from Hungary. The northern route was used exclusively by US aircraft for strikes above the 44th parallel, and the others for the other NATO and USAF strike packages.[23]

During the first week of OAF, almost 80 percent of the strikes were carried out against RV i PVO targets, including 33 strikes on air bases, 18 on missile air defence positions and 10 on air surveillance/radar positions. In this phase, the night of 28/29 March was notably 'heavy', with six airstrikes carried out, combined with cruise missiles launched from B-52 bombers.

Most of the combat missions in Operation Allied Force were carried out by night. Kosovo was an exception, since it was covered with daily strike missions from 26 March. The largest and most spectacular missions around the capital, Belgrade, were carried out during the night. In the beginning, there was one sortie in the late evening and another in the early dawn. They were soon expanded throughout the night, and greatly intensified during May, after a decision made at the NATO summit in Washington. This was a turning point in the increase in the number of airstrikes.[24]

Strike packages which included all types of combat aviation (fighters, fighter-bombers, bombers and SEAD) was the standard form of attack. Such packages could consist of 20–50 aircraft. The RV i PVO registered 622 strike packages, including around 400 over Kosovo and southern Serbia, with the remaining sorties north of the 44th parallel.

Meteorological conditions caused a lot of problems in the execution of airstrikes and other missions, although the weather patterns that NATO encountered were not unusual, either in the Balkans or much of Europe. Cloud cover of 50 percent was registered for 70 percent of the duration of OAF. Only 24 (out of 78) days of the operation were registered as undisturbed by weather conditions. In the first phase of Allied Force, most of the strike aviation aiming to carry out attacks on Kosovo (USAF A-10s and RAF Harriers) returned to their bases with their ordnance. There were only seven favourable days of weather in the first three weeks of the air campaign, and 10 days in which at least half of the strike sorties had to be cancelled. General Short later commented that the weather "just kicked our butts for the first 45 days".[25]

Other sorties included dropping propaganda leaflets over Belgrade and causing sonic booms, which started from the beginning of May. The first sonic booms had an enormous psychological effect on the citizens, but they later lost their impact once the Serbians in the capital and surrounding area became used to them. The authors found evidence for 28 sonic booms being heard in 16 days in Belgrade during this period.

Technological Gap Between the US and Allies

During the air campaign and in later years, Serbian state propaganda frequently claimed that the FRY/Serbia was attacked by the "19 most powerful countries in the world". Actually, 13 NATO armed forces contributed to Operation Allied Force, with the United States dominant by a scale of 7:3. Most of the NATO European allies provided only limited, even symbolic, contingents. The old powers, Great Britain and France, had contingents which covered most aviation types, but in vastly smaller scale than the United States. Some of them had maintained aviation contingents in Italy from the time of the Bosnian War, from 1992–95, and now simply continued with their engagement. New allies such as Hungary and the Czech Republic allowed their airspace to be used for the operation.

Britain's Royal Air Force remained the only one of the NATO allies that was able to deploy all types of combat and support aviation in OAF, albeit in significantly fewer numbers than the USAF could

A Luftwaffe Tornado, serialed 45-33, of Aufklarungsgeschwader 51 seen at Aviano Air Base during a routine visit. The German Air Force carried out SEAD and reconnaissance missions during Operation Allied Force. (Author's Collection)

A detailed view of the underwing weapons load on an F-16A Falcon from the Royal Netherlands Air Force as it takes on fuel from a 100th Air Expeditionary Wing KC-135R. (NAC)

provide. Rising tension in Kosovo during the summer of 1998 led to the deployment of a detachment of RAF Harriers of No. 3 Squadron, and in January 1999 another from No. 4 Squadron, to Gioia del Colle Air Base in Italy, to give NATO an intervention capability. In March 1999, the Harriers of No. 1 Squadron were at the forefront of the first attacks of OAF by launching Paveway bombs against a range of targets.[26] To boost the RAF's contribution to the NATO effort, the Tornado force was ordered to start flying attack missions from RAF Bruggen in Germany. By mid-May, the RAF had at last got into its stride and daily strikes were being made in Kosovo and Yugoslavia. An MoD study concluded that 60 fixed targets were badly damaged or destroyed by the RAF and 75 tactical targets hit, during a total of 1,008 RAF attack sorties. By early May, the RAF component in Allied Force had increased to 16 Harrier GR7s, 12 Tornado GR1/GR4s, three E-3Ds, four Tristars, four VC-10s, a Nimrod and a Canberra PR9.[27] RAF Wing Commander Andrew Brookes wrote a year after the campaign: "During the 78 day air campaign NATO aircraft delivered 23,614 munitions against 421 static targets and over 520 tactical targets in Kosovo, with 99.6 [percent] accuracy. Only 30 of these caused collateral damage, but their political impact was nonetheless massive." He pointed out that 34 percent of weapons launched during Allied Force were precision guided.[28]

To a certain extent, the French Air Force, Army and Naval aviation (ALA, ALAT and Aeronavale) could compare with the RAF's capabilities, but France actually deployed the largest number of aircraft – 88 – to the operation of any of the allies, compared to 45 RAF aircraft. The French part of OAF was named Operation Trident. By deployed assets, one could say that France wished to show that it had an "efficient and coherent military structure". France engaged assets from all three of its military branches: the *Foch* aircraft carrier group, aviation elements from the French Army (12 Puma and Gazelle helicopters based in Macedonia) and various units of the ALA. Their units were based in theatre, flying from Macedonia,

F-15E Eagles from the 492nd Fighter Squadron, 48th Fighter Wing, prepare to launch during a NATO tactical evaluation exercise. (NAC)

on the Adriatic Sea and from Italian air bases, with some of the assets operating from home bases in France. The ALA already had a contingent at Italian air bases from the days of the Bosnian air war, comprising eight Mirage 2000C fighters plus four Mirage 2000Ds (a fifth arrived on 15 March) and four Jaguar strikers. Four Puma helicopters were based in Macedonia for the CSAR role. French aviation logged over 3,600 operational sorties, including 1,200 for transport and support, 1,263 strikes, 476 CAP missions, 518 tankers, 277 recce, 112 electronic combat missions, 47 AWACS and 12 C-SAR missions.[29]

The Italian Air Force (AMI, Aeronautica Militare Italiana) was the third largest contributor among the European allies with its air assets. Its contribution was the 17 air bases used by NATO air contingents, which were the backbone for the whole operation.[30] The workhorse of the AMI during Allied Force was its Tornado units, which were part of the first ATO on the night of 24 March 1999. In total, during the operation, Italian Tornado IDS/ECRs completed 338 sorties with the equivalent of the 1,285 flying hours. The principal types of armament used were the AGM-88 HARM missile, of which 115 were launched, and the GBU-16 bomb, 79 of which were dropped. The Italians operated for the first 20 days of OAF exclusively by night in support of Battlefield Air Interdiction (BAI). They later flew only daylight missions, supporting CAS or free-hunts for Serb SAM systems. Analysing the role of the Italian Air Force, Dr Riccardo Niccoli proudly stressed that: "American crews of the F-15 Strike Eagles, preferred the support of the Tornado SEAD to their own F-16CJ with [the] HARM Targeting System."[31]

The German Air Force (Luftwaffe) was the next largest NATO contributor with its 14 Tornados, engaged only in SEAD and recce missions. The Germans also deployed an aerial recce unit equipped with CL-289 UAVs, which significantly improved the picture of VJ/MUP activities in Kosovo as well as BDA (Bomb Damage Assessment). Besides air assets, Germany provided four air bases on its territory for the operation.

Lesser contingents included Canadian (RCAF) and Spanish Air Force F/A-18 Hornets, which carried out a significant number of combat sorties. The Canadians launched 679 missions, of which 588 were strikes. They carried out a total of 2,527 flying hours, dropping 361 GBU-10s and GBU-12s, as well as 171 Mk-82 'dumb' bombs.[32] The Spaniards, meanwhile, carried out 269 missions with EF-18s, 66 with KC-130 tankers and 67 transport missions with CASA Aviocars.

The Belgian and Dutch Air Forces operated their F-16MLUs at Amendola in a single unit known as B-D DATF. One of the Dutch pilots flying an F-16 claimed an RV i PVO MiG-29 on the first night of the campaign, thus making history for the RNLAF. A joint B-D contingent was engaged in the initial strike missions, but after the changes of ROE, they switch to CAP missions only. From mid-April, RNLAF F-16s were engaged in recce missions, carrying MARS containers. The Dutch also provided a KC-10 tanker for air refuelling. Dutch F-16s logged 1,252 combat sorties during OAF, while the Belgians made 620.[33]

Four other NATO air forces contributed with their older F-16As in CAP missions. The Danish and Norwegian Air Forces established their joint fighter unit at Grazianese Air Base. Unlike B-D DATF, Danish and Norwegian pilots flew their CAP missions separately. The Turkish Air Force deployed to Ghedi Air Base a fighter unit which was equipped with brand-new AMRAAMs (Advanced Medium-Range Air-to-Air Missiles). They were able to provide CAP missions over the theatre. A Portuguese unit operated alongside the USAF's 31st AEW in Aviano. Since their F-16As were not upgraded to MLU standard and were equipped with AIM-9 Sidewinders, they carried out CAP missions outside the combat theatre, logging 107 combat missions and accumulating almost 470 combat hours, with an average mission length of almost 4.4 hours.[34]

With the exception of the RAF and Armée de l'Air, which were backed by their own national aviation industries, the Europeans lacked most of the modern equipment such as precision/laser-guided munitions and various pods for targeting, altitude measurement or jamming. Consequently, most of the smaller allied air forces carried out only CAP missions, which represented 16 percent of the whole operation. Knowing that most of the RV i PVO fighter and strike assets were neutralised in the early stages of the campaign, the engagement of the smaller allied fighter contingents represented an important contribution to the wider common cause.

The campaign showed that some kind of consensus among the allies on certain issues was difficult to reach, such as approval for targeting or the level of applied air power. The Europeans had their own interests and perceptions and, in many cases, insisted on legalities such as UN approval for certain actions rather than NATO's. This led to a different dynamic among the allies: the Americans acted fast, insisting on air power and a high tempo of operation, while the Europeans were slower, demanding breaks for diplomatic efforts and being very sensitive to the impact of the media. The decision-making process was actually carried out between the United States, Great Britain and France, although in many cases the United States acted independently. The Americans started to introduce their own separate ATOs and limited the flow of intelligence, which they feared may reach the Serbs. Despite this being a NATO-led campaign, it is obvious that the United States was dominant in planning and executing Allied Force, and that whole operation had an excessively American character.[35] CIA analyst David C. Isby commented: "Perhaps the most significant single lesson in this area was that Operation Allied Force showed a widening gap between the technology and operational capabilities of the US and its NATO partners."[36]

Serbian Chain of Command

The Serbian chain of command was much simpler than that of NATO, since it was a national body and was politically linked to leader Slobodan Milošević. As the president of the FR Yugoslavia, Milošević was also the supreme commander in case of war. In peacetime, the main defence body was the Supreme Defence Council, which coordinated all of the nation's defence and military activities. The council consisted of the three presidents of the FR Yugoslavia, Serbia and Montenegro, while the federal prime minister, defence minister and Chief of the General Staff and the council secretary took part in the decision-making process but were not members. Since the President of Montenegro, Milo Djukanović, had shown his opposition to the war with NATO in October 1998, he took no further part in the decision or command process. The peculiarity of the FRY defence system was the separation between the Vojska Jugoslavije (VJ) General Staff and the FRY Ministry of Defence, which had existed since May 1992 when the FR Yugoslavia was created. The General Staff was directly subordinated to the FRY President, while the Ministry of Defence acted as a kind of support or political institution.

When Operation Allied Force started, the VJ General Staff became the Supreme Command Staff, with FRY President Milošević as its head. The Chief of the General Staff acted as his assistant. The commanders of the three ground force armies (the First, Second and Third), RV i PVO and Jugoslav Navy were the next level in the chain of command.[37] But as events during the campaign showed, in many cases Milošević directly communicated with the commanders of the Third Army (which had Kosovo and Metohija as its AOR) and RV i PVO. In many cases, the army and air force commanders bypassed the Chief of the General Staff and asked for assistance from or the opinion of the supreme commander.

The commander of the RV i PVO, General Spasoje Smiljanić, relied on his two commanders of the Air Defence Corps and the Air Corps. Due to the type of air campaign in Allied Force, the main responsibility lay with the Air Defence Corps and its Operations Centre (OC). The deterioration caused by the NATO air attacks on the air defence systems produced several organisational problems. Damage to the air defence system led to the merging of the Air Surveillance Brigade OC and its Sector (Battalion) OCs, which were tasked with command of the air defence units in their respective area of responsibilities, with the Air Defence Corps OC. This remained the main command and control body during the air defence operations, alongside General Smiljanić as the RV i PVO commander.[38]

Previous RV i PVO commander General Ljubiša Veličković (who had resigned from the post after the Milošević–Holbrooke agreement in October 1998) also appeared on the scene, using his

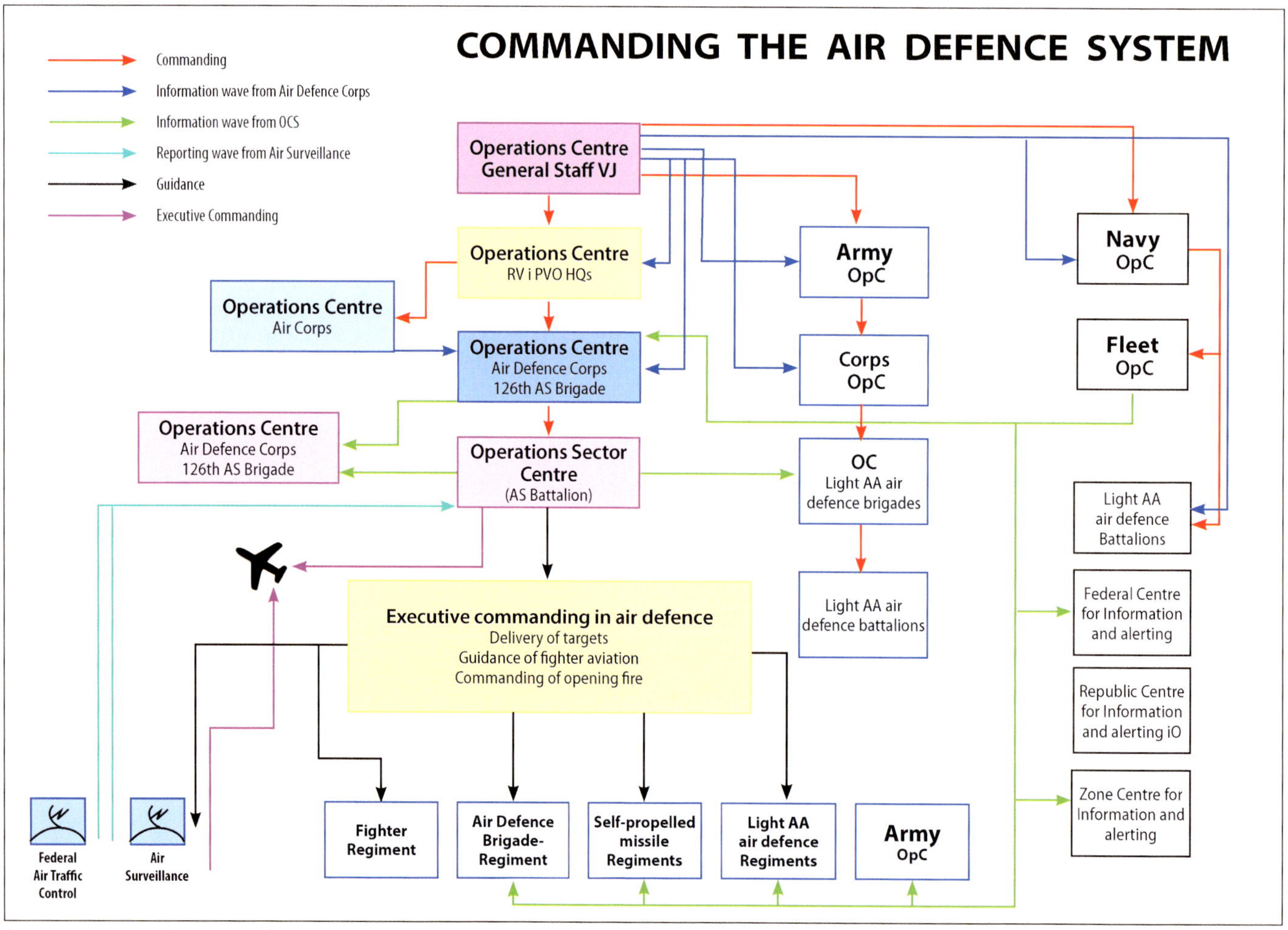

Structure of the Serbian Air Defence command during Operation Allied Force.

The Operations Centre of the Air Defence Corps at underground Object 909 at Straževica Hill in the suburbs of Belgrade. This location was targeted many times but remained operational throughout the conflict since it was in a well-chosen position deep in the hillside. (Komanda RV i PVO)

authority as the former chief and as assistant to the minister of defence. Veličković remained as Milošević's informal advisor for the air force, and even issued orders to air defence units at the tactical level. He was killed in one such appearance, together with the crew of the missile unit where he had suddenly arrived, ordering them to engage one of the SEAD groups that were orbiting in the area.

Different Number of Combat Sorties

Despite modern evidence and the high level of military bureaucracy, the total number of NATO missions/sorties are difficult to precisely determine. There were differences caused by various parameters within NATO and the USAF, including differences in the date which marked the end of nations' engagement in the operation.

The facts as stated by NATO officials are that there were a total of 38,004 combat sorties, among which were 10,484 strike missions, with more than 15,000 of these sorties being carried out by NATO allies. On the other hand, the US Joint Staff revealed the following statistics: a total of 37,200 sorties, of which 23,208 (62 percent) were carried out by US aviation and 13,992 (38 percent) by NATO allies; 9,500 strike/fighter-bomber sorties, with 5,035 (53 percent) by US aircraft and 4,465 (47 percent) by NATO allies; and 1,200 recce missions, of which 948 (79 percent) were US and 252 (21 percent) NATO allies. There were also some 26,500 other missions in support of the air war, with 17,225 (65 percent) involving US platforms and 9,725 (35 percent) those of the NATO allies.[39]

Belonging to the 494th Fighter Squadron based at RAF Lakenheath, but deployed to Aviano, an F-15 Strike Eagle is seen before a night mission flown against targets in Yugoslavia on 19 April 1999. (NAC)

Monitoring NATO activities with a high level of reliability, the 280th ELINT Centre of the RV i PVO provided the following statistics: between 24 March and 10 June, they identified a total of 26,095 sorties, with 21,683 involving combat aviation, of which 18,168 were combat missions over the FRY. The following number of missions were identified: 3,903 fighter, 10,004 fighter-bomber, 4,104 SEAD, 173 bomber, 74 recce and 3,515 air refuelling. Notably, these statistics did not count (or reveal) the number of other missions identified, such as AWACS, ABCCC, J-STARS, etc. These statistics testify that the RV i PVO monitored all SIGINT/ELINT communications in an attempt to provide a complete picture of the air war to its leadership.[40]

No matter the high degree of air superiority maintained by the US and NATO from the first moments of Operation Allied Force, the RV i PVO still managed to carry out a number of combat sorties and to keep its helicopter fleet active throughout the conflict. The RV i PVO carried out 25 strike missions over Kosovo, flying Oraos and G-4s, and 11 interceptions with MiG-29s – plus two which were terminated during take-off. There were 14 overflights between air bases carried out by the fighter and strike aviation, plus 19 transport sorties with An-26s. Yugoslav helicopters also carried out a total of 179 missions, ferrying 94 wounded, 113 passengers and five tons of cargo. They completed five CSAR missions rescuing downed RV i PVO pilots during the first night of OAF. These make a total of 248 (plus two terminated) sorties, with a total of 122.20 flying hours, conducted by RV i PVO aircraft during the air campaign.[41]

A B-1B Lancer is marshalled to a stop at RAF Fairford. (NAC)

2
NATO COMBAT EXPERIENCES

Newly Used Weaponry

Operation Allied Force was an opportunity for the introduction into combat service or testing of many new types of ordnance, as well as other military technological improvements. Nearly all of these belonged to the USAF, confirming the previously mentioned technical gap within NATO between the United States and its European allies.

Some of the systems, such as Unmanned Aerial Vehicles (UAVs) or Joint STARS, had their operational debut with IFOR in the air campaign that ended the Bosnian War in 1995. The large-scale use of satellites in aerial reconnaissance, BDA and guidance of smart bombs was another important feature of Allied Force. The other types of ordnance used in Bosnia – laser-guided Paveway bombs, AGM-88 HARM missiles, CBU-97 cluster munitions and LANTIRN (Low Altitude Navigation and Targeting Infrared for Night) targeting pods – also proved their reliability in combat.

There were two notable aspects of the strike operations. First, there was a heavy use of standoff and Global Positioning System (GPS) in guiding munitions to attack targets throughout the FR Yugoslavia. Second, the operation was marked by the introduction of new weapons and systems, including the B-2A stealth bomber equipped with JDAM (Joint Direct Attack Munition) and new applications for Standoff Land Attack Missiles (SLAM).[1]

The most spectacular new entry to the USAF inventory that took part in OAF was certainly the B-2A Spirit stealth bomber. It was used for the first time in combat missions during the operation, flying historic global missions from Whiteman AFB in Missouri to Serbia and back. They were using brand-new ordnance, the JDAM,

Armourers of the 509th Operations Group at Whiteman AFB work to remove a tie-down strap on a trailer load of Mk 84 2,000lb bombs during day 27 of OAF. (NAC)

This Joint Standoff Weapon AGM-154 remained almost in perfect shape after launching against a target in Serbia. After OAF, it was taken to the Yugoslav Air Force Museum at Belgrade International Airport. (B. Dimitrijević)

which were standard bombs fitted with a GPS guidance device which turned them into high-precision projectiles, independent from meteorological conditions, with accuracy to within 9.6 metres of the target. Usage of JDAMs added to the precision of targeting, which was earlier possible only by using cruise missiles (C-ALCM, TLCM). Black-grey stealth B-2As with JDAM were used to strike some of the most important targets in Serbia.[2]

Other types of air-to-surface guided ordnance used for the first time during OAF included AGM-142 HAVE NAP and AGM-154 JSOW (Joint Standoff Weapon). They were generally known before but had never been used in combat. On the usage of HAVE NAP, a spokesman for the 2nd BW at Barksdale AFB said that the missiles failed to hit their targets: "HAVE NAPs skewed off into space like a golf ball sliced off a tee." The JSOW was a 1,065lb glide bomb that could be dropped 40 miles from its intended target and be guided there by a low-cost inertial navigation system that used satellite coordinates to locate the target. This enabled the aircraft which dropped it to stay outside the range of enemy air defences.[3]

Unknown to many was the BLU-114/B bomblet, which soon became known in Serbia as the 'Graphite bomb'. It was cluster type, non-lethal bomblet used to disable an electrical grid. The bomb worked by spreading a dense cloud of extremely fine, chemically treated carbon filaments over air-insulated high voltage installations such as transformers and power lines, causing short-circuits and subsequent disruption of the electricity supply in an area.[4] By using BLU-114/B, NATO switched off the electricity supply in Serbia on eight occasions, as spokesman Jamie Shea commented at one NATO press conference.

To this day, most of the attention in Serbia and Kosovo has been focused on the use of depleted uranium munitions by the A-10 strikers, and its consequences on people's health and the environment. There is still a huge public dispute and many accusations about the use of such munitions during the 1999 campaign. The PGU-14/B API ammunition fired by the GAU-8/A 30mm gun had much more destructive power than traditional aircraft gun munitions. These munitions containing depleted uranium have caused uncontrolled radiation in the area where they were delivered, with airborne levels up to 900 times higher than usual.[5]

Equipped with ammunition with depleted uranium, A-10s became an important tool in targeting armoured vehicles, artillery and radar vehicles. (NAC)

According to the VJ's estimations, published in *Vojska* magazine, the use of this depleted uranium munition was registered for the first time on 30 March in the area around Prizren:

> During the war, evidence was gathered that in eight locations below the 44th

parallel were 'spread' 3,000 to 5,000 such bullets. In Kosovo and Metohija, according to the same estimations, 50,000 bullets were fired at around 100 locations (NATO admits 31,000 of such munitions). Chemical protection units of the VJ made a survey of the areas where A-10 strikers fired this type of munition (out of Kosovo), and discovered depleted uranium munitions in the wider area of Bujanovac (18 April), at cape Arza on the Luštica peninsula on the Montenegro coast (30 May) and in the wider area of Vranje.

After the campaign, it was stated that there were 112 such strikes on 91 locations, with 12 at nine locations in Serbia proper, two at one location in Montenegro and 98 at 81 locations in Kosovo. Most of the depleted uranium munitions were used against individual targets, such as VJ tanks, APCs and artillery or various types of strongholds. A few years after the campaign, VJ NBC (Nuclear, Biological, Chemical) units worked to decontaminate nine micro-locations in southern Serbia and one in Montenegro.[6]

Fighter Aviation

As each type of NATO/USAF aviation had its particular experiences during Operation Allied Force, we shall try to outline most of the characteristic details for each of them, from combat to support aircraft.

NATO fighter aviation was used throughout the campaign in two main ways: to escort the strike packages which entered FRY airspace and performed combat missions, or as part of CAP missions outside FRY airspace. When air superiority was achieved during the later stages of OAF, the number of deployed fighters was downsized.[7] There were around 80 sorties daily at the beginning of OAF, but that number had declined to around 50 in the later stages of the campaign, once air superiority was gained in FRY airspace.[8]

A system was established from the first day of the campaign for the continuous presence of NATO fighter aviation along the FRY's borders with Macedonia, Albania and Bosnia and Herzegovina. Temporary patrols were carried out in front of the FRY's borders and near the borders with Hungary and Croatia. CAP missions were carried out away from the combat zones to protect the non-combat NATO aviation that operated in this part of Balkan airspace. The latter included air tankers, AWACS, ABCCCs, ELINT and recce assets. The CAP missions also had the task of covering 'dead spots' in the FRY airspace, which AWACS were not able to monitor, mostly at lower levels. These lower altitudes were used by RV i PVO helicopters, and in many cases NATO UAVs which were not showing proper identification. The fighters which orbited in CAP missions were dispatched by AWACS to intercept and check these unidentified aircraft. After visual identification was made, fighter pilots would report back that they were friendly objects.[9]

The following CAP zones were in use during the campaign: 'North' and 'South' over eastern BiH in the area Tuzla–Sarajevo–Mostar; 'FYROM-E/W' over eastern and western Macedonia; 'Alby' over northern Albania in the area between Skadar (Shkodra) and Peskopeja; 'Hung' over Hungary in the area Pecs–Siklos; and finally 'Sabre' in front of FRY territorial waters. The usual altitude for patrol missions was 30,000ft. Fighter pairs would remain orbiting an area for around three hours, including air refuelling, maintaining contact with AWACS. They were armed with standard AAMs such as the Sidewinder, AMRAAM and other types to a lesser extent. Some of the patrols were armed with LGBs, which they used after their CAP mission upon given targets on the ground.[10]

USAF fighter aviation was engaged as escorts to the strike packages. In the earlier stages of OAF, a fighter escort usually consisted of around 10 fighters, mostly F-15Cs or F-16Cs. Fighter cover was mostly carried out with two pairs of fighters. At the beginning of Allied Force, four-ship F-15C detachments carried out 'offensive counter-air missions' flying in front of the strike packages. On the first night of OAF, three Yugoslav MiG-29s were claimed while confronting the fighter cover. USAF pilots noted that encounters with RV i PVO pilots were at close range and that it was an unpleasant experience, as they were trained to fight at much longer distances. Another two MiGs were claimed on 26 March by a USAF fighter pair carrying out a standard CAP mission (DCA type – Defensive Counter Air) in the Tuzla–Sarajevo zone – without any warning from orbiting AWACS. One final Yugoslav MiG-29 was claimed by an F-16CJ belonging to the SEAD group, which was headed out of FRY airspace for refuelling. One of the F-16 HARM shooters simply turned back and claimed the Yugoslav

The AIM-120 was the main Air-to-Air missile used to combat the Yugoslav MiG-29s during Operation Allied Force. Here, a load of AIM-120s are seen before being transported to an aircraft by a crew of the 31st Maintenance Squadron at Aviano Air Base. (NAC)

The 493rd FS deployed with its F-15C Eagles to Cervia Air Base in Italy, where they joined the 501st EOG. (NAC)

Another F-15C Eagle belonging to the 493rd Fighter Squadron, 48th Fighter Wing, at RAF Lakenheath. The squadron claimed a total of four RV i PVO MiG-29s in aerial combat on 24 and 26 March 1999. (NAC)

A French Air Force Mirage 2000C drops away from a KC-135R Stratotanker after refuelling during a combat patrol mission in Operation Allied Force. (NAC)

fighter with an AMRAAM from distance.[11] This was the last fighter encounter during the operation.

The European allies carried out most of the CAP missions during the campaign. The French part of Allied Force, entitled Trident, led to an overstretching of the ALA units. A typical Mirage 2000C mission lasted between six and seven hours, with three air refuellings. Each of the engaged fighters needed at least three available pilots, which caused fatigue among the pilots and airframes. Fatigue was also registered with the missiles (Magic-2 and Super 530D) that were carried during the patrols. French estimates noted that fatigue with AAMs was equal to the launching (or loss) of 28 Magic-2 and 18 Super 530D missiles, at a cost of US$20 million.[12]

The Italian AMI used their Tornado ADVs belonging to the 12th and 21st Gruppo based at Gioia dell Cole for CAP missions. Typically, there were two sorties in a standard fighter configuration of this type (four Skyflash or Sidewinder AAMs). The most serious engagement involved rushing two AMI Tornados on 26 March to replace a pair of F-15Cs which left the CAP station and claimed two Yugoslav MiG-29s. During OAF, Italian pilots had their first experience of air refuelling. There was also an Italian contingent of modernised but obsolete Lockheed F-104 Starfighters kept on alert at Amendola, Cervia and Gioia del Colle, and occasionally used for CAP missions.[13]

Fighter-bomber and Strike Aviation

During the operation, fighter-bomber and strike aviation had a pivotal role in attacks on targets in the FR Yugoslavia. Strike aviation assets carried out missions mainly in Kosovo, which may be regarded as CAS – Close Air Support missions. The paradox of these CAS missions was that there were none of their own forces on the ground and that Close Air Support was not that 'close', since the rules of engagement ordered that combat sorties should be carried out more than 5,000 metres above the ground north of the 44th parallel, and only at lesser altitudes south of it, mostly over Kosovo province.

The average number of daily sorties was around 100 at the beginning of Allied Force, later growing to 200–300 sorties per day. The list of participants in those missions is a long one, but they mostly comprised F-16CGs and F-15Es belonging to various USAF units. Lockheed F-117A stealth fighters were also used during OAF strikes, delivering mostly precision munitions and several different types of LGBs on targets in Serbia, north of the 44th parallel.[14]

The basic formation of fighter-bomber and strike aviation was the strike package, of which the RV i PVO ELINT Centre registered a total of 622. Each strike package consisted of between 10 and 20 aircraft. Initially there were between two and four such groups, but later, towards the end of the operation, there were around 10 strike packages per day. The targets were military in the early stages of Allied Force, but then expanded to other targets, mostly infrastructure. The strike packages were carried out at a higher altitude, around 30,000ft. When they entered into FRY airspace, they would turn off the IFF (Identification Friend or Foe) and maintain radio silence. The strikes were carried out from a distance of 20,000–25,000ft. Strike package would remain in FRY airspace for around one or two hours; prior to and after leaving FRY airspace, they would carry out mid-air refuelling.

During the early stages of OAF, the strike packages entered FRY airspace from Hungary or Macedonia at night, but later by day. After 11 April, they started to use a third entrance via Bosnia and Herzegovina airspace. The three main entrances established were: from Hungary, in the Sombor–Subotica sector; from Bosnia and Herzegovina, in the Višegrad–Zvornik–Bijeljina area; and from Macedonia, in the sector between Kačanik and Kumanovo. The northern entrance was used exclusively by USAF strikers (F-15Es, F-16Cs and F-117As), mostly by night. They used secure radio channels with voice crypto-protection, so Serbian ELINT experienced difficulties in successfully monitoring their activities. This northern entrance was used by the USAF to attack targets north of the 44th parallel. The European NATO allies used the other two points of entry. The middle entrance (BiH) was used to attack targets on both sides of the 44th parallel, whereas the southern path was used exclusively for attacks on Kosovo and southern Serbia. Strikes on targets in Montenegro were carried out from the sea or via Albanian airspace, while targets to the north of Montenegro were attacked after entering from Bosnia and Herzegovina.[15]

Most of the strike sorties north of the 44th parallel during OAF were carried out by F-15E Strike Eagles, which used standard bombs such as the Mk-82, as well as GBU-10/12/24 LGBs and CBU-87 cluster bombs. Besides the standard missions in strike packages, the F-15Es orbited in 'CAP-regime'. Loaded with GBU-12s (and standard AMRAAMs and Sidewinders for protection), they orbited in the 'waiting areas' for targets which would show on the ground suddenly or unexpectedly. Such missions could last up to nine hours

A pair of Lakenheath-based F-15E Strike Eagles return from a mission during the OAF campaign. (NAC)

USAF airman Kevin Hart attaches a GBU-24 laser-guided bomb to an F-15E Strike Eagle at Aviano Air Base, Italy, on 24 March 1999. Two squadrons equipped with F-15E Strike Eagles flew combat missions from separate locations at Lakenheath (UK) and Aviano. The 48th Wing's crews led almost 50 percent of strike packages and dropped 2.7 million pounds (1.2 million kg) of ordnance during the 78-day OAF campaign. (NAC)

USAF ground crew stop an F-15E Strike Eagle of the 48th Fighter Wing as other ground crew run out to give the aircraft final checks before it takes off on 29 March 1999. (NAC)

and proved difficult and stressful for the pilots. The F-15Es of the 494th EFS were used as the platform from which AGM-130 missiles were launched, guided by the Weapons System Officer behind the pilot. These launches were out of the range of the Serbian SAM systems and were carried out no matter what the weather conditions, targeting Serbian air defence firing positions as well as MiG-29s and MiG-21s dispersed around Batajnica Air Base (even on the nearby highway, as was the case on 17 May). Strike Eagles of the 494th EFS were used to drop 4,600lb GBU-28 'bunker buster' bombs from 26 April. Their use had not been planned, and a special ordnance team had to be sent to Aviano to prepare the bombs and train the ground crews for using them. The 492nd EFS entered the fray on 3 May, in the first combat missions to be flown direct from Lakenheath since the airstrikes against Libya in 1986.[16]

During the period between 9 May and 7 June, the RV i PVO ELINT Centre registered 10 launches of standoff missiles. Launching was carried out during the night using F-15E Strike Eagles, and in one case an F/A-18 that took off from a carrier. They flew on 22 May in a two-ship formation, and strike packages launched a single missile each. The distance between the launching point and the target was between 50 and 70km. Usually, the airspace of BiH was used, from the area Višegrad–Bijeljina–Brčko, and they would fire AGM-154 JSOW missiles from an altitude of around 30,000ft.

Stealth F-117As were protected by fighter aviation and SEAD groups during their missions. They had a computer system for mission planning which measured the optimal route through the holes in the enemy radar network.

Kosovan territory was split into two zones: 'NFL' west of Pristina Air Base and 'NBA' east of it. During strikes in each of these zones, NATO aviation used different radio channels, which enabled Serbian ELINT to monitor their operations a little more easily than in the northern FRY. In some cases, the targets were chosen beforehand and pilots were briefed pre-flight. In other cases, the ABCCC (EC-130E) or 'small AWACS' (E-2C) would send the order while the strike units were over Kosovo. Selection of targets and the order to attack them were in both cases approved by the CAOC in Vicenza.[17]

Rules of engagement for the strike aviation over Kosovo were limited at the beginning of Operation Allied Force to intrusion no deeper than 10 miles inside the province, and from altitudes not lower than 17,500ft. During the first week of the operation, the lower limit was reduced to 15,000ft, and later to as low as 10,000ft. After the first week of the operation, the strikes were approved over the whole of the province, but exclusively with an entry point across the Albanian border. From 15 April, strikes were allowed with entry from Macedonian airspace. After several incidents of collateral damage, commencement or continuation of airstrikes was forbidden if anything was spotted which it was thought may lead to unintended casualties or damage.[18]

From 12 April, the second phase of attacks on targets in Kosovo was launched, with intensified strikes on VJ forces and battle interdiction strikes in the border area with Albania. This coincided with a series of clashes between UCK and VJ forces around the army

Stealth F-117A fighters were forward deployed from Holloman AFB to Aviano in Italy, from where they flew 337 combat missions during the OAF campaign and accumulated 942.1 combat flight hours, with an average of 2.8 hours per sortie. (NAC)

Avionics specialists monitor a Laser Destination Calibration test through the Heads-Up Display of an F-16CG of the 510th EFS/31st AEW at Aviano Air Base on 26 April 1999. (NAC)

border post at Košare. To begin with the strikes were carried out by RAF Harrier GR.7s, USMC (US Marine Corps) AV-8B Harriers (aboard an amphibious assault ship) and USAF A-10s. Later, all other types of aviation were introduced. The increase in A-10 activity came after the transfer of the 81st EFS from Aviano to the much closer Gioia del Colle on 11 April.[19] The veteran A-10s were used as a multitasking platform during OAF. Besides strike missions in which they used standard ordnance, they were used in Combat Search and Rescue (CSAR) for two downed US pilots and for A-FAC (Airborne Forward Air Controller) missions. The A-10s were used to illuminate targets over Kosovo, southern Serbia and occasionally in Montenegro. After the usual A-FAC tasks, they would finish the mission by joining the strike package and firing their ordnance. The usual A-10 formation comprised two aircraft. No matter what their combat capabilities, they were always backed by SEAD groups.

Discovery and tracking of Jugoslav Army or MUP targets in Kosovo was undertaken by reconnaissance aviation, various UAVs and several command and control platforms that orbited in the area, and by the continuous searching by the strike aviation that was flying over the province (USAF A-10s, F-16s and USN F-14s). Images were transferred from UAVs (with the note 'picture only from UAV') to ABCCCs and then to crews in the combat aircraft. Targets included armoured vehicles, artillery and missile or radar positions, and strikes were carried out with guidance from another aircraft and, to a lesser extent, independently. Target guidance was carried out by A-FACs flying in O/A-10As, F-16s or later F-14s. Laser

Fully loaded with ordnance, this A-10A of the 81st EFS, with its home base at Spangdahlem Air Base in Germany, pulls away from a tanker. This squadron moved from Aviano to Gioia del Colle on 11 April, from where it continued to carry out strike missions over Kosovo and Metohija until the end of the air campaign. (DoD)

designation of the targets was carried out by F-16s and F-14s. After refuelling, A-FAC crews reached the target zones prior to the main strike package, together with fighter cover and a SEAD package. They would identify the targets by orbiting around the zone, flying a little higher than the strike package. Occasionally they also carried out strikes to indicate more clearly the position of the target for the pilots in the strike package.

From mid-April, the strike packages included F/A-18 Hornets and F-14D Tomcats from the carrier USS *Theodore Roosevelt*. This marked the start of continuous strikes over Kosovo until the end of Operation Allied Force, with between 20 and 50 different targets daily.[20]

A pre-flight inspection of an A-10 Thunderbolt II on 12 April 1999. The aircraft and technician were part of the 81st Expeditionary Fighter Squadron, which had deployed to Gioia del Colle on the previous day. (NAC)

Allied Force confirmed the concept of the use of F-14s with LANTIRN navigation/targeting pods and usage of this type in an A-FAC role (nicknamed Fast-FAC), which was a great success. It was no doubt strange for the USAFE pilots to see the Navy Tomcats in such an unusual role. The US Navy estimated that almost 50 percent of the FAC missions were carried by its F-14s.[21] For example, the VF-41 squadron dropped around 350 LGBs. USN aircraft in general accounted for 30 percent of destroyed targets with the use of the Fast-FAC concept. Both carrier-borne F-14 squadrons (VF-14 and VF-41) worked closely together in this concept. Tomcats used ordnance such as GBU-10/12/16s and even GBU-24 'Deep Penetrators'. The robustness of the F-14 enabled more ordnance to be used, and even the safe return to the carrier of the bombs not dropped on the targets. LANTIRN pods performed better than the pods used on F/A-18s, which enabled a much more precise drop and from higher altitudes. US Navy strikers (F-14s and F/A-18s) had tremendous success in hitting and destroying the facilities at Podgorica Air

The Harrier GR.7 serialed ZG 477, with the code '67' on the fin, of No. 3 Squadron at Laarbruch, taxiing on a strike mission during OAF armed with four BL755 cluster bombs. This Harrier was based at Gioia del Colle with a detachment of the No. 1 (F) Squadron RAF and took part in at least seven combat missions in Kosovo and southern Serbia using BL755 and Paveway II/III LGBs. (Brit. MoD)

An F-14A Tomcat prior to launching from USS *Theodore Roosevelt* during OAF. Tomcats of VF-14 and VF-41 squadrons mostly operated over Kosovo and Montenegro in strike and A-FAC missions. (DoD)

A US Navy F/A-18C Hornet of VFA-15 is prepared for a catapult launch from the flight deck of USS *Theodore Roosevelt* during Operation Allied Force. The Hornet is armed with AGM-88 HARM missiles. (NAC)

Flightdeck personnel prepare an F/A-18C of VFA-87 for a catapult launch on board USS *Theodore Roosevelt* during the OAF campaign. (NAC)

Base. "I am particularly proud of the same-day devastating strikes, for example, again Podgorica Airfield conducted by Air Wing 8," remarked Vice Admiral Daniel J. Murphy Jr, commander of the Sixth Fleet, US Navy.[22]

Beside other specialised variants of the standard C-130 Hercules transport, AC-130 gunships, armed with 40mm and 105mm guns, were used during OAF. The Serbs located 23 of their missions, 21 by night and two registered as overflights. They orbited in the zones of their bases or over the Adriatic Sea. Gunships were only engaged in SAR missions for two downed USAF pilots. Their crews always used coded/cyphered communication, which made the monitoring of their activities very difficult.

Some of the airstrikes were provided by the US Marine Corps. Their AV-8Bs operated from amphibious/assault ships, which were introduced a little later during OAF. For the first time they were using LGBs and CBU-99 cluster advanced munitions, while laser guidance to the targets was carried out by USAF F-16Cs. Useful experience was gained during the AV-8B missions. The USMC Harriers operated against targets in Kosovo without refuelling. The aircraft showed the excellence of the maintenance crews, reaching 90 percent airworthiness throughout the deployment.[23]

The use of RAF Harriers during the first 20 days of OAF was particularly frustrating, about which personnel openly spoke in front of British TV cameras. After the first six sorties from Gioia del Colle carried out over Kosovo and southern Serbia, which were labelled as the forerunners of the NATO strikes, bad weather caused the missions over Kosovo to be halted. On 27 March, RAF Harriers returned to base after jettisoning their ordnance. After two days of

An F/A-18C Hornet belonging to VFA-87 seemingly glides in for a precision landing on the flight deck of USS *Theodore Roosevelt*. (NAC)

Armourers of the the 81st EFS arming their A-10s for a mission. They are preparing an AGM-65 Maverick for attaching to the aircraft. (DoD)

renewed missions (by day and night), more successful strikes started to be carried out from 5 April. The other strike asset of the RAF was the Tornado. Operating from RAF Bruggen in Germany, an average package of six Tornados were launched between 1930 hours and 0130 hours. Each of the aircraft was loaded with either a pair of Paveway II 1,000lb bombs or a single Paveway III 2,000lb bomb, for missions averaging seven hours. The aircraft were refuelled twice enroute to their targets, and once on the return leg, spending, in the words of one pilot, "twenty minutes being shot at" over the target. At least one Tornado is known to have returned with damage from anti-aircraft fire. As the campaign drew to a close, the strike operations transferred to Solenzara, a French Air Force base in Corsica.[24] The following British munitions were used: 230 1,000lb LGBs, 226 Paveway II 1,000lb general purpose bombs, 18 Paveway III 2,000lb LGBs, 532 BL755 cluster bombs and six ALARM missiles.[25]

Until the start of the air campaign, the French ALA had not been able to launch night strike missions with its types: Jaguar As, MirageF-1CTs and even the latest Mirage 2000Ds. Prior to the commencement of the operation, a batch of 22 PDL-CT and CTS laser targeting pods was received for the AS-30L missile on the Mirage 2000Ds, which enabled their launching at night. Indeed, during a night sortie on 26 May, two Mirage 2000Ds launched up to eight AS-30Ls. The GBU-12 and GBU-22 LGBs were also integrated on the Mirage 2000D, and the first adapters were introduced by the beginning of OAF. Guided GBU-12/Paveway II bombs were dropped against targets which were designated by the ATLIS (Automatic Tracking Laser Illumination System) container carried by veteran Jaguar As or the Mirage 2000. The Jaguars, as a strike platform, carried LGBs up to 1,000 kg. Both types were used in daily missions, but in each of them only a single Jaguar had use of the ATLIS laser

A weapons load team use an MHU-83 B-E lift truck to load an AGM-65 Maverick missile onto an A-10 Thunderbolt II on 10 April 1999. The 81st EFS would move on the next day to Gioia del Colle, continuing operations from this base until the end of OAF. (NAC)

designator. PDL-CT and CTS pods were not integrated on Super Étandards which were on the aircraft carrier *Foch*, so they continued with their 'classic' operation. Older Mirage F-1CTs from Colmar deployed to Istrana Air Base between 16 May and 25 June, carrying out 70 missions with over 300 flying hours, dropping 77 GBU-12 bombs on Serbian targets.[26] Each French package was systematically preceded by German ECR Tornados or American F-16CJs, which cleared the way of SAMs for the 'French mud-movers'.

French strike aviation had to carry out three refuellings during each mission over the FRY. The exception was the carrier-borne Super Étandards, which only needed a single refuelling. The withdrawal of the *Foch* on 1 June due to problems with its catapult launching system had the effect of downsizing the French aviation contribution in the last 10 days of OAF. Its aircraft fleet undertook 878 operational sorties over Serbia, Kosovo and Montenegro, with around 15 sorties a day on average.[27] In around 420 strike missions, French pilots dropped up to eight laser-guided air-to-surface missiles, 314 LGBs and 398 unguided bombs.[28]

Ground crew of the 494th EFS prepare to attach the guidance system to a GBU-24 laser-guided bomb at Aviano Air Base, Italy, in the early stages of Operation Allied Force. (NAC)

After Operation Allied Force commenced, French Air Force authorities discovered that LGBs were missing in their inventory. There were no 1,000lb bombs, and only limited numbers of 500lb and 2,000lb bombs in stock. A number of LGBs had to be borrowed from the French Navy. The French military authorities concluded that they had been caught out because the air campaign had lasted longer than expected. During OAF, additional LGBs to the value of US$130 million were ordered.[29]

In general, NATO fighter-bomber (strike) aviation used bombs ranging from 250–1,000kg. Various types were used to attack the targets on the ground: standard Mk-82, Mk-83 and Mk-84 bombs, GBU-12/14/16/22/24 and Paveway (GBU-27/28) laser-guided bombs, GBU-31/32 JDAM, CBU-87/89/97 and most likely CBU-102 cluster bombs, British BL755s (used also by the RV i PVO), and various air-to-ground missiles such as the AGM-65 Maverick, AGM-88 HARM, AGM-130 and AGM-154 JSOW. The most often used were Mk-82 and GBU-12 bombs.[30]

Staff Sergeant Barry Muller (left) and Airman Joseph Sirek prepare to attach a GBU-24 laser-guided bomb to an F-15E Strike Eagle at Aviano Air Base. (NAC)

In the early days of the operation, A-FAC missions were carried out with unguided munitions with white phosphorus. However, the practice showed that using the AGM-65 Maverick or 500lb bombs was much more effective for spotting targets for the strike aviation that flew from higher altitudes and were able to see the targets much easier. The use of such ordnance destroyed the target, and the visual effect was much better for the other pilots to carry out further strikes. The A-10s belonging to the 81th EFS developed the practice of flying such missions in pairs.[31]

Although it was estimated that around 1,500 tons of 250–1,000kg bombs were dropped, the RV i PVO ELINT Centre claimed that this

A munitions crew load scores of MK-82 bombs into a B-52H Stratofortress at RAF Fairford in the United Kingdom on 4 May 1999. (NAC)

Armament personnel for the 31st Air Expeditionary Wing load bombs on a transport trailer at Aviano Air Base, Italy, on 29 March 1999. The 31st AEW was the largest expeditionary force of its kind in US Air Force history. The total score for the whole Wing, with all American and NATO assets, was 8,241 combat missions, with a total of 37,886 combat hours for all types. The two squadrons of the original 31st FW flew 2,403 of the combat sorties. (NAC)

figure was probably higher.[32] In the earliest stage of the campaign, some of the NATO pilots were not able to discover and identify the target due to bad weather conditions in the area, mostly heavy cloud cover. In cases where the target remained impossible to locate, unused ordnance – along with wing or underbelly fuel tanks – was dropped, upon orders from the ABCCC, in the border area toward Albania or over the Adriatic Sea.

The European allies achieved different levels of success in ground attack missions. Hitting static targets proved very successful, but in the case of mobile targets, results were poor. Even overestimated NATO figures on the destruction of such targets were poor compared to the results of US strike aviation. Besides the US only the RAF and ALA had the capability to use precision munition (LGBs). Bad weather over Kosovo often provoked frustration, especially with the RAF crews.[33] This was clear confirmation that new weaponry had not managed to solve the problems caused by bad weather conditions or poor visibility over the targets, and that the enemy could use such conditions for the manoeuvre of its forces on the ground.[34]

The other problem for the NATO strike (and bomber) aviation was the absence of a strict military task, such as taking a certain position or perimeter, holding a defence or front line, supporting its own forces, or destroying the enemy forces or part of it. There was no proper verification of the effects of strike/bomber aviation on the ground. It was evident that Serbian/VJ forces changed their tactics and operations according to those of the NATO aviation. The only task of the NATO strike aviation was to destroy as many Serbian/VJ systems or vehicles as they could discover. Nobody could actually say during the whole course of the operation what 'victory', in a military sense, would consist of.

Bombers

During the air campaign, only the USAF used classic strategic bombers, for the simple reason that the European allies did not have such assets. The Americans used three types: the B-52 Stratofortress, B-1 Lancer (Bones) and, making its debut in this operation, the stealth B-2A Sprit. The USAF bomber units were based in CONUS air bases, the USAFE having not had any bomber units since the peak of the Cold War.[35]

The average number of bomber sorties was between two and four per day. The most active were the B-1B crews, who flew almost every day from the beginning of OAF. B-1s were part of the wider strike packages, with SEAD group protection. They were attacking targets throughout FRY territory. There were usually two Bones in each strike package, and their crews used voice and/or radio communication crypto-protection. When they were used against targets in the northern part of the FRY, they arrived through the airspace of Germany and Hungary. In the case of attacking targets in southern Serbia and Kosovo, they flew via the airspace of Italy and Albania.[36]

A typical B-1B combat load comprised 84 Mk-82 bombs. Other types of ordnance were not used by this type. The airframes, marked

Five B-1B Lancers were forward-deployed from CONUS to RAF Fairford in the United Kingdom to take part in OAF missions. The Lancers could carry up to 84 Mark-82 conventional 500lb bombs. (DoD)

B-52H Stratofortresses gathered from several bomber squadrons, seen here at RAF Fairford during the early stages of Operation Allied Force. A total of 25 airframes from 11, 20 and 96 BS from 2nd BW, Barksdale AFB, and 23BS from 5th BW, Minot AFB, were deployed at Fairford under the control of 20th EBS, 2nd Air Expeditionary Group. All of the missions against Serbia, using either cruise missiles or classic ordnance, were undertaken from this base. (DoD)

USAF ground crew manoeuvre an AGM-86 air-launched cruise missile toward the bomb bay of a B-52H Stratofortress, belonging to the one of the Barksdale-based squadrons, at RAF Fairford on 25 March 1999. (NAC)

as Block D, used in OAF were modified using the programme for conventional munitions and had improvements for encountering air defences.[37] The B-1s were also fitted with the Raytheon AN/ALE-50 fibre-optic towed repeater jammer and decoy system stored in launchers scabbed on the rear fuselage. Crews of B-1Bs received facts and figures on targets directly from the CAOC, while already flying close or inside of FRY airspace. One of the 37th Bomber Squadron 'Bones' was used as the source for spare parts, nicknamed 'Canbird'. It was the practice not to wait long for the delivery of spare parts from CONUS, since the latest Block D modification was used.[38]

A true veteran of the Cold War, the B-52H Stratofortress was used from the start of the OAF campaign. Their primary task was launching C-ALCM AGM-86C conventional cruise missiles on the first night of 24 March 1999. Each AGM-86C was armed with a conventional blast fragmentation warhead, designed specifically to provide precision strikes against long-range, strategic 'soft' targets, guided by an onboard GPS. Enroute to launch areas, the bombers received updated weather, target and threat information courtesy of the Multi-Source Tasking System. Once released, a second missile could not be fired for at least one minute after its predecessor. Two nights later, following the completion of a massive cruise missile attack mission over the Balkans, four B-52s continued to their home bases in the United States. During the following days, RAF Fairford became host for many B-52s from different bomber wings from CONUS. In this period, the problem was transport of the C-ALCM missiles, which were ferried directly on B-52s to Fairford. In one case, they were brought even from an air base on Diego Garcia in the Indian Ocean. Such problems and the duration of OAF led to a decision that the role of the B-52s had to be changed. Instead of a cruise missile launching platform, the B-52s started to be used as conventional bombers until the end of the campaign. They thereafter appeared in the FRY skies loaded with 45 Mk-82 500lb bombs or 18 Mk-84 2,000lb bombs, or with a combination of both types. These were classic 'dumb' bombs, without any guidance, except for the GPS which was used by the crew. A few B-52s arrived at Fairford armed with GBU-10 LGBs, but there is no evidence that they were ever used.[39]

From 23 May 1999, B-52s became active on a daily basis in continuous bombing of VJ targets in Kosovo's border area with

Members of the 393rd Bomb Squadron use an MB-2 tow tractor to push a B-2 Spirit stealth bomber back to a hangar at Whiteman AFB to conduct post-flight maintenance checks upon its return from successfully performing a combat sortie on day 30 of Operation Allied Force. (NAC)

Albania, between the city of Prizren and Mount Paštrik. B-52s operated in pairs, approaching Kosovo through Albanian airspace. Each bomber had a separate target, but all were in the same area. They bombed targets from altitudes between 38,000ft and 41,000ft, sometimes without visual contact through clouds or fog. During several missions they went for 'carpet bombing' using a full load of 45 Mk-82 bombs.[40] On 3 June, one of the B-52s carried out a 'carpet bombing' attack with 45 M-117 Minol bombs. Any bombs which remained inside the bomb-bays after the strikes were dropped in two zones of the Adriatic Sea – EJA-5 (Middle Adriatic) and EJA-3 (North Adriatic) – or else off the coast near Bristol in the UK, at a location designated as 'Danger area D-112N off Lundy Island'. B-52 bombers operated over Kosovo with the mandatory protection of SEAD groups. For increased security, B-52s used the same callsigns as their strike packages they were assigned to, which were only decided on the day.

B-52s were used to launch AGM-142 HAVE NAP standoff missiles, built on the same basis as Israeli Popeye missiles. These had a range around 50 miles and had an 800lb fragmentation or penetrating warhead. AGM-142s were mounted on the fuselage side of the B-52, coupled with the AN/ASW-55 data link pod. During Operation Allied Force, only two AGM-142s were launched. It was reported that B-52s carried AGM-129 cruise missiles, but there was no confirmation from either side that this weapon was used during the operation.[41]

Doubts have been cast on the enthusiasm shown by USAF bomber unit commanders regarding the effect the B-52s had on Jugoslav Army troops in the border area with Albania, some having even said they killed up to 800 VJ soldiers. Historian Tim Ripley pointed out: "British intelligence officials who have visited the site, say those figures are exaggerated and that the Yugoslav soldiers in question saw contrails of the approaching B-52s and were able to make a quick exit from the target zone."[42] American national security analyst Anthony Cordesman also commented that "no evidence has since surfaced to support such claims".[43]

A total of 25 B-52 and nine B-1 bombers were engaged during the OAF campaign. Fluctuation in the number of B-52s deployed was high, with the largest number deployed at one time being 14. Several of the airframes flew back to their CONUS bases before returning to Fairford to take part in the campaign again. On the contrary, B-1s were not rotated, with the best available airframes being chosen for participation in the operation. Using information gathered from SIGINT/ELINT, the Yugoslav RV i PVO estimated that both these types dropped around 500 tons of bombs. USAF figures reveal that both types flew over 400 sorties from Fairford, dropping a total of 11,000 Mk-82 and 20 Mk-84 bombs and firing 75 C-ALCM and two AGM-142 missiles.[44]

The B-2A Sprit stealth bombers made their operational debut in Operation Allied Force, being an impressive illustration of the USAF strategy of 'Global Reach – Global Power'. Stealth B-2As were the first type to use GPS guided standard bombs, by using the guidance kit mounted over the bomb. It was a Joint Direct Attack Munition, or JDAM. Initially, the B-52s and F/A-18s were to be the first aircraft to carry JDAM, but Pentagon officials decided that the B-2As, then going through operational tests to develop non-nuclear capabilities, would be the best choice.[45]

At the start of Allied Force, the 509th BW at Whiteman Air Force Base, Missouri, had 19 B-2As at its disposal. Of these, 10 were currently under modification to Block 30. USAF official figures showed that during OAF, only six B-2A airframes were used in combat missions. For a single sortie, B-2As usually deployed 16 JDAM 2,000lb bombs, but there were also other payload configurations. USAF figures reveal 656 JDAM bombs (1.3 million pounds) were dropped in 49 missions from Whiteman.[46] Among these were 609 GBU-31/1 Mk-84s, 43 GBU-31/3 BLU-109s for fortified targets and four GBU-37/B 4.700lb penetration bombs, or 'bunker busters'. It is important to note that B-2As were used against static military or civil infrastructure targets but were not employed against VJ/MUP targets in Kosovo. USAF estimations stated that 87 percent of the GBU bombs dropped hit their targets. The facts show that B-2s carried out just 1 percent of the total number of missions, but the quantity of ordnance used was 11 percent of the total dropped on the FRY and Serbia. US officials remarked that the B-2 had been successfully tested in "very hard combat zone". It was noted that in many cases, changes of the targets occurred prior to entering FRY airspace.[47]

The B-2A missions were exclusively nocturnal. No matter what their stealth capabilities regarding radars, the RV i PVO SIGINT/

ELINT Centre managed to monitor B-2A activity through constantly listening to air traffic in Europe. They noted that B-2s had an attached fighter escort while flying over Europe and carried out several air refuelling 'stops'. B-2s were flown at altitudes over 40,000ft, to avoid any air traffic and to remain outside the maximal altitude range of Serbian air defence missiles, during the combat phase of the sorties. During talks between RV i PVO and USAF representatives in 2005, Colonel Vujić, commanding officer of the 280th ELINT Centre, explained: "We registered 14 B-2 sorties, always flying in pairs." According to Vujić, his operators identified B-2s over Serbia on several dates, including: 24 March and 17, 18, 19 and 22 April. On 15 May, he said, missions were unable to be carried out due to bad weather over the targets. He added that B-2s were only used against targets in northern Serbia (above the 44th parallel). When asked how they managed to discover such details of B-2 missions, Colonel Vujić told the USAF officials:

> As every other aircraft, [the] B-2 had to report to some air traffic control, when it enters its area. They had specific callsigns, [using a] tremendously powerful radio. For experienced listeners who monitor air traffic for 30 years there were no dilemmas that this was [a] B-2, which fly by night. [Then] it reported to district air traffic control at Brindisi, but it continued north and entered our air space from [the] north. It attacked the targets north of the 45th parallel, in the Belgrade area, upon already ordered specific targets.[48]

These included targets of high importance which had to be destroyed with minimal collateral damage. Such targets were in Belgrade, including the Federal Ministry of Defence, General Staff, Ministry of Interior/HQ of the MUP forces, Federal Directorate for Supplies (which turned out to be the Chinese Embassy), HQ of the Socialist Party and Serbian state television. In some missions, B-2s were used to finish off targets which standard fighter-bomber strike packages had been unable to destroy, including bridges over the Danube, an oil refinery in the Novi Sad area and some of the targets at Batajnica Air Base.

It was later said that JDAMs were used in other ways which had not been anticipated. For instance, one mission took out the Žeželjev bridge which spanned the Danube at Novi Sad. "We didn't expect [the weapon] to be used against bridges," said Louis Cerrato, chief engineer of the JDAM Squadron at Eglin AFB, Florida, who worked on the weapon from its earliest days, but "the pinpoint accuracy amazed all of us". During the Balkan air war, he said "they used almost the whole first lot" of JDAMs.[49]

Flying in this type of bomber was an enormous challenge for its pilots. They would take off from their base in Missouri, make their way over the eastern United States, Atlantic Ocean and Western Europe, then carry out the strikes over Serbia in night conditions, under pressure from the Serbian air defences, before making their way back using the same transatlantic route. Typical missions lasted for around 29 hours, of which 14 hours were taken in reaching Serbia. Sometimes, the mission could last up to 34 hours due to the developing situation over the targets. The B-2s used to operate in pairs or as a single ship against designated targets, using different directions of attack. In a quite traditional looking aircraft cockpit, and with a crew of only two, missions caused the most extreme psychological and physical strain, leading to numerous complaints by B-2 crews. At the beginning of OAF, B-2s were flown by only the most experienced pilots. Later, upon the instigation of the 509th Wing commander, other pilots were also used. By the end of Operation Allied Force, of the 509th BW's 54 pilots, 51 had managed to carry out at least a single B-2 combat mission. A number of them logged two missions, and one pilot even managed three missions from Whiteman to Serbia and back.[50]

The USAF revealed that the 509th Wing maintained six airworthy airframes at any given time. During the campaign, one mission was cancelled due to malfunction, a second because of bad weather over the target (which confirmed the claims of the RV i PVO 280th ELINT Centre) and a third because the target was cancelled. After each mission, upon its return to Whiteman, each B-2 needed between four and seven days to be prepared for another sortie. The B-2s mainly went through checks to renew their special anti-radar coating.[51]

During their missions, B-2As were backed up by a SEAD group and fighter escort. Without them, a B-2 would not enter into Serbian airspace. However, the 509th BW HQ claimed that escorts were not needed, and that B-2s were fully capable of independent operations from take-off to return to home base. The support of the EA-6B Prowlers was only used because "they were available". During the mission launched on 14 April, B-2s attacked targets around Belgrade, escorted by a SEAD group from the 22nd EFS at Spangdahlem. The SEAD group was engaged in fierce fighting with the Serbian air defences, with a large number of SAM missiles fired during the early hours of 15 April. As well as this standard protection carried out by the other types of aviation, the B-2A had its own electronic warfare system, AN/APR-50, which was considered an effective device to enable independent operations by the bomber.[52]

The commander of the RV i PVO 280th ELINT Centre noted: "All facts concerning B-2 appearance we send to Operations centre. But the conditions for claiming it were very unfavourable."[53] Despite the lack of any evidence, some of the air defence personnel still believe that they managed to bring down one B-2 during Allied Force.[54]

SEAD Aviation

'Suppression of Enemy Air Defence', or simply SEAD, was defined by the US Department of Defense (DoD) as "That activity that neutralizes, destroys, or temporarily degrades surface-based enemy air defenses by destructive and/or disruptive means."[55] SEAD aviation became a very important NATO/USAF asset during the Allied Force campaign. SEAD groups were engaged from the very beginning of the operation, tasked to discover, jam, neutralise or destroy the radar and SAM systems of the RV i PVO. The basic platforms used for SEAD were USAF F-16CJ Fighting Falcons and USN/USMC EA-6B Prowlers, operating from Aviano, Spangdahlem and USS *Theodore Roosevelt*, armed with AGM-88 HARM missiles. Some European allies also contributed in SEAD missions, mostly with their Tornados, but to a much lesser extent compared to the American assets. As RAF Wing Commander Brookes summarised in a short but succinct sentence, "Europe depended on the US for EW expertise and for most suppression of Serb air defences."[56]

Rules of engagement during OAF did not allow for strike packages to enter into FRY airspace without escort by SEAD groups. Such groups were thus engaged as mandatory participants in every strike package that entered FRY airspace, with the task to protect the strike package by neutralising Serbian air defences. SEAD groups were looking out for the Neva and Kub (SAM-3 and SAM-6) firing positions. Prior to their entrance to FRY airspace, SEAD groups would receive information on the latest known positions of Serbian radar and missile systems, which had been gathered by crews of RC-135s or AWACS. The SEAD group would enter FRY airspace some 10–15 minutes prior to the main strike package and maintain

Two HARM shooters, F-16CJs belonging to the 52th Fighter Wing (from their home base of Spangdahlem in Germany), during refuelling on 9 March 1999, some two weeks prior to the start of Operation Allied Force. F-16CJs were the basic SEAD platforms during the operation. The F-16CG above is equipped with an unusual payload that consisted of an AGM-65 Maverick (starboard side) and AGM-88 HARM (port). (NAC)

their cover while orbiting in the area where the strike package was engaged. They usually flew at altitudes from 20,000–25,000ft. SEAD groups usually provoked a response from missile units of the Serbian air defence systems and if any of those units should make a wrong move by turning on their radar and radiating for longer than a couple of seconds, the SEAD groups would immediately fire their HARM missiles. Their time of reaction was a matter of seconds. Communication was conducted through the IDM modem and secure channels. The RV i PVO counted some 40 sorties by the SEAD groups per day, with that number later increasing to 80. This serves as confirmation that Serbian air defences remained active until the end of campaign. Difficult weather conditions did not influence the SEAD operations, and they continued whenever the other types of combat aviation were not engaged. The usual composition of a SEAD group was between two and four Prowlers and between four and eight F-16CJs.[57] A SEAD group would enter FRY airspace first, and was also the last to leave it. Despite the reinforcements that occasionally arrived from the US, there was always a shortage of SEAD aircraft due to their constant need to protect the strike packages. In several cases, the SEAD group would abandon FRY air space for refuelling and return to cover the next strike package that entered the fray.

The basic SEAD platform within the USAF was the F-16CJ. The core of the SEAD fleet were two squadrons (Nos 22 and 23 EFS) belonging to the 52nd Fighter Wing at Spangdahlem Air Base in Germany. At the start of OAF, from the first night on 24 March, No. 23 EFS was at Aviano with 19 (later 20) 'CJs'. After the unplanned extension of the OAF, on 6 April the 22nd EFS joined SEAD operations directly from Spangdahlem, marking the first time that such sorties had been launched from German soil since the Second World War. These lengthy sorties involved F-16CJs flying in packages with F-117As of the 9th EFS that had deployed to Spangdahlem on 4 April, reaching Serbia via Germany and Hungary. A week later, they would be supported by the 78th EFS deployed from the 20th FW at Shaw AFB, which arrived at Aviano on 13/14 April and took part in SEAD missions two days later.[58]

F-16CJs carried two AGM-88 HARM missiles and an AN/ASQ-213 HARM Targeting System (HTS), a small pod mounted on the

Equipped with AN/ALQ-99 ECM pods, an EA-6B Prowler belonging to the USMC VMAQ-1 squadron takes off for a mission over Serbia. (DoD)

right chin station used for precision strikes on targets and displaying the data directly to the pilot's Head-up-Display. Experience from OAF showed that HTS could display the information to the pilot from the 180-degree forward field of the aircraft. For better cover of enemy territory, CJs used to operate in four-ship formations.[59]

The other American SEAD platform was the EA-6B Prowler. During Allied Force, a total of eight USN/USMC Prowler squadrons were engaged, operating from Aviano Air Base (VAQ-134, 138, 140 and 209 and VMAQ-1, 2 and 4) and USS *Theodore Roosevelt* (VAQ-141).[60] Prowlers, which had been in the theatre since 1994 and were used in the Bosnia air campaign, were employed in 1999 as jammers and 'window openers', meaning that they could break into the Serbian RV i PVO electronic space and enable the entrance of the larger SEAD groups or strike packages. The Prowler was slower than the earlier EF-111 Raven and was a standoff jammer rather than a plane that escorted strike aircraft into defended areas. Prowlers would later join the SEAD groups by firing their AGM-88 HARM missiles against various targets on the ground.

Prowlers usually used three AN/ALQ-99 ECM (Electronic Countermeasures) containers below the wings and/or fuselage, coupled with the AN/ALQ-149 communication jammer and AN/ALQ-126 air defence radar jammer, both mounted in a housing on the tail. Those Prowlers which operated from USS *Theodore Roosevelt* were mounted with two HARM missiles, while those flying from Aviano did not have HARM in their inventory, instead carrying underwing fuel tanks because of the greater distance they had to cross to the area of operations. The Aviano Prowlers were usually paired with SEAD groups equipped with F-16CJs or European Tornados. According to the estimations of the RV i PVO ELINT Centre, when they entered FRY airspace, the EA-6Bs would jam Serbian systems in a VHF range between 118 and 150 Mhz.[61]

The usage of the Prowlers was considered to be one of the best episodes of the whole campaign for the allies. The constant need for their use led to the engagement of 50 percent of the whole available Prowler fleet. As noted earlier, they were needed to provide protection for each strike package. Any aircraft which entered FRY airspace without their protection were much easier prey for the Serbian air defences, as was the case with two USAF aircraft that were claimed on 27 March and 2 May. Many of these daily repeated missions caused fatigue among the already aging fleet of Prowlers.

The fleet of Prowlers, the only tactical jamming platform then in the US inventory, was heavily overtaxed, and there was also a shortage of flight crews. Undertaking electronic jamming, US Navy Prowlers flew 671 combat missions and logged 2,997.4 flying hours, whereas Marine Corps Prowlers flew some 377 missions[62] and amassed 1,713.4 flight hours. Both services thus had average mission times of approximately four-and-a-half hours.[63] Facts and figures are available for the tempo of use of Prowlers belonging to the US Marine Corps. Each of their EA-6B Prowlers had an average of 95 flying hours per month – one even logged 123 flying hours in a single month. The planned average had been 36 hours. USMC statistics insisted that they managed to maintain 100 percent airworthiness during Operation Allied Force. Their Prowlers fired a total of 57 AGM-88 HARM missiles. A few of the platform's shortcomings were also noted, such as the inability to use the night vision devices and lack of Link 16 and Wideband data reception. Nevertheless, the Prowler proved to be a useful and widely used platform, which influenced the decision for its modernisation and further use until 2015.[64]

Some of the SEAD missions during the operation were carried out by European NATO allies, using the Tornado as their only available platform for such a task. This type was used by the German and Italian air forces, and later by the RAF. The Germans and Italians carried out 8 percent of the total of SEAD missions and fired 35 percent of the missiles. Later analysis of missile debris discovered all over the theatre cast a shadow over the practice of firing a large number of HARMs as the most successful method for protection of the strike packages.[65]

As a part of OAF, the German Air Force was used solely in SEAD and recce missions. A detachment from the German 32nd JaBo was based at Piacenza-San Damiano with 10 Tornado IDS, tasked to act as a SEAD unit and also equipped with recce containers. The Italian AMI took part in SEAD missions for the first time in their history. They were operating both versions (ECR-IT and IDS) belonging to the 155 Gruppo at Piacenza-San Damiano Air Base. Italian pilots used to carry out up to four sorties in SEAD groups, and occasionally IDS Tornados were equipped with HARM missiles.[66] The RAF used their Tornados operating from Bruggen Air Base in Germany, and later from Solenzara Air Base in Corsica. They were used in the later stages of the operation, firing their MATRA/BAe ALARM (Air-Launched Anti-Radar Missile) munitions and having

A Tornado of JbG-32, based at Piacenza AB in Italy (with a home base at Lechfeld in Germany), approaches the refuelling drogue of a USAFE KC-135R during OAF. (NAC)

a secondary role as a SEAD platform.[67] In an *AFM Magazine* article, Jon Lake pointed out that the RAF fired six ALARM missiles during the operation, stressing their "much greater accuracy" than of the AGM-88 HARM fired by the USAF and German Air Force.[68]

The main missile used in SEAD missions during OAF was the AGM-88 HARM, which was carried by all types of SEAD aircraft. HARMs were fired from middle altitudes and usually outside or at the edge of the effective SAM combat radius. After the detection and identification of radar signals (and receiving the authorisation to fire), the pilot would fire his HARM against the identified target. Operation Allied Force showed that HARM's extreme speed was a serious advantage in combating the Serbian air defences. On the other hand, it became obvious that HARM did not possess the power to destroy the target radar or nearby equipment if the hit was not direct. Although the RV i PVO estimated that AGM-88 HARM missiles "did not show a great efficiency", most of the neutralised SAM units and casualties were actually caused by HARM missiles.[69]

Once RV i PVO radar units became aware that HARM missiles quickly caught the electromagnetic signal from their radars and subsequently arrived very fast at the target, they soon started improvising to downgrade the threat from this source. Using IRZ (Imitators of Radar Illumination) and improvised angle reflectors, they managed to defend their radar positions with a degree of success: HARM missiles would hit the imitator or angle reflector, or even the empty space between the radar and angle reflector. A curiosity in this matter was the case of the 1st Radar Company of the 20th AS Battalion, which was deployed at Rupov Salas farm. During an attack on 30 March, a HARM missile hit a plough which was 100 metres behind the radar, which the missile warhead most likely mistook to be the target. It is also worth noting that a couple of HARM missiles fired upon Serbian air defence targets were later discovered in neighbouring Bulgaria.[70]

Other types of unguided and guided munitions were used for the destruction of SAM firing positions in the next phase of combating the Serbian air defences, which was titled 'Destruction of Enemy Air Defence', or DEAD. Information on the current location of certain Serbian PVO missile units would be passed to the strike package when it was already in the air – mostly F-15Es and F-16CGs. They would then attack the discovered SAM position with PGMs (Precision Guided Missiles) or cluster bombs in an attempt to destroy it completely.

According to RV i PVO figures, there were 222 strikes on 98 locations of the Serbian air defence units, with more than 250 HARM missiles fired. They said there were 210 'confirmed' firings – but it was estimated that the actual "number was certainly higher" – and that a total of 14 attacks were carried out on 13 SAM units with 36 guided and unguided bombs as part of DEAD missions.[71] NATO claimed a much higher number of AGM-88 HARMs launched by the USAF and European allies: a total of 743. The 52nd Wing stated that more than 300 HARMs were launched by their F-16CJs. Moreover, the

Sent from its home base at Shaw AFB, South Dakota, the 78th EFS strengthened the SEAD capacities engaged in Operation Allied Force. Here, ground crew mount an AIM-120 missile on the wing of an F-16CJ on 19 April 1999. (NAC)

German Air Force revealed that it had carried out 394 Tornado missions with total of 244 HARM missiles fired. Post-campaign US analysis noted that HARM missiles were fired on a much lower number of confirmed targets, and that in many cases they were fired as a precaution.

USAF SEAD pilots were also engaged in other missions, such as battle interdiction, A-FAC, patrolling the CAP system (Defensive Counter Air) and assistance in Combat SAR missions. Most notable were two CSAR missions on 27 March and 2 May to rescue downed USAF pilots. SEAD groups remained in the air for 10 hours and more. In other cases, SEAD groups acted as fighter protection for the strike packages.[72] On 4 May, for example, one of the SEAD pilots claimed the commander of the 204th Fighter Regiment over Valjevo by firing an AMRAAM missile while the strike package was abandoning FRY airspace.

For most of the 52nd FW pilots, these were their first combat SEAD missions. Night missions were a novelty for the whole SEAD community engaged during OAF, since their previous SEAD missions over Iraq had been carried out in daylight. There were many new procedures to be carried out, such as night refuelling and recognition of friendly strike packages during the mission, especially in the attack phase. Finally, they had to learn how to avoid any SAM missiles fired at them. SEAD pilots later praised the Serbian air defence for its sustainability and skilled manoeuvring. As the SEAD pilots became more experienced, the Serbian air defence also became more skilful in avoiding their missiles.[73] SEAD missions comprised 21.5 percent of all NATO combat missions during OAF (4,538 out of 21,111). Nevertheless, the Serbian air defence managed to remain a threat until the end of the campaign.

Some of the leaflets dropped over Belgrade by USAF PSYOPS during the campaign. They warned Serbs "Why don't you ask Milošević?", "No fuel, no electricity, no market, no freedom, no future – Milošević" and "NATO Strikes". (Author's collection)

Electronic Countermeasures and PSYOPs

Throughout the campaign, NATO and the USAF carried out constant ECM operations against the VJ (RV i PVO) forces all across the FR Yugoslavia. Jamming was carried out by the attacking formations or in certain zones as part of the preparations for the airstrikes.

The 280th ELINT Centre registered the ECM at the VVF-UHF OPSEG between 118 and 150 Mhz. Jamming of VVF-UVF frequencies was carried out by EC-130H Compass Call which orbited in Bosnian airspace.[74]

According to RV i PVO ELINT/SIGINT, the EC-130E Commando Solo which was used for special operations and PSYOPS started from 3 April and continued its operations on a daily basis between 1100 hours and 1700 hours. After taking off from Ramstein for a mission, it was occasionally refuelled and was escorted by a couple of fighters.

EC-130H Compass Call arrived from Aviano and usually operated in the airspace of BiH, where it orbited for around six hours with refuelling. Monitoring its work, the Yugoslavs noted that strike packages waited for this aircraft to arrive and start its ECM. The start of its jamming was announced with the signal 'Music' or 'Noise'. A total of 75 Commando Solo missions and 68 Compass Call missions were identified.[75]

As a part of PSYOPS, a number of different leaflets were dropped over Serbia. According to the USAF, this leaflet operation started on 3 and 4 April. They were noted some time later over FRY capital Belgrade. Leaflets were small in size and their text was adjusted according to the particular phase of OAF. There was some archaic language in certain messages written on the leaflets. A total of 104.5 million leaflets in over 30 different versions were dropped from MC-130H Combat Talon, belonging to the 7th SOS. Such operations were invented and coordinated by the Joint Psychological Task Force, a unit formed in Ramstein in February 1999 among the personnel of several PSYOPS units.

Besides the leaflets, PSYOPS included what were thought to be a better way of informing Milošević's opponents in Serbia about certain information, namely a TV programme that was broadcast on television channel 21 and a radio programme at several frequencies. The television programme and signal were emitted from EC-130E Commando Solo, belonging to the 193rd SOW.[76] It took off from Ramstein and orbited in Hungarian airspace. The TV programme, titled 'Allied Voice Radio and Television', could be seen two to four times per day when the aircraft was in the air. The programme continued to be transmitted after the war, and the final TV broadcast was registered on 27 June.[77]

Reconnaissance

Aerial reconnaissance was only ever carried out in daylight. According to RV i PVO figures, there were 74 identified missions by NATO's reconnaissance aviation. The average number of sorties were between two and four per day, but the recce aircraft did not operate on a daily basis during Allied Force. The RV i PVO stated

A fleet of the RC-135 Rivet Joints of the 55th Wing, whose home base was at Offut AFB, Nebraska. This wing maintained a detachment of its aircraft at RAF Mildenhall in the UK during Operation Allied Force. (DoD)

that "recce aircraft were not noted in every strike package and they operated upon certain need. In the last days of the Operation, they used to fly independently."[78]

Most of the (tactical) reconnaissance missions were carried out over Kosovo, and in most cases these were BDA missions, flown by the French and German air forces, using Mirage F-1CRs and Tornados. It was normal practice that they were attached to the SEAD groups. They usually flew at altitudes from 3,000–5,000 metres. In the northern part of the FRY, recce missions were carried out by the ALA Mirage F-1CRs flying in single or two-ship formation at altitudes above 7,500 metres. Besides the regular set of aerial photo cameras (Raphael/SLAR pod) and containers used in standard, IR or radar mode, they used the Desire digital aerial photo container, which could deliver top-quality images to the ground station in near real time. The other French type flown in these missions was the naval Étandard IVP, which was used in standard aerial photo operations.[79] The RAF deployed a single Canberra PR.9 of No. 39 Squadron from RAF Marham to Gioia del Colle, which started operating over the theatre in late January 1999.[80]

Looking back at the experience of tactical reconnaissance during OAF, it is clear that the USAF did not make great use of tactical recce platforms. It mostly relied on UAVs, strategic recce types or satellite imagery. It is worth noting that General Jumper, a commander of the USAFE, refused to introduce into operations the Virginia ANG 192nd FW, which had F-16s equipped with TARS (Theater Airborne Reconnaissance System) recce containers, despite the positive experience gained by this unit flying from Aviano over the Balkans in May and June 1996.[81]

Contrary to the USAF, the USMC tested the latest recce system in the combat environment, ATARS (Advanced Tactical Airborne Reconnaissance System), using a couple of F/A-18Ds operating from Taszar Air Base in Hungary. The Hornets from VMFA(AW)-332 ('The Moonlighters') and VMFA(AW)-533 ('Hawks') were usually engaged in strike and bombing missions, but they also tested the new system in their flights over Serbia. The system, mounted in the nose of the aircraft, produced numerous digital and multispectral images, which were used for tactical reconnaissance, location of the position of targets and BDA. Until the end of the campaign, ATARS-equipped F/A-18s logged a total of 22 missions. The USMC remarked that the use of this system was successful, as was the general usage of the Hornets flying from Taszar.[82]

Strategic reconnaissance was much in favour among the USAF top brass. It was carried out by the Lockheed U-2R/S in 167 missions, with a usual daily schedule of two to four missions per day. According to RV i PVO SIGINT/ELINT monitoring, the U-2, upon taking off, would report to an AWACS using HAVE Quick – an ECM-resistant system. They then continued up to 60,000ft, which was they standard operational altitude during OAF. While close or inside FRY airspace, the U-2s maintained complete radio silence, which caused a problem for RV i PVO monitors trying to identify details of flight, zones or the objects of their aerial photo activities. Interestingly, the U-2s operated even during the missions carried out by the different strike packages, only flying twice as high as the strikers. They would then abandon FRY airspace simultaneously with the strike packages.

The other strategic reconnaissance platform used during Allied Force was the French ALA Mirage IVP, which contributed the aerial imagery received by the French Helios satellite. They logged a total of 79 missions, operating at altitudes between 42,000ft and 54,000ft. In most cases, they entered FRY airspace from BiH, with Višegrad as their entry point. They used three Omera 36 aerial photo cameras in their missions, which achieved a better performance than the Helios satellite imagery, no matter that they could not transfer the imagery in real time. On 12 April, Mirage IVs operated jointly with tactical Mirage F-1CRs at an altitude of 25,000ft. Mirage IVs performed sonic booms over cities in Serbia during several other missions.[83]

NATO naval aerial reconnaissance assets were also included in Operation Allied Force. Most of the 191 missions (180) were carried during 64 'flying days' by the US Navy EP-3 Orion. Other missions were conducted by Dutch P-3s (10) and an Italian Breguet Atlantic (a single mission). They operated from Sigonella Air Base in Sicily (used also by the USAF U-2s), operating above FRY territorial waters or in the airspaces of Macedonia, Albania and parts of Croatia and BiH. The aircraft mostly flew at medium altitudes between 14,000ft and 29,000ft. They recorded the position of potential targets, and the RV i PVO estimated that they were also used for BDA in real time.

Finally, naval patrol aviation was engaged during OAF too. The US Navy and Dutch Naval Aviation Service operated the standard Lockheed P-3 Orion. They operated in the Strait of Otranto in the southern part of Adriatic or near FRY territorial waters. The RV i PVO registered 41 such missions (40 USN and a single Dutch), but it was believed that more missions than this were carried out. Patrolling P-3s were active in supporting the launching of cruise missiles from ships, and later in the observation and control of sea traffic that that was heading to FRY ports. Since there were no clashes with the Yugoslav Navy, which remained inactive in its ports, the patrol aviation was used against other VJ targets. In such missions, a total of 14 AGM-84 SLAM missiles were fired.[84]

An S-3 Viking attached to the Air Anti-Submarine Squadron VS-24 on USS *Theodore Roosevelt.* (NAC)

Another S-3 Viking returns to the busy flight deck of the same carrier following a strike mission over Kosovo. On the left side, a single E-2C Hawkeye, belonging to VAW-124, is moving slowly over the deck. (NAC)

ELINT

ELINT aviation was heavily tasked, being the most engaged among all the recce platforms in OAF with 552 registered missions during the campaign. The missions were almost continuous, without a break, in a 24-hour regime. ELINT aircraft operated in several standard zones: 'Golly' in Albania and Macedonia, 'Lobster', 'Jenny' and 'Sally' in Bosnia and Herzegovina, and occasionally 'Pam' in FRY territorial waters. Most of the missions were carried by USAF RC-135s and RC-12s, as well as US Navy EP-3s and several different French types.[85]

The Boeing RC-135s belonged to the 55th Wing based at Offutt AFB. Taking off from RAF Mildenhall, they operated independently in ELINT missions. Two 15-hour missions were flown each day during OAF from this air base. During the conflict, the 55th Wing's Rivet Joints flew a total of 232 operational missions. It was revealed that they participated in identifying the take-off of RV i PVO MiG-29s on the first night of Allied Force and that they played an important part in the rescue of the stealth pilot from FRY territory three nights later.[86] Their main task was monitoring the work of the Serbian air defence missile units, and sometimes providing support to the SEAD aviation during their missions. They logged 125 sorties, operating at altitudes between 29,000ft and 35,000ft and remaining in the air for six hours, and even up to 10 hours with refuelling. RV i PVO SIGINT operators noted that the RC-135s during their operational work used different callsigns to those used for flying into the theatre. In communication with other types of combat aviation, RC-135s used two separate callsigns, one during their arrival in the theatre and another during operations, to confuse Serb ELINT operators. Serb monitors admitted that this type had "high accuracy in identifying the activities of the Air Defence and in communication with SEAD groups".[87]

Smaller ELINT platform Beechcraft RC-12s were engaged in the two- or three-ship formations. Belonging to the 1st Battalion of the 205th Military Intelligence Brigade, US Army, based in Germany, the RC-12Ks operated from Taszar prior to the start of OAF, and later from Brindisi and Napoli air bases in southern Italy. They had deployed ground stations for receiving and processing the data. RC-12s operated in pairs to gather and cross the ELINT data from different positions. Their main disadvantage was the need for optical contact with ground stations. The US Army RC-12s logged a total of 203 missions during OAF. Usually, they remained airborne for around five hours, operating at altitudes between 30,000ft and 31,000ft.

Operating from Souda Bay Air Base in Crete, US Navy EP-3s logged a total of 123 missions. They performed their ELINT missions from Macedonian, Albanian and occasionally BiH airspace, usually maintaining altitudes between 20,500ft and 26,500ft and remaining in the air for around six hours. The RV i PVO also registered the Lockheed ES-3 Viking carrier-borne ELINT platform on five operational days, with a total of 10 sorties. They operated in the Adriatic, near FRY territorial waters and from the airspace of Macedonia and Albania. The Vikings remained in the air for some six hours, without refuelling, at altitudes of 24,000–25,000ft.

European allies also contributed to ELINT operation during the Allied Force campaign. The RAF operated with their Nimrods from Practica di Mare in central Italy, with a total of 33 day and night missions. The German Navy used its Bregeut Atlantics in 30 missions, during which they usually changed their callsigns. European ELINT platforms mostly used BiH airspace, maintaining an altitude between 20,000ft and 30,000ft.[88]

The French ALA contributed significant resources to recce and ELINT missions during OAF, accounting for over 20 percent of all recce missions and 8 percent of ELINT missions. The ALA operated many types of platforms in these missions: UAVs, aircraft equipped for ELINT and SIGINT, aerial photo-recce platforms, AWACS and Helios 1A satellites, which operated daily in clear-sky conditions. There were two types of aircraft used in ELINT-SIGINT missions: the DC-8 Sarigue from Evreux Air Base in France and C-160G Gabriel from Istrana Air Base in Italy.[89] The RV i PVO identified Gabriels in 28 missions. The ALA operated just a single aircraft of each type, and it became a burden for the French Air Force in its intention to remain constantly present over the theatre of operations.

Airborne Early Warning

Airborne and Early Warning (AEW) missions were equally important as the combat missions during Operation Allied Force. They were carried out by Boeing E-3 Sentry AWACS types belonging to NATO, the USAF, RAF and ALA. The US Navy operated its Northrop Grumman E-2 Hawkeyes in the same role. The NATO air component at Geilenkirchen in Germany was arguably most recognisable for its AWACS unit. During OAF, the base temporarily hosted the three USAF E-3s from Tinker Air Base in Oklahoma. Geilenkirchen operated around the clock, as did the NATO and USAF crews which orbited in the AWACS in theatre.[90] The RAF engaged its E-3D AEW 1 Sentries from Nos 8 and 23 Squadrons. It was noted that a RAF Sentry crew assisted in the successful rescue of a downed US pilot during OAF.[91]

Among 957 registered sorties, over 50 percent (554) were carried out by the NATO AEW element at Geilenkirchen, and others by the RAF at Aviano (184), the USAF (95), the US Navy (72) operating from Trapani, Preveza, Konia and aircraft carriers, and the French ALA at Avord (52).[92] The average number of missions was around 12 per day, with seven from NATO and the remaining air forces contributing a single aircraft per day. NATO and RAF AEW units operated each day of Allied Force. The ALA launched operations on 50 days during the campaign, the USAF on 46 days and US Navy on 33 days.

The AWACS orbited in the following zones: 'I-5', 'I-5E' and 'I-5S' over the Adriatic Sea, 'Bikini' over Croatia, 'Bluto' over Bosnia Herzegovina and 'M-1' over Hungarian airspace. From the zones over the Adriatic, AWACS controlled air operations south of the 44th parallel, mainly in Kosovo. From the other zones they controlled operations north of the 44th parallel, around Belgrade and in northern Serbia. The presence of AWACS was constant, without cessation. Sometimes there were even four AWACS platforms orbiting over Hungary, Bosnia, Croatia and the Adriatic. The RV i PVO monitors noted that in cases where cruise missiles were prepared for launching and then launched from ships in the Adriatic, AWACS maintained radio silence.[93]

The RV i PVO SIGINT monitors registered the use of several data/communications systems between AWACS and combat aviation, such as HAVE Quick, Quick Draw, Improved Data Modem IDM and IDT. Such communications with the fighters were called 'Candy Data'. Particular systems of communication were used with different types of aviation: Ram Road code with daily combination changes for F-15 crews, an unidentified protected channel for crews of B-1s and a short-wave frequency range for US Navy EP-3s, as well as communication with a ground station based in Hungary which controlled the combat theatre air space.[94]

The work of the AWACS crews was intensive during OAF. The missions were much longer than in peacetime, since the presence of the AWACS was mandatory during all moments of the campaign. A typical Allied Force AWACS mission lasted between 14 and 18 hours, including transit time, mission preparation and debriefing. They controlled a number of take-offs, various sorties in theatre, combat missions and returns to air bases, the total ranging from 300 sorties per day at the beginning of the operation but numbering "by the end no less than 800". The crews had to be strengthened with additional personnel on the missions to allow for continuous operating and tracking of the increased number of simultaneous sorties.[95] American sources insisted on there being differences between the effectiveness of USAF and NATO AWACS, such as communication equipment and different ways of training, which led to lesser capabilities in the NATO AEW units compared with those of the USAF.

Finally, the 606th Air Control Squadron was deployed from the 52nd FW at Spangdahlem to Galatina in southern Italy. The unit, strengthened by personnel from Eglin, Moody and Hurlburt Field units, carried out the longest march in the history of the USAFE, with a total of 88 vehicles travelling over 1,600 miles in five days

A Boeing E-3A AWACS belonging to the NATO air component at Geilenkirchen in Germany. This joint unit carried out over 50 percent of the AWACS missions during the campaign. (nato.int)

to arrive in theatre and provide an additional radar picture with its long-range radars.[96]

Airborne Command and Control

Command of NATO strike and fighter-bomber aviation during the Allied Force campaign was undertaken from an Airborne Battlefield Command and Control Center (ABCCC) that operated inside an EC-130E fuselage which was stationed at Aviano Air Base, and to a lesser extent from carrier-borne E-2C AWACS, which commanded strike packages that were active over Kosovo. The RV i PVO monitors registered that on a couple of occasions, other platforms took over the command role, twice with E-8 J-STARS and in a single case with an E-3 AWACS.[97]

The ABCCCs directly commanded strike packages and received reports from them after the strikes. There were 230 missions registered by the RV i PVO: 157 by EC-130s and 73 by E-2Cs. The US Navy E-2C Hawkeyes started operating from 8 April (when USS *Theodore Roosevelt* arrived in the Adriatic) and continued for another 38 operational days, with two missions per day. The Hawkeyes mostly coordinated the operations of the carrier-borne US Navy strikers over Kosovo.[98]

The presence of the ABCCCs were constant on every day of OAF. They usually remained in the air for around six hours, and up to 10 hours if refuelled. They orbited in two zones: 'Claw' over Albania and 'Crab' over Croatia. During the rescue operations for two downed USAF pilots, on the night of 27/28 March and on 2 May, they used a zone named 'Puffy' in BiH airspace. RV i PVO monitors noted that on 30 May, an ABCCC which orbited in the 'Claw' zone received real-time imagery from a UAV that flew over Kosovo. They also noted that the ABCCC warned the strike packages about "prohibited areas", in which Kosovan UCK forces were believed to be operating.[99]

Boeing E-8 J-STARS of the 93rd Air Control Wing (based at Robins AFB, Georgia) were used for the control of movements on the ground, surveillance, identification and guidance of the strike packages. They were maintained with a crew of 21, with the possibility of a reserve crew on board. The J-STARS had the capability to identify combat vehicles on the ground at a distance of 100km. The aircraft had a compatible communication system for coordination of all types of aviation, and could deliver data on targets to strike aviation in real time. They could also operate as a kind of airborne operations centre. They usually operated at altitudes between 29,000ft and 31,000ft, staying in the air for six to eight hours with additional refuelling. RV i PVO SIGINT/ELINT monitors registered a total of 88 E-8 missions in 74 days of Operation Allied Force. J-STARS usually operated in zone 'Duke' in Macedonian airspace, from where they monitored the movements of the VJ/MUP forces in Kosovo province and guided NATO strike packages against identified targets. During their mission, the E-8s communicated with the leading airplane in a strike package and with tankers during refuelling. The E-8 crews maintained strict discipline in communications, using the HAVE Quick or Ram Road systems to contact strike aviation.[100] At the beginning of OAF, a large amount of data obtained on VJ movements was used by the A-10 crews. After couple of incidents involving civilian casualties, however, it was discovered that VJ/MUP forces had been using refugee convoys or regular civil traffic for protection against attacks from the air. Refugee columns consisting of civilian vehicles or tractors were mistakenly taken for troop movements. After several such tragic mistakes, the information gathered was taken with caution. The E-8s were used throughout the daytime, and when Serb/VJ forces started to carry out night movements, it was considered that J-STARS could be valuable asset flying by night. Despite such requests, the CAOC did not change their pattern of work and consequently the E-8s kept flying only in daylight.

During the operation, the French Army tested a radar system similar to the one that was used on J-STARS but mounted on a helicopter. This was done on two army aviation (ALAT) AS.532 Cougars belonging to Escadrille EHOR, 1st Regiment of Combat Helicopters, based at Phalsbourg. They were equipped with the Horizon radar, which was intended to identify and monitor troop movements on the ground. They were sent to Macedonia on 9 April with a data receiving station and personnel from various French military intelligence units, as well as from the manufacturers. This small unit subsequently became operational on 26 April. The helicopter, which was overloaded with equipment, took a while to reach its operational altitude between 3,600 metres and 4,500 metres. The radar could efficiently operate for two hours, and the helicopter flew inside Macedonian airspace, maintaining a distance of 25km from the FRY/Serbian border. Operating from that distance, the Horizon radar could monitor the situation up to 125km inside Serbian territory. There was, however, a problem with linking up with the CAOC in Vicenza, the gathered data being used only by the French contingent. After 18 days of operations, the CAOC allowed the French Army to have their Horizon representatives in the CAOC, but without permission to exchange any gathered information. Incidentally, on 19 May, SACEUR General Clark was visiting the CAOC and discovered the French team there. They showed him a real-time picture from Kosovo. At that moment, a RV i PVO helicopter was seen carrying out a very low-level flight. Clark asked for confirmation from a USAF E-8, but they did not manage to discover or identify the VJ helicopter. Another check with an RQ-1 UAV which was orbiting over Kosovo confirmed that the French indeed had a clearer picture of events as they happened. On the following day, a decision was made that imagery from the French Horizon radar should be included in support of that provided by the E-8 J-STARS. During the campaign, there were 49 missions involving the Horizon radar, among them 14 nocturnal, with a total of 110 hours in operation.[101]

Unmanned Aerial Vehicles

NATO forces used a variety of Unmanned Aerial Vehicles, or UAVs, for tactical reconnaissance missions during Operation Allied Force. These included types such as the Predator, Hunter, Pioneer and CL-289 Piver, which were launched from bases in Macedonia and operated over Kosovo and Montenegro.[102] UAVs had been flying over Kosovo and Metohija province since mid-October 1998, under the terms of the Milošević–Holbrooke agreement, and monitoring all VJ and MUP movements (as described in Volume 1 of this work). During the winter of 1998/99, RQ-1 Predator UAVs were withdrawn from the region and were replaced by the Bundeswehr 100th Drone Battery equipped with CL-289 UAVs. This unit was the only NATO UAV unit deployed in the region between December 1998 and 24 March 1999.[103]

After the OAF campaign started, more UAV units were deployed into the theatre. These included the 11th RS USAF with Predators, a US Army combat team with Hunters and part of the 61st Artillery Regiment of the French Army equipped with SAGEM Crecerelles and CL-289 UAVs. The Germans sent further UAVs to strengthen their already deployed 100th Battery. All of the NATO UAV units were based in Macedonia, except for the 11th RS USAF, which was based at Tuzla Air Base but also had a detachment in Macedonia.

The most recognisable UAV in the Balkan conflicts during the 1990s was undoubtedly the RQ-1 Predator. During Allied Force, they were operated by the USAF 11th RS from different bases in the Balkans. (US DoD)

The British Army sent their Phoenix UAVs to the theatre much later, and they carried out 20 flights during the period after 6 June.[104] The US Navy deployed a detachment of its only one UAV squadron, VC-6, with RQ-2 Pioneers. These were launched from ships in the Adriatic and were used to control the activities of the Yugoslav Navy and to seek possible targets upon which SLAM missiles could be launched from P-3C Orions.[105]

Predator UAVs were employed in the border area with Albania day and night. Sometimes they were launched to monitor certain targets or convoys, and they were used during missions in Montenegro over Golubovci Air Base and the Berane civilian airfield. The 11th RS Predator unit passed its gathered data on to the CAOC. According to historian Tim Ripley:

Another American UAV was the IAI RQ-5 Hunter, which was operated by the US Army from its bases in Macedonia during OAF. The Hunters belonged to A Company of the 15th Military Intelligence Battalion, based at Fort Hood, Texas, but while in theatre they were under the control of Task Force Hunter. Here, Staff Sergeant Dale Pierce, flight line operator, performs a final maintenance check before its flight to capture aerial images. (NAC)

> At that time Predators, were flying over Kosovo 24 hours a day, trying to identify hostile forces. The current rules of engagement called for a visual identification of any potential target by a forward air controller before a strike could be made. A major problem was [that] similarity of terrain, housing and other features made it difficult to convey to an attacking pilot exactly where the target was. Pilots spoke of being told to use a building with an orange roof as a landmark, while they were flying over a figurative sea of orange-roofed buildings.[106]

The US Army had deployed its Task Force Hunter to Macedonia, which, by the April of 1999, operated four Hunter UAVs that provided 12-hour coverage to a radius of 180 nautical miles. Upon the deployment of Task Force Hawk to Albania in mid-April, TF Hunter became a part of it, tasked to gather information on possible targets that would be attacked by the AH-64 Apaches based at Rinas, near Tirana in Albania. By late April, TF Hunter was sending imagery and other data to the CAOC and started to operate under its request, as well as upon that of the US Navy.

The RV i PVO identified the Hunter UAVs by monitoring communications of the NATO pilots who orbited over the theatre in CAP missions, mostly in the area of southern FRY and the Serbian–Macedonian border towards the city of Tetovo. The 280th Centre concluded that they were operating from Ohrid airport. This type was identified over Kosovo and Metohija province, and all over the Montenegrin coast, from Ulcinj to Herceg Novi. Their operational altitude was estimated at 10,000–12,000ft.[107]

German CL-289s, operating from a base in the vicinity of Tetovo, were flown on a programmed route, mostly between 3,000ft and 10,000ft. A total of 237 such missions were carried out.[108]

European UAVs were subordinated to their national HQs or to the highest army unit HQ that was deployed in the theatre (Macedonia). Their gathered data was not sent to the CAOC, but their missions were coordinated with the CAOC and were noted in the daily ATOs. This was necessary to avoid them being brought down by friendly fire. Data transfer from American UAVs to the CAOC was not in real time, but images from CL-289s were praised as being very sharp, while those obtained from the Predator were highly valued because they were in colour.

By the beginning of Allied Force, it was expected that two Predator and two Hunter UAVs would be airborne at all times. But due to the rising tempo of OAF, it soon became obvious that such a number of UAVs was not sufficient. The American UAVs now managed to send imagery in near real time to the CAOC and into the Pentagon's global information system. SACEUR, General Clark, could also receive the imagery from UAVs in his office in his Mons HQ throughout the campaign. He even frequently intervened in their usage on certain targets over Kosovo province. However, the CAOC did not use the imagery from the European UAVs, as although being useful, they were not in real time. The fascination with real-time data within the US and NATO leadership led to a situation where the strategic level of command started to become involved in micro-level control.

After several strikes resulted in the loss of civilian lives during April, UAVs were thereafter used for additional verification of the targets that were to be attacked. This was especially so in cases where there was no A-FAC present over the target. This practice especially irritated the combat pilots, due to the limited performance of UAVs and high expectations among the higher HQs. In several cases, before UAV verification worked its way through the chain of command to the pilots, targets would move, AA fire would open up from the ground or the strike aircraft would reach the bottom line in their fuel tanks. In the latter case, after refuelling and returning to the target scene, the same verification procedure would have to be repeated. This caused a lot of tension and disappointment in the combat pilot community. The British suggested that this problem could be solved by adding a FAC officer to the cabin from where the pilot operated the UAV, but this proposal was not accepted and taken into practice.

RV i PVO SIGINT/ELINT monitors had a lot of difficulties in identifying and confirming the operations of NATO UAVs. They identified 111 day and night sorties, but through indirect means: by monitoring AWACS communication, when the UAV was spotted by other types of aviation or when warnings were given that they were

A C-130 Hercules receives fuel from the boom of a 100th Air Expeditionary Wing KC-135 Stratotanker during the OAF campaign. (NAC)

operating in a certain area. The usual altitudes they were operating at was between 14,000ft and 20,000ft. The UAVs were covering the activities of different types of strike packages and carrying out after-mission BDA, but they were also monitoring the movements of VJ/MUP forces and marking targets. Transfer of imagery from UAVs to combat aircraft in real time was confirmed several times. However, the RV i PVO ELINT/SIGINT did not manage to confirm the exact locations where the UAVs were based in Macedonia, neither the way of directing and controlling them from the ground, nor the means of data transfer in real time. On several occasions and in their general conclusions after the campaign, RV i PVO officials were misled by assuming that UAVs were used for laser guidance to targets on a large scale.[109]

Actually, there were attempts to use the UAVs to laser-mark targets for combat aviation. But these were pioneering attempts and were hampered by many problems. For example, the pilot of an A-10 was over the target, as well as the UAV, but its operator/pilot was miles away from the combat zone, somewhere in Macedonia. There was no direct link between them, since communication was carried out through the ABCCC. The presence of an intermediary – the ABCCC – merely prolonged the process of identification and coordination, and the strike aircraft thus remained longer in the air, exposed to Serbian air defence fire.[110]

At the behest of the CAOC, a single Predator was modified to carry a laser designator. The modification was tested in a single sortie with an A-10 striker, tests from which showed that information and laser designation from the UAV was recordable and usable on the A-10. There was only one test in combat, on a target in Kosovo, on 11 May 1999. The Predator imagery went through the ABCCC and CAOC, but the attempt to coordinate with strike aviation did not work well: the targets changed their position during the data

A KC-135 Stratotanker from the 19th Air Refuelling Group of the Kansas Air National Guard, seen on the ramp at RAF Lakenheath on 28 March 1999. (NAC)

transfer. The whole concept was further developed during the years after OAF.[111]

Both RV i PVO and NATO statistics showed that the number of the UAVs lost in action was unexpectedly high. The Serbian air defence had claimed their first Predators in the summer of 1995 over Bosnia and Herzegovina. For example, among 13 French Army UAVs, five were lost (three Crecerelles and two CL-289s). By mid-April 1999 during OAF, the Germans ceased use of their CL-289 UAVs after they lost three of them, but the need for the UAVs led to the continuation of operations with another 18 CLs. The Americans lost a total of three Predators, four Pioneers and six Hunters.[112]

There were many factors that accounted for the large number of UAVs lost, such as rugged terrain in the theatre, the same entry points being dictated by the composition of the terrain at the FRY/Macedonian or Albanian border, and of course the constant activity of the Jugoslav Army AA artillery. For many weeks in the earlier stages of Allied Force, the Germans used the same route and the same time of launching their UAVs. Such routine led to several losses, with the VJ forces setting up AA or MANPADS ambushes. The loss of over 20 UAVs in combat missions was high. But in estimations after OAF, it was pointed out that it was much better to suffer such losses than to lose the same number of combat or recce aircraft and their crews if classical aviation had been used instead.

As RAF Wing Commander Brookes pointed out, UAVs "were another Allied Force success story, with the US and European UAVs conducting important reconnaissance operations and battle damage assessments".[113] There were no evidence that the Serbians had a favourite anti-UAV tactic such as using armed helicopters against them, as occasionally claimed in different media.[114]

Air Refuelling

Despite air refuelling not being a pure combat mission, it became one of the most necessary and critical aspects of the Operation Allied Force campaign. Air refuelling missions were demanding and their presence in the air was needed 24 hours a day, without stop, throughout the whole campaign. Air tankers were located on the periphery of or outside the theatre, since the combat aviation was deployed at the air bases closer to the FR Yugoslavia. NATO tankers supported airstrikes from more than 16 air bases in Germany, Greece, France, Italy, Hungary, Spain, Turkey, the UK and United States. Some 175 KC-10A Extenders and KC-125E/R Stratotankers were deployed by the USAF – including AFRES (Air Force Reserve) and ANG (Air National Guard) – four Tristars by the RAF, three KC-135FRs by the French ALA, two KC-130s by the Spanish Air Force, and two Boeing 707T/Ts and a single KDC-10 by the Dutch RNLAF.[115] The average workload for the air tankers was around 40 daily missions at the beginning of OAF, which grew to around 80 missions by the final stage of the operation. Air tankers fuelled all types of engaged aviation, with their operations and usage coordinated by a dedicated tanker cell within the CAOC at Vicenza.

Seen from a 100th Air Expeditionary Wing KC-135R Stratotanker is another air tanker, a KC-10 Extender, after taking on fuel and proceeding on its further mission on 31 March 1999. (NAC)

The USAFE had a single refuelling squadron equipped with KC-135s at its disposal, the 351st ARS belonging to the

100th ARW at RAF Mildenhall. During OAF, many tankers from USAF CONUS units were deployed to the theatre. A significant proportion of the personnel and airframes were from the ANG or AFRES, ranging between 40 and 60 percent, depending on the period. Two air expeditionary wings were formed to control such assets deployed on TDY (Temporary Duty) basis: the 60th AEW at Ramstein Air Base in Germany and 92th AEW at Morón Air Base in Spain. Both wings controlled around 110 KC-135s and KC-10s. At Sigonella Naval Air Station in Sicily, the 99th ERS was deployed with KC-135s; this was the closest USAF tanker base to the theatre of operations.[116] The RAF operated Tristar tankers from Ancona, carrying out over 200 air refuelling missions involving a total of 6,250 tons of fuel.[117]

Several zones were dedicated for air refuelling during the campaign. Three were over Bosnia and Herzegovina – the closest to the operations theatre: 'Total' in the Banja Luka–River Sava area, 'Agip' between Banja Luka and Mostar, and 'Elf' around Mostar. There were also two over Hungary – 'Conico' in the Budapest-Kecskemet area and 'Golf' around Kaposvar–Pecs – and the same number in Macedonia, 'Amoco' and 'Sinoco' in the western and eastern part of the republic, while Croatia had 'Texaco' and Albania 'Exon'. Finally, over the Adriatic Sea, was 'Speedy' in the north, 'Sunny' in the central area and three in the south – 'Shell', 'Mobil' and 'Johnson'. One tanker was constantly on duty in 'Agip' (BiH) and another in 'Amoco' and 'Sinoco' (Macedonia) for the refuelling needs of the fighter aviation.[118]

During combat operations, the number of tankers increased in the zones which led to the areas where the airstrikes were to be carried out. Depending on the size of the strike package, refuelling could be undertaken in two or three refuelling zones simultaneously. Combat aviation could refuel prior to entry into FRY airspace or when they finished the mission and were preparing to return to base. One refuelling zone could sometimes have between three and five deployed tankers at the same time. They operated at altitudes between 10,000ft and 20,000ft, depending on the type and the weather conditions. An increase in their number and their presence in certain refuelling zones indicated to RV i PVO monitors where the path of the next air strike may be. It is interesting that during the campaign, the USAF used callsigns for their tankers using the names of different currencies: even the Serbian Dinar was allotted as a call sign.[119]

Transport and CSAR

Besides combat missions against VJ/MUP Srbije targets, NATO and the USAF engaged their transport assets in providing humanitarian and other assistance to the stream of refugees that arrived from Kosovo province from the end of March (a number of them even before the start of Allied Force). Transport airplanes started to be frequent guests at Tirana-Rinas (Albania) and Skopski Petrovac (Macedonia), where most of the Kosovar Albanian refugees arrived. The humanitarian operation was entitled Allied Harbour. The token

Staff Sergeant John Enns washes the refuelling boom of a USAF KC-135R Stratotanker, belonging to the 351st ARS/100th AEW, in the wash rack at RAF Mildenhall on 12 May 1999. (NAC)

US Air Force personnel from the 86th Contingency Response Group unload relief supplies from the rear of a C-130 Hercules cargo plane on 1 April prior to a mission to Tirana in Albania. (NAC)

Two Albanian children watch as relief supplies are unloaded from US Navy MH-53E Sea Dragon helicopters at Camp Hope near Fjer (Fieri) in Albania on 13 May 1999. (NAC)

C-17 Globemasters were deployed from the 437th Airlift Wing at Charleston AFB to Ramstein Air Base, Germany. Their crews prepared for the Operation Sustain Hope mission to Tirana in Albania on 11 April 1999. (NAC)

A Charleston-based C-17 Globemaster III departs after delivering its cargo to Rinas Airport near Tirana. Flight-line operations continued around the clock during Operation Sustain Hope to assist refugees from Kosovo. (NAC)

The 37th Airlift Squadron of the 86th Airlift Wing at Ramstein was the main USAF airlift unit throughout the Balkan wars in the 1990s. Here, a symbol of the squadron, known as the 'Blue Tail Flies', is shown in the squadron premises. (B. Dimitrijević)

NATO forces deployed to Albania were titled AFOR, with a HQ of the Allied Command Europe Mobile Force (Land) commanded by Lieutenant General John Reith.

For humanitarian transport/cargo operations in Albania, the USAFE deployed the 86th Contingency Response Group from the 86th Airlift Wing at Ramstein, Germany. The 86th Group was activated on 20 March and, after the start of the humanitarian crisis, reached Tirana on 3 April. It was engaged to unload and distribute the humanitarian assistance that was taken by NATO (also by Austrian, Swiss and UAE air force) transport planes. Initially there were a dozen or so sorties per day, but by the end of the conflict this grew to the enormous number of 400 daily flights. The 86th CRG organised the acceptance of and initial support for Task Force Hawk, that arrived at Rinas, Tirana, in mid-April.[120]

Rinas, near Tirana, was a serious problem for the allies, especially at the beginning of OAF, due to the unsuitability of the airport for intensive traffic. Later, the presence of Task Force Hawk complicated procedures further, since it operated under a different schedule to that of the transport aviation. NATO transport aircraft that were registered in Albania and Macedonia by RV i PVO monitors used the callsigns 'KSV' and 'KOO'. The RV i PVO noted a total of 943 aircraft landing at Tirana, with a further 874 at Skopski Petrovac.[121]

The basic transport unit of the USAFE was (and still is nowadays) the 37th Airlift Squadron of the 86th AW at Ramstein Air Base with its Lockheed C-130 Hercules transport aircraft. To offer support to this squadron from the early 1990s (during the operations over Bosnia), a provisional airlift squadron was formed in Ramstein, named 'Delta', or the 38th Airlift Squadron. This unit was formed with crews and airframes gathered from different CONUS units. From 20 May onwards, this unit was manned by the crews and C-130s from the 50th Airlift Squadron. Another temporary squadron was formed, known as 'Delta II', formed from the crews and aircraft of the AFRES and ANG. It was later remarked that, as with the air refuelling aviation, the success of the transport aviation was achieved by activating guardsmen and reservists into the service, no matter the TDY type of engagement. They created some two-thirds of the personnel involved. Nevertheless, it was generally acknowledged that the activation of whole units was much better than creating provisional units with different personnel on rotation.

Because the transport aviation was under serious pressure, maintenance became a problem, particularly due to waiting for spare parts from CONUS. To help cope with this situation, a temporary cannibalisation was introduced, transforming at least one 'cann-bird' into a source of spare parts. Despite the various problems encountered, a high level of airworthy aircraft – around 80 percent – was maintained.

Half of the strategic transport missions were carried out by the C-17 Globemaster IIIs. This type of aircraft, introduced into the units prior to OAF, was a great success. It could carry four times more cargo than the C-130 and land on a runway of the same length, Rinas in Albania, for example. Two of them could be simultaneously offloaded, with their engines running, unlike the C-130s, which had

A busy ramp at Ramstein Air Base, which was the hub for many USAF airlift and air refuelling units on TDY during the Operation Allied Force campaign. (B. Dimitrijević)

A 37th Airlift Squadron ramp at Ramstein Air Base, with a single parked C-130H. The unit was active over the former Yugoslavia in various different air transport, air drop and other missions from 1992. (B. Dimitrijević)

to shut down their engines because their prop wash distributed huge amounts of water, mud and other debris which littered the airfield. A C-17 could land, offload and depart within an hour, and because of its small turning circle and ability to reverse, it had no problems manoeuvring within the tight confines of the airfield. A detachment from the 437th AW (whose home base was at Charleston AFB, South Carolina) with C-17s was established at Ramstein AB in Germany to carry out flights to Albania. This small fleet performed 1,232 missions and carried 111 million pounds of cargo. The fleet of C-17s carried out over 60 percent of transport missions in OAF, despite accounting for only 10 percent of the USAF transport fleet. Meanwhile, the fleet of C-5 Galaxy transporters carried out 332 missions, mostly across the Atlantic and to the bigger airports or air

General Dynamics F-16AM, serialled FA-135 (USAF 90-0026), belonged to 1 Squadron, Belgian Air Force (FAB). It is shown as equipped with an AN/ALQ-131 ECM pod on centreline and AIM-120 and AIM-9 air-to-air missiles on underwing stations. The Belgian and Dutch air forces operated their F-16MLUs in a combined unit known as B-D DATF from Amendola AB, in Italy. The Belgian squadron flew some 620 combat air support sorties during the operation. (Artwork by Tom Cooper)

Another Belgian F-16A Block 15, this example is serial number FA-124 (USAF 89-0002) and is coded BL. It served with five different units during its career, including with 350th Squadron, which flew only air support sorties during Operation Allied Force. The aircraft is shown armed with AGM-65D Maverick electro-optically guided air-to-ground missiles and AIM-9M air-to-air missiles on underwing stations (the latter for self-defence), AIM-120 AMRAAM air-to-air missiles on wingtips, and an AN/ALQ-131 ECM pod under the centreline. (Artwork by Tom Cooper)

A General Dynamics F-16AM of the Royal Danish Air Force: serialled E-070 (USAF 83-1070). As of January 1999, this aircraft was operated by *Eskadrille 727* which was deployed at Grazzianise Air Base where the Danish and Norwegian air forces established their joint fighter unit during the conflict. Their aircraft were tasked with CAP missions, and this example is shown in such a configuration, including four AIM-120 AMRAAMs and two underwing drop tanks. (Artwork by Tom Cooper)

A French Air Force (*Armee de l'Air*) Boeing KC-135FR of the *Escadron de Ravitalliment en Vol* (ERV) 93 Bretagne. Six such tankers were engaged in Operation Trident, the French contribution to OAF operating from air bases in France. They provided fuel for AdA aircraft – including Mirage IVP reconnaissance bombers, Mirage 2000 interceptors, Mirage 2000, Mirage F.1CT, and Jaguar fighter-bombers – and for the fighter-bombers of allied air forces. (Artwork by Tom Cooper)

An *Armee de l'Air* Mirage 2000C of the 5th *Escadre de Chasse*, coded 5-OF (c/n 30). It is shown in its standard armament configuration as of 1999, including short-range, infrared homing Matra R550 Magic Mk.II (outboard underwing pylon) and Matra Super 530D (inboard pylon, and inset, lower left corner). French Mirage 2000Cs were engaged in CAP missions during OAF in 1999 operating from Istrana air base in Italy. A typical Mirage 2000C mission lasted between six or seven hours, with three air refuellings. (Artwork by Tom Cooper)

A Panavia Tornado IDS of the Italian Air Force (AMI), serialled 6-20. As of 1999, it was operated by the *155 Gruppo* of *6 Stormo*, home-based at Piacenza – San Damiano Air Base. It is shown armed with a targeting pod and a GBU-16 Paveway II laser-guided bomb. Italian Tornado ECR-ITs also took part in the SEAD campaign – for the first time in their operational history – and *155 Grupo* operated a mix of this sub-variant, and 'classic' IDS fighter-bombers. The Italians would conduct up to four sorties in SEAD groups, and occasionally IDS Tornados were also equipped with HARM missiles. (Artwork by Tom Cooper)

A Lockheed F-104S ASA-M of *22 Gruppo*, *51 Stormo*, Italian Air Force, based at Istrana AB. A contingent of modernised, but nevertheless obsolete, Starfighters were kept on alert at Amendola, Cervia and Gioia del Colle and occasionally used for CAP missions. In at least one case, they were vectored towards an unknown target apparently moving in the direction of the Adriatic Sea, but were eventually called off. This airframe, serial 51-22, is shown as painted at the time, in air superiority grey overall, and armed with AIM-9M Sidewinder and AIM-7 Sparrow (or, more likely, their Italian licenced version, Aspide) air-to-air missiles. (Artwork by Tom Cooper)

This McDonnell-Douglas AV-8B+ Harrier II was operated by the *Grupo Aerei Imbarcati*, 'The Wolves' of the Italian Naval Aviation, in 1999. Operation Allied Storm saw eight of them flying combat sorties for the first time ever – and from the aircraft carrier *Giuseppe Garibaldi* (C.551). This example is illustrated only armed with an AIM-9 Sidewinder air-to-air missiles, but during about 60 combat sorties mounted by Italian Harriers, they were usually armed with GBU-16 Paveway II laser-guided bombs, or general-purpose bombs of US-design, such as the Mk.82, Mk.83, and Mk.84. (Artwork by Goran Sudar)

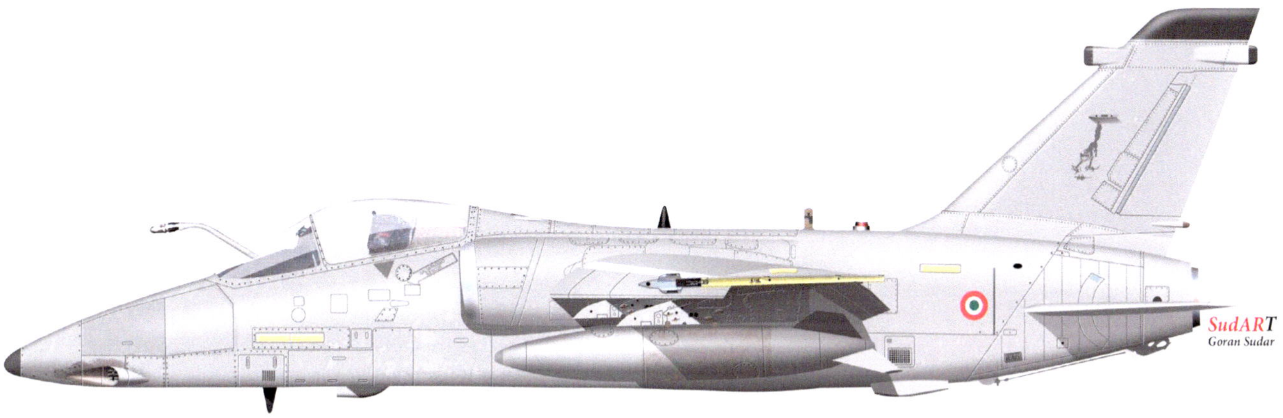

A total of 12 AMX lightweight fighter-bombers drawn from the *13 Gruppo* of *32 Stormo, 103 Gruppo* of *51 Stormo* and *132 Gruppo* of *51 Stormo*, Italian Air Force, took part in Operation Allied Force, all from Amendola AB. This example is shown as seen at that air base around the time, wearing the famous 51° Stormo badge of a black cat chasing three mice, but no visible serial on the side. This type primarily deployed general-purpose bombs of US-design, such as Mk.82s and Mk.83s in combat over Kosovo. For self-defence purposes, it was regularly equipped with wing-tip-mounted AIM-9M Sidewinder air-to-air missiles. (Artwork by Goran Sudar)

The Royal Norwegian Air Force initially deployed six General Dynamics F-16AMs to Grazzanise AB in Italy. Amongst the first aircraft noted were serials 677 (illustrated here), 686, 286, 288, and 293. They were supported by a single Lockheed C-130H Hercules transport, and drawn from Nos. 331, 334, and 338 Squadrons. Later on, they were replaced by aircraft from the same units and No. 332 Squadron, including serials 658, 670, 672, 674, 680, and 285. While initially flying CAPs in the armament configuration illustrated here – including four AIM-120s and two AIM-9s on underwing stations, and an AN/ALQ-131 ECM pod – they subsequently became involved in offensive operations, for which they were usually armed with GBU-12 Paveway II LGBs. (Artwork by Tom Cooper)

Optimised for air defence, four General Dynamics F-16As of *Esquadron 201* of the Portuguese Air Force were forward deployed to Aviano AB during Operation Allied Force. Serial numbers 15101, 15106, 150107 and another example arrived on 23 February 1999, and were replaced by four others, including 15113, 15115, and 15116, all of which were adapted for deployment of AN/ALQ-131 ECM pods under the centreline. Optimised for air defence, they flew combat air patrols away from the battlefield – essentially protecting NATO air bases in Italy – and eventually logged 107 combat sorties and 470 hours. (Artwork by Tom Cooper)

As of 1999, this General Dynamics/TUSAS Aerospace Industries (TAI) F-16CG Block 40, serialled 92-0003, belonged to *191 Filo*, Turkish Air Force, home-based at Balikesir AB. During Operation Allied Force it was one of 11 jets forward-deployed at Brescia-Ghedi AB in Italy. This number was bolstered by seven additional examples operated from bases in Turkey. Initially, the Turkish contingent flew CAPs only, armed with AIM-9M Sidewinder and AIM-120 AMRAAM missiles, but eventually these very advanced aircraft – equipped with LANTIRN targeting/navigation pods – also flew offensive sorties over Serbia. (Artwork by Tom Cooper)

This Lockheed U-2S (serial 84-329), was operated by 99th Expeditionary Reconnaissance Squadron of the 9th Reconnaissance Wing, home-based at Beale AFB. Modified to the Senior Trend standard, it carried a satellite-communication antenna in a giant pod atop of the central fuselage, enabling a real-time transfer of collected intelligence to the headquarters. U-2Ss had flown over Kosovo before the commencement of Operation Allied Force between mid-October 1998 and 24 March 1999, within the scope of Operation Eagle Eye. During Operation Allied Force, they operated from RAF Mildenhall in Great Britain and usually transited the combat zone at an altitude of 60,000ft – frequently during ongoing air strikes, so as to transmit the results of attacks in real time. (Artwork by Tom Cooper)

Once the Serbian air defences were sufficiently suppressed, the USAF began deploying three AC-130H/U Spectre gunships of the 16th Special Operations Squadron – forward deployed at Brindisi – for operations over Kosovo. In addition to their internal armament including two M61 Vulcan 20mm guns, one 40mm gun, and one 105mm howitzer, all aircraft were equipped with exhaust suppressors, and additional chaff and flare dispensers for the mission. This example was C-130H serial 59-6570, nick-named 'The Huff'. (Artwork by Tom Cooper)

During Operation Allied Force, Brindisi also served as the forward operating base for a detachment of three MC-130P special operations tankers of the 67th Special Operations Squadron. They were deployed in support of combat search and rescue operations, primarily those of MH-53J Sea Stallion helicopters that recovered two downed USAF pilots from within Serbia. For this purpose, and as well as the giant underwing fuel tanks carried between the engines on each wing, they were equipped with in-flight refuelling pods carried on additional outboard adaptors. (Artwork by Tom Cooper)

This Boeing KC-135R Stratotanker (serial 63-7991) of the 173rd Air Refuelling Squadron, 155th Air Refuelling Wing, Nebraska Air National Guard, is shown as representative of the large fleet of US, British, and French tanker aircraft without which the entire Operation Allied Force would have been entirely impossible to run. Deploying two aircraft and more than 80 personnel to Rhein-Main AFB, outside Frankfurt, the squadron was the first unit of the Air National Guard to become involved and flew its first mission in April 1999. Over the following weeks, no fewer than 36 KC-135E/Rs and crews from 22nd ARW, and 72nd, 74, 91st, 153rd 171st, 196, and 197th ARS were rotated in and out of Rhein-Main AFB. (Artwork by Tom Cooper)

A USAFE General Dynamics F-16CJ, serialled 91-406, of the 23rd EFS "Fighting Hawks", 52nd AEW, based at Spangdahlem, and forward deployed to Aviano AB for Operation Allied Force. The 23rd Squadron flew over 1,000 sorties during OAF and fired a total of 191 HARM missiles at Serbian radar sites. This airframe is equipped for a typical SEAD mission with eight underwing stations: two anti-radiation AGM-88 HARM missiles, four AIM-120 AMRAAM air-to-air missiles and two underwing fuel tanks. An underbelly station carries an AN/ALQ-131 ECM pod and at the starboard edge of the air intake is an AN/ASQ-213 Harm Targeting System (HTS). It served with the squadron from November 1993 to April 2010, after which was transferred to an ANG unit. (Artwork by Tom Cooper)

Another USAFE General Dynamics F-16CG, serialled 89-2029, belonging to the 510th EFS "Buzzards" of 31st AEW at Aviano Air Base in Italy. It is shown as equipped for the A-FAC mission armed with LAU-131 rocket launcher pods, two AIM-120 AMRAAM and two AIM-9 AAMs for air defence, two underwing fuel tanks, AN/ALQ-131 ECM pod on the centreline station and an AN/AAQ-13, which is part of the LANTIRN targeting system, at the port side of the air intake. Underneath the other wing, A-FAC F-16s usually carried two GBU-12 LGBs. (Artwork by Tom Cooper)

A Grumman F-14A Tomcat (AJ 101/162608), belonging to the VF-41 Black Aces, aboard USS *Theodore Roosevelt* during OAF. This Tomcat is equipped with a pair of GBU-16 Paveway II laser guided bombs installed on 'pallets' underneath the fuselage, and standard self-defence configuration including AIM-9M and AIM-7M air-to-air missiles. VF-41 initiated operations over Serbia on 6 April 1999, with an airstrike on targets in the Pristina area. Following the initial reluctance of the USAF-dominated headquarters in Italy, the unit eventually proved itself one of the most successful fighter-bomber assets involved and dropped about 350 LGBs. (Artwork by Tom Cooper)

This shows a Grumman EA-6B Prowler of the VMAQ-1 squadron of the US Marine Corps. Originally deployed at Incirlik AB in Turkey, and involved in Operation Northern Watch over Iraq, it was redeployed to Aviano for participation in Operation Allied Force. The aircraft is shown configured for its usual mission, carrying three AN/ALQ-99 ECM pod, and a pair of drop tanks. Inset is shown an AGM-88 HARM anti-radar missile: due to the availability of a large number of other 'HARM-shooters', these were rarely deployed by Prowlers. (Artwork by Tom Cooper)

This Dassault Breguet Super Etandard Modernise (SEM), of *Flotille 11F* of the French Navy was one of 14 aircraft of that unit embarked aboard the aircraft carrier *Foch* (R98) of the French Navy, in the Adriatic Sea. It is shown in a 'bomber' configuration: armed with two GBU-12 Paveway II LGBs (or *bombes guidees par laser* in French), and a Barrax ECM pod under the outboard underwing pylon. In this configuration, it required another SEM, equipped with a targeting pod, to deploy its laser guided bombs effectively. (Artwork by Tom Cooper)

A Sikorsky MH-53J Pave Low of the 20th Special Operations Squadron, USAF, serialled 66-14431, and based in Brindisi from 23 March 1999. Well-equipped for penetration of enemy airspace, MH-53Js – some of which were redeployed to Bosnia and, later on, Hungary – were the principal combat search and rescue asset during Operation Allied Force. Unsurprisingly, they extracted both of the downed US pilots, one on 27 March and the other on 2 May 1999. (Artwork by Luca Canossa)

This Sikorsky MH-53E Sea Dragon helicopter of HM-15 (Helicopter, Mine Countermeasure) Squadron of the US Navy, deployed at NAS Sigonella and Bari to provide rescue cover for the seas around southern Italy during Operation Allied Force. Later during the campaign MH-53Es became involved in support of humanitarian operations in Albania. (Artwork by Luca Canossa)

This Agusta Bell AB.212 of the Helicopter Unit, Department of the Public Security of the Serbian Ministry of Interior (*Resor javne bezbednosti MUP Srbije*) was one of three such helicopters operated during the 1990s. Examples in this livery wore registrations YU-HCD and YU-HC and were operated by the Public Security (Police), while the third, camouflaged AB.212 – registration YU-HCA – was operated by the State Security. The example illustrated here was intensively involved in supporting the police and special anti-terror units of the *MUP Srbije* during clashes with the KLA in Kosovo province in 1998–1999. (Artwork by Luca Canossa)

This 2P25M1 or 2P25M2E transporter-erector-launcher (TEL) of the 2K12 Kub-M SAM-system (ASCC/NATO-codename 'SA-6 Gainful') belonged to the 240th Self-Propelled Missile Air Defence Regiment. Since around 1992, this unit was home-based in the Novi Sad area, in northern Serbia. Originally painted in olive-green-grey overall, by 1999 the vehicle received a 'home-made' camouflage pattern in black, dark brown and light blue, which covered its military registration number, usually applied in white on the side of the hull. (Artwork by David Bocquelet)

The heart of each Kub battery was the KAKAV radar system, officially designated the 1S91 Kvadrat (ASCC/NATO-codename 'Straight Flush') – and known as 'R-SION' in Yugoslav and then Serbian service (standing for Radar Station for Surveillance and Guidance). Each SA-6 SAM battery was equipped with one Straight Flush and four TELs. (Artwork by David Bocquelet)

The 9K35 Strela 10 (ASCC/NATO-codename 'SA-13 Gopher') self-propelled air defence missile system comprised the chassis of an MT-LB armoured personnel carrier/multi-purpose tracked vehicle, atop of which was a small turret and pedestal with four containers for missiles. In service with the Yugoslav Army since the late 1980s, it served in limited numbers with the Serbian armed forces: one battery was attached to the 453rd Mechanised Brigade, home-based in Sremska Mitrovica, deployed to Kosovo as of 1999. This launcher – military registration 22747 – survived Operation Allied Force and in 2006 was assigned to the 1st Brigade of the Serbian Army. (Artwork by David Bocquelet)

Introduced to operational service in the mid-1970s, the 9K31 Strela 1M (ASCC/NATO-codename 'SA-9 Gaskin') self-propelled air defence missile system saw widespread service with armoured formations of the Yugoslav National Army. It consisted of the hull of the BRDM-2 armoured reconnaissance car, with a small turret and pedestal carrying four missile containers that acted as launchers. Each Serbian Army brigade had a battery of four in its Light Anti-Aircraft Missile Regiment. As of 1999, the example shown here, registration 22343, was operated by the 211th Armoured Brigade, home-based in Nis. (Artwork by David Bocquelet)

While all the military vehicles of the former Yugoslav National Army wore the same livery in olive-green-grey overall, by 1999 many of the vehicles inherited by the Serbian Army wore very different camouflage patterns. This example – registration 22260 – served with an unknown unit in Kosovo in 1999 – and wore two 'kill markings' in the form of white silhouettes of NATO aircraft, claimed as having been shot down by its crew. (Artwork by David Bocquelet)

The former Yugoslav National Army was one of the major export customers for the Czechoslovak-made twin 30mm M-53/59 self-propelled anti-aircraft gun, installed on a lightly armoured chassis. Numerous examples were inherited by the Serbian Army, but many were either withdrawn from service, or on the way into retirement by 1999. This example received a camouflage pattern in two shades of green, brown, and black atop of its original olive-green-grey livery, and was operated by the Djakovica-based 52nd Light Anti-Aircraft Air Defence Brigade of the LII Corps of the Serbian Army. Following withdrawal from Kosovo, this unit was relocated to Nis. (Artwork by David Bocquelet)

In 1999, this M-53/59 Praga was rebuilt into an improvised *raketni lanser* (rocket launcher, RL), for deployment of Soviet-made R-60 air-to-air missiles (ASCC/NATO-codename 'AA-8 Aphid'). To improve their performance, missiles fired from this launcher were equipped with a 'booster', that fell off after burning out, some 2–4 seconds after the launch. (Artwork by David Bocquelet)

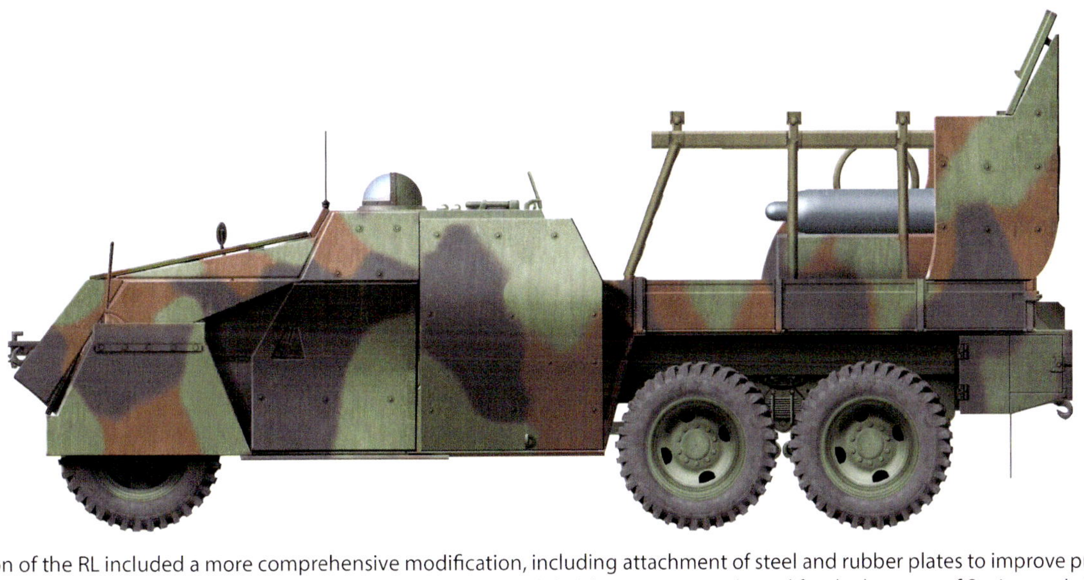

Another version of the RL included a more comprehensive modification, including attachment of steel and rubber plates to improve protection against rocket propelled grenades, and a camouflage pattern in black and dark brown. It was adapted for deployment of Soviet-made R-73 air-to-air missiles (ASCC/NATO-codename 'AA-1 Archer'). (Artwork by David Bocquelet)

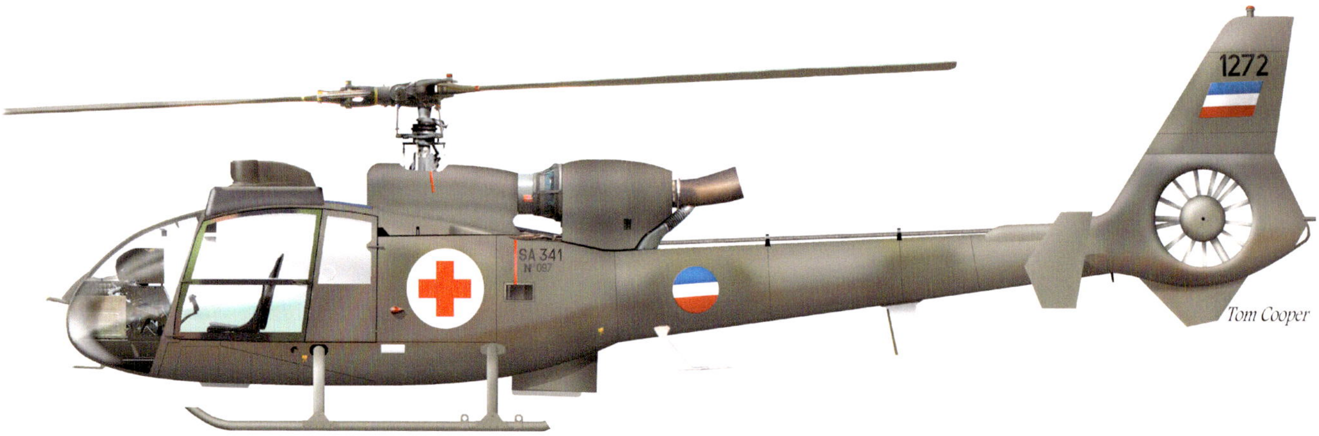

Soko HI-42 Hera (Gazelle), no 12721 (c/n 100, the last SA.341 ever manufactured by the Soko Works in Mostar, in Bosnia and Herzegovina), was operated by the 119th Helicopter Regiment from Nis AB in 1999. It was marked with Red Cross insignia to make it clearly distinguishable during MEDEVAC operations over Kosovo in 1998 and 1999. (Artwork by Tom Cooper)

A BOV-3 self-propelled AAA vehicle, serialled 13009, of the 52nd Light Anti-Aircraft Air Defence Brigade of the LII Corps, based at Djakovica barracks, but deployed almost all over Kosovo province during the 1998–1999 clashes. This BOV-3 belongs to the latest production series of the type at the beginning of the 1990s, from the TAM factory in Maribor, Slovenia. (Artwork by David Bocquelet)

Another BOV-3, without any serial number, belonging to the 124th Intervention Brigade of the *MUP Srbije*. Serbian MUP took over a number of BOV-3 vehicles and used them as fire-support vehicles for their units deployed in Kosovo province in 1998–1999. This example was withdrawn from use after the conflict and was stored at Smederevska Palanka barracks. Part of the police blue colour scheme was still visible on the wheels. (Artwork by David Bocquelet)

MiG-21bis (L-17), serial number 17163, of the 123rd Fighter Squadron of the 83rd Fighter Regiment at Pristina Air Base had served in this unit since 1990. It is shown in interceptor configuration, armed with R-13M (ASCC/NATO-codename 'AA-2c Atoll', inboard underwing pylon) and R-60MK (outboard pylon) air-to-air missiles – in which it was evacuated from Pristina AB to Batajnica AB during the afternoon of 11 June 1999. In 2006, this MiG-21, No 17163 was the first aircraft to receive new Serbian Air Force markings. (Artwork by Tom Cooper)

This Soko J-22 Orao, serial 25204 (c/n 078), of the 98th Fighter-Bomber Aviation Regiment, with HQ at Ladjevci, belonged to the last series manufactured at the Soko Works in Mostar in 1991. It is shown armed with four locally-manufactured FAB-250 bombs, based on a French design. This aircraft was destroyed on the ground at Ponikve AB during Operation Allied Force in 1999. (Artwork by Tom Cooper)

As of 1999, this Soko G-4 Super Galeb (N-62T), serial 23601, served in the III Detachment, 252nd Fighter-Bomber Squadron, 98th Fighter-Bomber Aviation Regiment, based in Batajnica. At the front of the fuselage, it carried the symbol of the 252nd Squadron ('Wolves from the Estuary') and a crudely painted symbol "IR" which under the terms of the Dayton Agreement meant "*Istrazivanje – Razvoj*" or "research and development" – identifying it as not used as a combat aircraft. Indeed, as of 1999, it served as a target tug. 23601 survived the war and is currently the oldest airframe still serving with the unit. (Artwork by Tom Cooper)

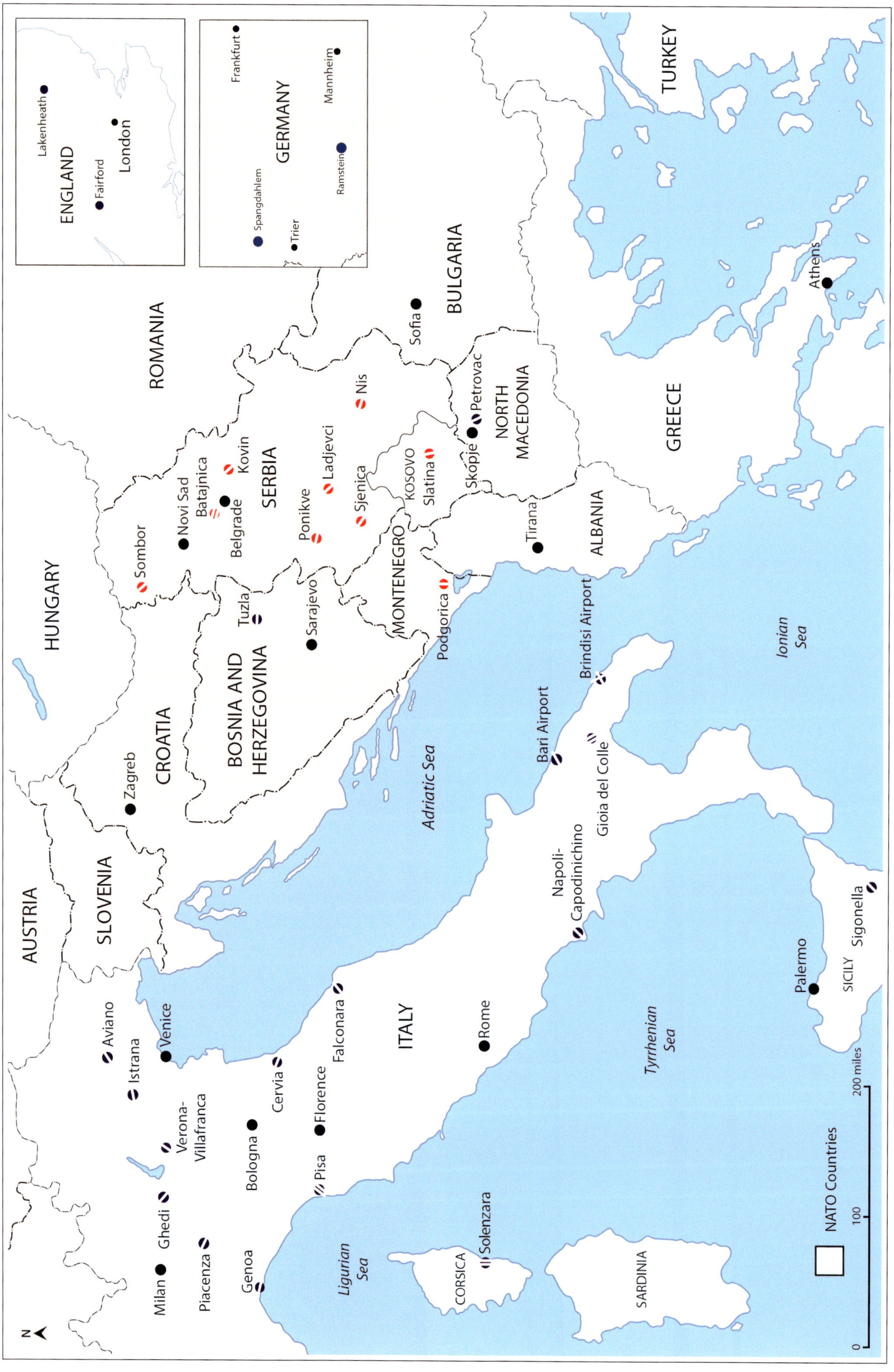

(Map by Tom Cooper)

bases in the theatre, while the C-130 Hercules fleet completed 288 missions.[122]

Up until 5 June, 4,809 sorties by NATO transport aviation were carried out. Of this number, 66 percent were completed by USAF transport aircraft. Their missions were twofold: humanitarian flights to Albania and Macedonia, and 'intratheatre' airlifts. Management of the transport sorties was run by the Regional Air Movement Control Center within the CAOC in Vicenza. Command of American transport assets went through the Air Mobility Operations Control Center of the USAFE, which passed the tasks through the Operations Groups HQs of the permanent and temporary expeditionary airlift wings. An additional coordinator of transport activities was the Director of Mobile Force, the commander of the 437th AW, General Bishop, whose unit deployed 12 brand-new C-17s to OAF.

The helicopter transport elements based in Macedonia took part in the deployment of Kosovo Force (KFOR) from 12 June, using the already deployed helicopters of the RAF and French ALAT.[123]

The Combat Search and Rescue (CSAR) aviation was active during OAF, based at Brindisi Air Base in southern Italy. The RV i PVO registered 59 sorties (among them 30 overflights) of MC-130H/Ps and 65 MH-53Js (36 overflights). Part of CSAR aviation was deployed to Tuzla or Skopski Petrovac, for quick reaction if necessary. This type of aviation was active when two USAF pilots were downed (on the nights of 28 March and 2 May). It was noted that they occasionally flew over BiH and Hungarian airspace. It is worth mentioning that among 11 USAF members decorated with the Silver Star, six received it for involvement in rescue missions of the two downed USAF pilots.[124]

Radio and Other Communication

NATO air forces used different radio communication networks in the VF or VVF/UVF range and satellite communication – SATCOM. The most-used were those in the frequency range from 118–144 MHz and 225–400 Mhz. Those frequencies had a 25 MHz interval. An amplitude modulation was used in voice transfer. Frequency division was set according to the types of aviation: each type had its own communications channel. The change of callsigns was frequent, nearly one every day. The system on which callsigns were changed was not identified by the RV i PVO SIGINT. Usage of crypto-protection devices to protect voice and information was standard at all levels of command. Different ECM-resistant or frequency-hopping systems for protection of communications were also used, such as HAVE Quick, Quick Draw or Improved Data Modem. These were used between the aircraft and ground-based stations.

It was very difficult for the RV i PVO SIGINT operators to monitor such secure communications. In several cases, demasking was helped by the situation where US and European NATO communications were not compatible. It was also noted that members of ANG and AFRES, usually commercial or other civilian pilots or crew members in their 'normal' life (nicknamed 'weekend warriors' by active personnel), were much more relaxed in their radio communication than the active pilots or crew members. They flew on tankers, transporters and A-10 strikers. Their 'open' radio communication became a valuable asset for the RV i PVO monitors.

Long-lasting missions also played a part in the active pilots forgetting the rules and communicating between themselves in an open manner, to discover what was going on in their vicinity. As the commander of the 280th ELINT Centre RV i PVO, Colonel Vujić, explained:

> Most of the information we obtain from the fighter pilots in 'Combat Air Patrol' zones. They were patrolling in the same zone for three hours, [which] became very boring and they had to talk about something. They were talking about women, telling jokes and commenting [on] their colleagues from other types of aviation. That is how we found out the facts on F-117s.

USAF counterparts, in mutual exchange of OAF experiences in 2005, commented on this practice by praising the job of gathering information through intensive listening to NATO and USAF communications: "We did not think about it too much… We were aware, but nobody could assume that you will obtain so much information."[125]

3
RV i PVO COMBAT EXPERIENCE

Combat Aviation

Notwithstanding NATO air superiority, RV i PVO aviation units managed to carry out missions throughout the air campaign. Combat aviation was active in the initial days of OAF, but after losses and the destruction of runways and infrastructure, they ceased to operate. However, helicopter units continued to fly missions until the end of the conflict, mostly in liaison, MEDEVAC and transport roles. The RV i PVO logged a total of 248 missions, with some 122 flying hours, as Table 1 shows.

As noted before, the RV i PVO only used MiG-29 fighters in combat on the first night of Operation Allied Force and a few other occasions. They operated in pairs or alone, with questionable reliability of their radars. The usual peacetime RV i PVO fighter training mostly relied on the close-in dogfight. However, during OAF, Serbian pilots were mostly brought down through the use of long-range AMRAAM missiles, in most cases not even seeing their enemies. Their performance had an impact on the morale of the RV i PVO and the wider nation, with limited success in producing short-term disruption to the NATO strike packages. The fleet of MiG-21bis remained grounded, except for a couple of overflights from Pristina to other air bases to disperse them from the frequently targeted Pristina Air Base.[2]

As was the case with Serb aviation after Deliberate Force in Bosnia during the autumn of 1995, the RV i PVO strike aviation showed that airstrikes could be carried out even in conditions of total enemy air superiority. They did this by operating in small formations against targets in their tactical radius. Sorties were carried out in radio silence, in the so-called 'low-low' regime and with only one sweep over the target, without any BDA.[3]

Reconnaissance aviation units operated over Kosovo in 1998 but were not engaged during OAF. Transporters were active in ferrying the personnel of combat units prior to the launching of the air

Table 1: RV i PVO Sorties and Flying Hours[1]

Types of aviation	Combat missions		Transport			Overflies		Total	
	Sorties	Flying hours (h)	Sorties	Flying hours (h)	Ferried cargo and persons	Sorties	Flying hours (h)	Sorties	Flying hours (h)
Fighter aviation	11	5.10	–	–	–	8	3.55	19	9.05
Strike aviation	25	15.25	–	–	–	6	3.00	31	18.25
Helicopters	–	–	104	59.15	94 wounded, 113 passengers, 5 tons cargo	75	29.55	179	89.10
Transport aviation	–	–	2	2.00	8 passengers, 3 tons cargo	17	3.40	19	5.40
Total	36	20.35	106	61.15	94 wounded, 121 passengers 8 tons cargo	106	40.30	248	122.20

No. 18101, one of the 16 MiG-29s operated by the RV i PVO from late 1987. This particular aircraft survived the airstrikes on Batajnica Air Base during OAF and remained there in the inventory of the 127th Fighter Squadron. (B. Dimitrijević)

Sporting the Socialist Yugoslavia red star roundels that appeared below the new FRY 'Pepsi' markings is the Super Galeb serialed 23745 of 252nd FB Squadron. It is shown taxiing prior to a mission with an underbelly pod for a GSh-23 gun. Most of the G-4s were dispersed from Batajnica and survived the airstrikes in the OAF campaign. (252. lbae)

campaign. Later, most of the transport missions were undertaken by Mi-8 and Gazelle helicopters, which remained active throughout the conflict, none of them being lost during missions.[4] The latter fact is even more astounding when one considers that most of the missions were carried out over Kosovo and southern Serbia, in low-level flight, with UCK guerrillas below and NATO aviation above.

Air Defence

The backbone of the RV i PVO activities against NATO aviation during OAF was supplied by the missile air defence units.[5] The missile units equipped with Neva (SA-3) (12 battalions) and Kub (SA-6) (20 batteries) systems remained as the sole opponents to the NATO strike packages. Numerous light AAA units which were part of the air bases or ground forces were also active throughout the conflict, equipped with MANPADS (Strela 2M, Igla/Silo), light missile systems (Strela 1M/SA-9 and Strela 10M/SA-13) and AA artillery ranging from 20mm to 57mm. During the conflict, more than a dozen improvised SAM systems marked as 'RL', with AA missiles mounted on vehicles or static launchers, were introduced in service. There was also one battalion of the obsolete S-75 Dvina (SA-2 Guideline) system.[6]

Command of missile units was centralised from the Operations Centre of the Air Defence Corps (OC KoPVO). Information on NATO strike packages was received through air surveillance and SIGINT/ELINT. In the later phases of the campaign, after the neutralisation of some 80–90 percent of air

Pilots of the 252nd Squadron prior to take-off for an overfly mission from Batajnica. (252. lbae)

The 252nd Squadron deployed all of its J-22 and NJ-22 Oraos from Batajnica to Ponikve Air Base. The NJ-22 Orao serialed 25529, its two pilots and ground crew are shown prior to take-off from Batajnica. (252. lbae)

RV i PVO V-601 Neva missiles at the improvised firing positions in the village of Drazenovac, Barajevo district, south of Belgrade, during the OAF campaign. (250.rbr PVO)

The 240th Self-propelled Missile Regiment, equipped with Kub (SA-6) missiles, based at Novi Sad, is seen here on the move to another position. (240.srd PVO)

The crew of an M-53/59 2x30mm AA gun, widely known as the 'Praga', of the 401st Light AA Artillery Brigade open fire during a daytime attack at Jakovo, north-west of Belgrade. (B. Dimitrijević)

surveillance units, a 'picture' of the air campaign was maintained by using the radars of the SAM units and a network of visual observing stations. The OC KoPVO ordered a certain level of combat readiness of the missile units depending on the situation in the air. Opening fire was on the orders of the commander at the level of the firing unit (whether Neva battalion or Kub battery). Occasional 'SAM-bushes' were organised with the Kub system, based on experiences in the Bosnian War of 1992–95. Synchronisation of the Neva and Kub missile systems or coordination with light AAA units from ground forces was said to be "weak".[7]

During OAF, the Air Defence Corps carried out 248 'actions' against the NATO aviation, with the following number of SAM firings: Neva, 50 with 93 missiles; Kub, 46 with 70 missiles. It was reported that 151 Strela 2Ms, 12 Strela 1Ms, 11 Silos and five RL-4Ms were also fired.[8] The AAA units of the RV i PVO opened fire 130 times with Bofors L-70 40mm guns, 57 times with 30/2mm Praga and 93 times with 20/3 M-55/Hispano AA guns. Since the majority of strikes above the 44th parallel were nocturnal, most of the Neva and Kub launchings were carried out by night, usually with a salvo of two missiles.[9]

It was estimated in post-war analyses that the number of Neva and Kub missiles fired was smaller than expected, with only two USAF combat aircraft claimed. However, there are several explanations for such a low number. The Serbian air defences were carrying out their operations in difficult conditions, with NATO air superiority and strict adherence to procedures, intensive ECM and jamming, SEAD and DEAD tactics, and constant degradation of air surveillance which forced SAM units to move their surveillance radars much further forward than envisaged to enable the creation of a proper radar 'picture'.

The experiences of the USAF in Bosnia regarding the Serbian use of Kub missiles led to an improvement in avoiding their effect by the usage of manoeuvres and towed decoys, such as the Raytheon AN/ALE-50 system. One such decoy was towed by Lieutenant Colonel Daniel Goldfein's F-16CG when it was claimed on 2 May.[10] The AN/ALE-50 decoy radiated a much bigger surface than the airplane and the Kub missile exploded some 300 metres from the aircraft, causing it no damage. The Serbian Kub 'rocketeers' were shocked by this since "all parameters were precise, guidance of the missile was correct, [and the radar] showed the missile hit the target, but there were no downed airplanes on the ground".[11]

The Serbian missile units performed well by remaining active for the whole duration of the campaign, forcing NATO (USAF) elements to remain cautious, careful and flying to strict ROEs due to the constant existence of the SAM threat.

Serbian air defences achieved such a level of combat readiness by shortening their procedures and keeping radiation to a minimum, reducing 'combat readiness No. 1' to a period from when strike packages were identified up to the moment of missile launching. They moved constantly, especially after a firing was carried out, avoiding so-called 'transfer of fire' or firing another volley of missiles from the same position. They were also aided by fortification and masking of the equipment at the next firing position, widening the deployment of the missile unit by using extended cables and installations, moving surveillance radars to a distance of several kilometres from the firing positions and using the IRZ imitators of radar radiation or other improvised jamming devices, mostly intended to confuse the warhead of AGM-88 HARMs. On several occasions, dummy firing positions were organised using damaged equipment, which became 'live' by using imitators of radar radiation.

The AAA units of the ground forces were deployed all over the FRY. There were eight light air defence brigades at each corps level, with numerous light AA battalions and batteries at brigade and regiment level. Using light missile systems, MANPADS and AA artillery, they were inferior to most of the NATO aviation. Light missile systems and AAA showed much better results in firing at and claiming UAVs and cruise missiles which were flying at low altitudes.[12] Their huge presence and constant firing forced NATO aircraft to fly much higher than expected throughout the campaign. They created a network of 'Triple-A' assets at several NATO aviation entry points or set up ambushes. Since the NATO pilots kept to strict ROEs, there was little threat for 'fast aviation'. In one case during a mission over Kosovo, an A-10 was hit from the ground by the 52nd Light AA Brigade but managed to make an emergency landing in neighbouring Skopje in Macedonia.[13]

Introduction of the Improvised RL System

The RV i PVO air defences were boosted by the introduction of the locally built improvised AA system known as 'RL' (Rocket or Missile Launcher). The basis of the system was mounted on a Praga V3S lorry instead of the M-53/59 30mm AA gun. The system consisted of a launcher which fired the AA missiles that were used on earlier MiG-21 models, mostly K-13 or R-3R AAMs. Later RL models used the R-60 and R-73 AAMs used by MiG-29s.[14]

The earliest improvisations/modifications of this kind were made in the opening stages of the war in Serbian Krajina and Republika Srpska, and were occasionally used in various locations until 1995. One such system was parked at the Aviation Test Centre ramp at Batajnica and was introduced into operational work on the evening of 27 March. Four days later, this earlier RL system was taken to Ponikve Air Base, where it was deployed to protect the Kub SAM battery which was in the wider area of the base. Its first launching was on 6 April at 2310 hours, followed by further launchings on 14, 17, 26 and 28 April and 3 May. The crew was ordered not to launch the missiles against the NATO helicopters that were seen across the border in Bosnia and Herzegovina (Republika Srpska). Despite its limited capabilities, the usage of the RL was a great boost to morale of the 252nd FB Squadron, whose ground crew operated this improvised system in situations where their aircraft were unable to fly. Local villagers were attracted by the presence of the army and the strange system and volunteered to guard it from NATO aircraft with hunting rifles.[15]

Serial production of the RL system started on 27 March 1999, at the premises of the ABM Eye Clinic in Nova Pazova and the Energoprojekt hangar on the road to Stara Pazova. Both locations were on the road north of Batajnica Air Base. The first location produced electrical systems, while the other was a technical/tooling workshop. The following RL systems were produced in such improvised manufacturing lines:

- RL-2 with R-60MK AAMs on Praga V3S, with APU-60-4M launcher
- RL-3 with R-60MK AAMs on BRDM-2 APC, with APU-60-4M launcher
- RL-4 with R-73E AAMs on Praga V3S, with APU-60-4M launcher

Testing of the new systems was carried out at the Nikinci test range in southern Srem. All three systems made direct hits on the target, a 120mm mortar illumination bomb.

After the first launching against targets in the air, it was discovered that the range was insufficient to endanger NATO aircraft operating at their regular altitudes. Booster engines to improve performance were thus added: an engine from a Grad multiple rocket launcher to the RL-2 and an engine from a Soviet S-24 AGM to the RL-4. The modernised RL-4M system carried out six test launchings on the Nikinci range, and the system was introduced into operational service on 18 May. A total of five launching were carried out by

Another wartime improvisation was photographed at Pristina Air Base: an R-60 (AA-8) missile and its APU-60 launcher taken from a MiG-21bis, mounted on the chassis of the M-55 20/3mm AA gun. (M. Špica)

The 'RL' Missile Launcher was a short-lived improvisation. Most of these launchers were removed, while their Praga vehicles were stored at 'Moma Stanojlović' Air Depot after the air war. (B. Dimitrijević)

A P-18 surveillance radar of the 250th Missile Brigade in the vicinity of Pančevo. (250.rbr PVO)

ground crews of the 204th Fighter Regiment and 250th Missile Brigade. Three night launchings were made by the 250th Missile Brigade from firing positions at Ripanj and Šimanovci on 26 May. Further launchings were made on 29 May and 2 June with single R-73 missiles. Until the end of the Allied Force campaign, the 204th Regiment maintained alert status with just a single RL-4M.[16]

RL systems were also deployed to Kosovo, where Prištinski Corps had a single combined battery consisted of RL-2s and RL-4s by early June. The unit was moved to the area around Pristina but made only two attempts at launching. The unit was then transferred to the Dragaš area at Mount Gora, where better conditions for launching were expected. Indeed, three launches were carried out (on 5, 7 and 8 June) from different positions, twice against A-10s and once against a UAV.

The RL system was an interesting episode in the air war. Although it did not score any claims, the Serbians believed that its employment confused the NATO aviation, mostly since it was passive, being resistant to systems with IC guided missiles because it created no electronic reflection. The RL's range was higher than that of other light systems, the R-73 missile was resistant to ECM jamming and it was simple to handle. Nevertheless, it had a lot of technical problems which burdened its use and launching. Furthermore, the missile did not self-destruct at the edge of its range, which caused a serious threat to the wider urban areas.[17]

Air Surveillance

The 126th Air Surveillance Brigade was responsible for all RV i PVO air surveillance assets. It was organised on three battalions with operations centres and a total of 17 radar units: nine companies and eight independent platoons. Each of these radar units was basic, and its size (company or platoon) depended on the radar type and location. Up until OAF, they operated from static positions, mostly on prominent mountains or hills. Most of the positions were abandoned on the eve of the campaign, including two operations centres. The 126th Brigade had its OC at the underground Object 909, below the Straževica hill in the southern Belgrade suburbs.[18]

Prior to the outbreak of the air campaign, RV i PVO air surveillance systems faced many problems: from lack of spare parts for the Ericsson and Marconi radars (the AN/TPS-63 in particular) to only 55 percent of the vehicles necessary to tow the radars and other equipment being available.[19]

The initial task of the Air Surveillance Brigade was to provide continuous control over FRY airspace and its approaches at over 500 metres above the Adriatic Sea, over 1,000 metres over the plains and over 2,500 metres above the hills and mountains, while avoiding casualties and loss of equipment as much as possible. The system was created with a main radar network in static positions and a reserve network which was created from radar units that were deployed in the open. There were also assets held in reserve.[20]

The 126th Brigade managed to survive the first wave of attacks, which mostly targeted its static positions and the radar units in them. The radar companies and platoons then started to operate from improvised radar positions, mutually exchanging in the operational work. As was the case with the missile units, the air surveillance units relied on manoeuvre as their most important practice to survive the air attacks. During the campaign, air surveillance units operated from almost 170 different radar positions. Among them there were 22 with different levels of fortification and 49 that were newly constructed, while the remainder were positions on which the radar was halted and operated for a short period of time before proceeding to another location. The 1st Independent Platoon of the

Another P-18 radar, also part of the 250th Brigade, at the Bozdarevac firing position. (250.rbr PVO)

at Bajina Bašta, both the MiGs being shot down; and on 4 May at 1247 hours for a MiG-29 to a group of USAF aircraft that were over Kosjerić, pilot Lieutenant Colonel Pavlović reporting a 'lock-on' but being shot down a moment later.[25]

ELINT Centre

A crucial position in the monitoring and gathering of facts and figures about NATO activities for the Yugoslav RV i PVO was undertaken by the 280th ELINT Centre. This unit was the 'eyes and ears' of the air force, providing the Intelligence Department within the RV i PVO HQ and Air Defence Corps with detailed information on all NATO activities in the wider region. The ELINT Centre had monitored all NATO air forces' activities since 1992 and had become very experienced in gathering and identifying the types, activities and procedures. It carefully monitored the rising number of NATO effectives from February 1999 and all activities during Operation Allied Force. Since the deterioration of the Yugoslav air surveillance capabilities, the 280th Centre became a vital asset in gathering facts on NATO activities, including the monitoring of strike packages, stealth aviation activities and rescues of downed pilots, as well as the activities of the RV i PVO units. All of the gathered data was transferred in real or near-to-real time to the Air Defence Corps Operations Centre.[26]

The 280th Centre had a HQ at '13 Maj' farm, a few kilometres south of Batajnica Air Base. It operated three ELINT stations with a US-produced system known by the Serbian abbreviation of 'ARTIS' (Automated Radio-Technical Reconnaissance System), located at Ski Centar, Varadin and Kamenički Vis. After some of its locations were attacked on the first night of OAF, the Operations Centre continued operations from stations based at Bukovac and Novi Beograd (which covered Serbia north of the 44th parallel, Croatia and Hungary – Taszar air base), Ski Centar (monitoring Serbia north of the 44th parallel and Bosnia and Herzegovina), Kamenički Vis (which monitored Serbia south of the 44th parallel, Albania and Macedonia), Valdanos (from where the Adriatic, southern Italy and Albania were monitored) and Dobre vode (which monitored activities in Macedonia, but was soon withdrawn due to the lack of secure communications).[27]

The 280th Centre monitored the complete process of NATO missions from take-off to gathering into strike packages, points of entries, combat missions, where they left FRY airspace, changes in working frequencies and tanker activities. Of special note was its monitoring of the activities of stealth bombers, E-8 J-STARS and EA-6B Prowlers. Its most spectacular findings were the monitoring of stealth aviation activities.[28] The centre thus became a kind of early warning unit. In 64 cases, it sent a warning to the Air Defence Corps about expected targets among its assets, of which 22 were accurate and carried out by NATO strike packages. In 937 further cases, other units of the VJ were warned regarding possible attacks via the RV i PVO HQ.[29]

The effectiveness of the 280th Centre's operations can be confirmed by the constant complaints from members of the CAOC

20th Battalion (equipped initially with the AN/TPS-63) operated from 39 different positions during OAF, making it the most manoeuvrable air surveillance unit of the RV i PVO. This practice showed that radars were much more secure at improvised positions, since any fortifications and fieldworks only attracted the attention of NATO reconnaissance assets. However, this produced a huge amount of strain on the personnel, who had to continually assemble radar and other equipment, operate it in various combat readiness levels (mostly No. 1), then dismantle the equipment and move on to the next location.[21]

After suffering casualties by the beginning of April (with two killed and one officer seriously wounded), the HQ of the 126th Brigade issued orders that instruments from control cabs should be removed, and that radars must be operated from a distance by using extended cables and other improvisations. This was particularly needed on the most sophisticated Ericson AN/TPS-63 and AN/TPS-70 radars. However, even this practice did not save the radars from destruction or damage, but it did save lives, with no more air surveillance operators killed until the end of Allied Force.[22]

During the last phase of OAF, instead of the damaged and destroyed 126th Brigade radars, the remaining surveillance radars (P-12s, P-15s and P-18s) from SAM missile units were used, separated from their units to provide an alternative radar picture. Using the civil meteorological service, the brigade established a network of visual observation stations, which provided a limited replacement for radar air surveillance. On several occasions, the data collected from visual stations was the only available information on NATO operations at the OC desk in the HQ of the Air Surveillance Brigade.

During the campaign, RV i PVO air surveillance managed to track 28,859 aircraft/sorties, among them 6,658 within FRY airspace marked as 'X' (unknown or enemy).[23]

Once the OC of the 20th Battalion was moved to Object 909 at the Straževica hill from Stari Banovci over the Danube (which was destroyed in the opening hours of the campaign),[24] there was no radar guidance for the RV i PVO fighters that took off from Batajnica that evening. During the campaign there were only three occasions where radar guidance was provided for MiG-29 interceptors: on 24 March for a MiG-29 that took off from Niš Air Base and was guided to a NATO formation over Kuršumlija, the pilot returning to Niš having suffered damage to his mount; on 26 March for two MiG-29s against a group of USAF fighters which were leaving FRY airspace to General Clark about "unconfirmed reports that the ATO was 'leaking' to the Yugoslavs, at least in the early part of campaign". Clark himself said that the leak "was as clear as the nose on your face". Later, in addressing the House Armed Service Committee (US Senate), General Jumper, commander of USAFE, said that because of the lack of standoff jamming gear and secure voice communication, "most communications between NATO aircraft were made in clear, providing the enemy with much warning and intelligence".[30] Analysts claimed that "NATO experts feel that Serbians regularly observed NATO air bases and facilities and would 'phone home' to warn [of] NATO take-offs and probable attacks", or as General Jumper commented, the "leaks [were] within the NATO targeting and command structure".[31]

Manoeuvre and Deception – Important for Survival

Coupled with masking and deception, manoeuvre was one of the main means of operating of the RV i PVO Air Defence Corps during the operation. Its units carried out a total of 689 different manoeuvres: 169 by Air Surveillance units, 142 with Neva missile battalions and 378 with Kub missile batteries. There were on average 60 units involved in movement/manoeuvre during each week of combat activities.[32]

The most difficult problem at the beginning of the operation was how to estimate the optimal length of radar illumination to identify a target and make ready for launching. Existing norms that were made in peacetime and according to earlier Cold War conflicts were abandoned or significantly changed. Remaining too long on a single radar or missile position could have grave consequences. For many commanders, it was an enigma how long a unit could remain on a certain position; for some it was a couple of hours, for others a couple of days, until another attack. The 230th SP AD Missile Regiment had to change location 38 times, and some batteries even switched positions up to 50 times. Everyone who did not meet or apply the new rules of engagement paid with his life and the destruction of radars and launching ramps.

As acting commander of the 250th Missile Brigade, Colonel Dragan Stanković explained that the manoeuvre of the Neva battalions was ordered immediately after the launching of their missiles, or if the illumination of the radar was too long and they received warning that it had attracted the attention of the NATO aviation. He said the movement of the Neva battalions:

> was one of the most complicated procedures … which [demanded] excellent training, good organization and tremendous effort of the personnel… Such exhausting work lasted for a month after OAF started, until the conditions were not improved with redistribution of personnel and organizing the work in shifts. Personnel of the missile battalions were at the edge of their psycho-physical capabilities… Manoeuvre was in the beginning taken, no matter day or night. Later, when the NATO airstrikes expanded into daylight, most of the manoeuvres were made during the night. Single missile battalion movement was limited with the crew capabilities, with a number of previously built firing positions at disposal or possibilities of certain fields and meadows to be prepared in due course. Due to the wider urban territory surrounding Belgrade it was difficult to discover free spaces for using as the Neva SAM firing positions. It was a limitation factor which influenced the manoeuvre of the Missile Brigade around this most valuable strategic target, the capital of FRY and Serbia.[33]

Manoeuvre of the Kub missile units, due to their self-propelled capabilities, was undertaken without serious problems. On the other hand, movement of the Neva units was difficult because the launchers were static. Frequent movements significantly influenced technical worthiness and fatigue among the crews. New firing positions were occupied during the night, straight from the march, or an area from where they were ready to deploy. In good weather conditions, the switching of a Neva battalion to another position took some 10–12 hours, and from 13–16 hours in difficult weather. A Kub battery needed much less time: for SP batteries around two-and-a-half hours, and for the regimental HQs in the region of four hours.

Due to the deterioration of the situation and the pressure of the SEAD and other strike aviation, the Kub regiments were deployed out of their pre-campaign area of responsibility, mostly to strengthen the air defences around Belgrade and in Kosovo, carrying out long-distance manoeuvres. The 60th Regiment, from bases in Montenegro, was sent to Kosovo (two batteries) and the wider Belgrade area (two batteries), whereas the 310th Regiment from Kragujevac sent its batteries to Mačva, Srem and Banat. On the contrary, the 240th Regiment remained in its AOR around the city of Novi Sad. There was a similar situation with the 450th Regiment (Neva), which did not move until the last phase of the operation when its crack units were sent to strengthen the Belgrade air defences. During the OAF campaign, a total of 74 new improvised

As part of deception activities, several dummy firing positions were made, using mock-ups or damaged equipment. A destroyed dummy Neva firing position is shown here. (250.rbr PVO)

An 'IRZ', or Imitator of Radar Illumination, being set up by its crew. (250.rbr PVO)

firing positions and two radar positions were built. There were cases where the Neva missile battalions remained only a couple of hours at one position, while other missile units stayed at one position for 12 days. More usually, the missile battalions remained between two and three days at the same location.

While at a new firing position, the missile units used shorter procedures for operating. In many cases, Neva battalions positioned only two (out of four) launching ramps, or with the Kub system, one or two missiles on a triple-missile launcher. The remaining part of the unit waited in the vicinity, staying in combat readiness or preparing for further movements. The illumination of the radars was shortened to a minimum level during the duration of the campaign. It is interesting to note that none of the RV i PVO missile units were caught in the open and attacked by NATO during their movement operations.

Air surveillance units also manoeuvred and masked their radar positions non-stop throughout the campaign. The choice of the new positions was burdened with many problems. New radar positions lacked the necessary fortifications, were open to enemy air attacks, and the personnel suffered from stress and fatigue. Reports from the 20th Battalion/126th AS Brigade showed that the NATO aviation did not change their pattern, which helped the air surveillance units to survive: "The aircraft were grouped at three points: over Tuzla, Timisoara and at the frontier triad between Hungary, Croatia and FR Yugoslavia/Serbia. According to the gathering of aviation and recognising the types, we knew that the assembling of the strikes on our radar positions needed at least two hours." Movement of the air surveillance units led to problems with operating on higher altitudes, hills and mountain peaks, where snow and heavy rain made life very difficult. Nevertheless, the air surveillance crews managed to cope with such problems. For example, they shortened the four-hour norms of assembling and disassembling of the S-600 radar to only 55 minutes.[34]

Use of dummy radar or firing positions as well as the creation and use of dummy MiG-29s, the practice of 'false launching' and use of Imitators of Radar Illumination (IRZ) were all part of the wider deception practice in the Air Defence Corps. It was recorded that NATO aviation units targeted abandoned or dummy firing and/or radar positions of the 250th Missile Brigade no less than 33 times. Furthermore, destroyed dummy MiG-29s were often taken to be real airframes.[35]

For electronic deception measures, the RV i PVO used different types of IRZ or 'angle reflectors', in many cases combined with false SAM launching procedures. The Air Defence Corps possessed 15 IRZs at the beginning of OAF. After the operation started, another eight were delivered to the units, with a further batch obtained during May. The power of the IRZ ranged from 4–65KW, with a frequency of 9.5GHz. A total of 506 'passive angle reflectors' were also used.

In the early days of OAF, the IRZs were successfully combined with 'false launching' practice and were used by one missile battalion with the assistance of neighbouring battalions, who also turned their IRZ and targeting radar (StVR, or NATO 'Low Blow') in the same direction. This caused the strike package to carry out an anti-missile manoeuvre and retreat out of the missile range, or even from FRY airspace altogether. After initial Yugoslav success, the SEAD groups and other strike packages started not to react to this practice, identifying it as a deception tactic. They instead focused on destroying the firing position of a missile battalion by using several SEAD groups against it. However, Serbian air defence units continued to turn on IRZs at the same time that the targeting radar was searching for the targets. In many cases, this provided some degree of safety for the radar, because the HARM missile fired from the SEAD groups missed the radar due to tracking the signal from the IRZ instead.

The other means of protection coupled with the use of IRZ was the building of dummy missile firing positions. A missile brigade or regiment would create the fake positions by setting up dummy or already damaged radars or launching ramps and using the IRZs and angle reflectors to make it look like an active unit. They were occasionally turned off and on, to resemble the practice of the active missile battalions or batteries. On five occasions, NATO strike packages or SEAD groups attacked such dummy positions made by the 60th, 310th and 311th Missile Regiments (Kub), and twice by the 450th Missile Regiment (Neva). The 250th Missile Brigade had nearly a dozen such cases, among them the 3rd Battalion which used dummy firing positions to avoided attacks by more than 10 AGM-88 HARM missiles. In an attack at 0311 hours on 23 April at Bumbarevo Brdo, the battalion used a previous firing position to create a false position with dummy launching ramps, radars and IRZ. The battalion activated the real P-12 surveillance radar from the vicinity, to imitate the observing of airspace, and then turned off the radar and abandoned the area, leaving the IRZ to further illuminate the signal. The position was attacked immediately afterwards.[36]

The practice of IRZ usage continued until the end of the campaign, with the introduction of new ones with better characteristics, including a remote system of turning off and on, which enabled the

IRZ to be set up 50–100 metres away from the battalion, and with simultaneous work with targeting and guidance radars.[37]

The air surveillance units and 450th Missile Regiment used angle reflectors to protect their radars from HARM missiles and the discover of their exact positions. Their crews used six reflectors around the radar, positioning a reflector every 60 degrees of a circle at a distance of some 150 metres. Their experiences showed that this kind of deception worked, since the use of reflectors in this pattern changed the radar reflection of their radars and consequently avoided HARM missiles.

The 250th Missile Brigade reactivated the single obsolete S-75 Dvina (SA-2) battalion. This system had been withdrawn from operational service in 1994. The acting commander of the 250th Brigade, Colonel Stanković, said that after several cases of sonic booms over Belgrade and Novi Sad made by French Mirages, he asked permission from the Air Defence Corps HQ to activate this antiquated, but long-range SAM system. His request was approved, and with the personnel of the 6th Missile Battalion, Stanković activated another '6th Missile Battalion', equipped with Dvina missiles taken out from storage. The Dvina battalion was manned by the combined personnel of the 6th Battalion and retired members of the brigade who had served on the Dvina system years beforehand. The Dvina battalion was deployed at Šimanovci, in Srem, a village close to the place where an F-117A was claimed on 27 March. However, the firing position was identified by NATO forces, and in one SEAD/strike attack its 'P' cab (guidance/targeting) was destroyed. Although everything resembled a dummy firing position, Colonel Stanković intended to use the Dvina against high-altitude sonic boomers.[38]

This practice also showed that classic terrain fortifications provide good protection for the missile or air surveillance units. The 250th Missile Brigade had its own Engineers Platoon which provided fortification works for the formation. Experience showed that wooden logs (some 7–9 metres long and 15–25cm in diameter) offered the most effective protection to cover the radar cab, generator or other cabs that were used by the missile or radar unit – except, of course, in cases where the missile hit was direct.

Air Technical Maintenance

The technical branch of the RV i PVO played an important role during Operation Allied Force, although most of its efforts remained outside public knowledge. The RV i PVO air technical branch started to deal with its shortcomings in the months that preceded the air campaign. Its primary effort was to improve the level of air worthiness of the RV i PVO by repairing everything that could be repaired and returned to the front-line units. During 1998, "the realisation of the overhauling" fell to 48 percent,[39] but despite this low figure, the effort made in the months prior to OAF are clear to see as shown in Table 2.

As can be seen in Table 2, most of the efforts of the air technical branch were in repairing and returning to the units as many airframes and radars as possible. Two of the four most modern radars in use, the Ericson AN/TPS-70, were repaired, but the emphasis was on repairing the MiG-29 fleet. Four of the MiGs were repaired and returned to the 127th Fighter Squadron, resulting in an improvement in the airworthiness of this type from 44 to 69 percent. It was remarked that this was the highest possible airworthiness that was achievable in the circumstances prior to the start of the air campaign. Vital spare parts which were missing included engines for MiG-29s, transmitting tubes for radars and various different kinds of batteries and tyres. The economic embargo that had been placed on the FR Yugoslavia since June 1992 and a general lack of state finance made such purchases more difficult. Nevertheless, prior to the air campaign, five Klimov RD-33 engines for the MiG-29s were purchased.[41]

The actual problem, which was obvious but not taken seriously, was the introduction of the unusual category 'functional airworthiness'. This meant that certain combat aircraft could be used (i.e. flown), but lacked combat capability. This mostly involved radars and other electronic devices that remained out of service on the aircraft which could fly. This was a particular problem with the MiG-29 fighters: they could take off and fly, but could not engage in fighting. Although 'functional airworthiness' for the whole RV i PVO reached 88 percent, 'technical worthiness' (i.e. those assets truly combat capable) was only up to 76 percent.[42]

The air technical branch had another serious task: to organise and carry out the dispersal of fuel, munitions, armament, spare parts, tools and other equipment from storage and workshops to other locations to avoid destruction in the forthcoming airstrikes. This task badly affected regular maintenance and overhauling work. Lack of additional premises for accommodation of the equipment and shortages of transport vehicles were serious problems. Another problem was that the RV i PVO HQ ordered only a partial dislocation, and not a general dislocation of the whole air technical service assets.[43]

After OAF had started, the dislocation continued through the use of available personnel and transport vehicles. Maintenance was put under severe pressure by the airstrikes, and any wide level of general maintenance of aviation assets became impossible. Aviation maintenance was possible at only the first and second level (squadron and regiment), while at the third and fourth levels (air base workshop and air depot) it proved impossible. In the air defence (missile and radar) units, maintenance was slightly better, and included two levels (company/battalion and brigade), with a third level at a temporarily created centre for maintenance of the air technical equipment (COVT). This was organised by the Air Technical Department of the VJ General Staff from the personnel of air depots: 'Moma Stanojlović' at Batajnica, 'Kosmos' at Banja Luka, technical personnel from the RV i PVO Training Centre, the specialised INFIZ enterprise and several retired officers and NCOs from the air technical branch. Many private owners of local factories simply offered their premises and personnel to join the overhaul and repair efforts of the RV i PVO units, without any contracts of payment. Such practice greatly helped the general effort to maintain the air defence equipment to the highest possible level of worthiness.[44]

Table 2: RV i PVO Air Worthiness[40]

Air Worthiness	Aviation and helicopters	Missiles and missile technical equipment	Radars and air surveillance equipment	Other technical equipment
Beginning of 1999	61%	90%	68%	73%
24 March 1999	72%	93%	70%	78%

For the repair of damaged air defence equipment, two centres (SOT, or *Sabiraliste ostecene tehnike*) were created. SOT-1 was formed in the southern Belgrade suburb of Rakovica for damaged equipment that belonged to the air defence

Table 3: RV i PVO Airworthiness at the end of Operation Allied Force				
Air Worthiness	**Aviation and helicopters**	**Missiles and missile technical equipment**	**Radars and air surveillance equipment**	**Other technical equipment**
End of campaign	14%	83%	40%	74%

units in the northern FRY: the 20th Battalion of the 126th Air Surveillance Brigade, 250th Missile Brigade and 240th SP AD Missile Regiment. SOT-2 was organised in Kraljevo for equipment from the units in the centre and south of Serbia, Kosovo, Metohija and Montenegro, which included the 60th, 230th, 310th, 311th and 450th Missile Regiments, and 31st and 58th Air Surveillance Battalions. Each of the SOTs had an electronic and technical workshop and other facilities run by neighbouring civilian factories and works.

Damaged equipment, once repaired in the SOTs, was returned to the units. Such repairs were counted as the return of the whole unit into service. These included eight Neva missile battalions (following the repair of eight StVR-125M targeting/guidance radars and a RKU-N cab for dispersion of electric energy), three Kub missile batteries (three 1RL128 surveillance radars, five R-StON or 1S91M2 targeting radars and three launching 2P25M2 vehicles being repaired), three radar companies and 27 air surveillance platoons (with the repair of 14 Soviet 'P' radars, 12 British S-600 radars and four American AN/TPS-63 and AN/TPS-70 radars). Important support was given by the Air Technical and Maintenance Battalion of the 126th Air Surveillance Brigade.[45]

For the maintenance of aviation throughout the whole territory of the FRY, a total of 22 temporary workshops were established. Within the aviation units and part of the destroyed 'Moma Stanojlović' air depot, only 17 damaged aircraft (including two helicopters) were repaired. Minor damage was fixed on 30 aircraft, with regular checks on 10 others and further work on 10 more aircraft. All of these repairs were undertaken in extremely dangerous conditions at different locations. NATO aviation was a constant threat, causing breaks in the repairs and occasional changes of location, while movement of the dismantled or damaged aircraft in the open was a dangerous endeavour.[46]

In the middle of May, the Supreme Command HQ decided to allow the dismantling of combat aircraft and their removal from air bases to nearby civilian areas. The RV i PVO HQ decided to disassemble 24 airworthy and all damaged aircraft. Between 24 May and 6 June, 20 dismantled airworthy aircraft, and another nine that were damaged, were taken out of air bases, with J-22 Oraos from the 252nd Squadron moving from Ponikve Air Base to the Sušica railway tunnel, and Galeb G-4s relocating from the Aviation Test Centre to locations in nearby Banovci or the distant village of Surduk. The aircraft were dismantled by the crews from the units and technicians from air bases and 'Moma Stanojlović' Air Depot. This operation was halted on 6 June, when the ongoing peace talks resulted in the RV i PVO authorities believing that the campaign would soon be over.[47]

At the end of Allied Force, the air technical branch estimated levels of technical airworthiness as shown in Table 3.

Most of the destroyed or damaged equipment comprised aircraft and air surveillance radars. The dismantling of airworthy aircraft also reached a very low percentage by the end of campaign. On the contrary, missile units showed high levels of skill and effort to keep their equipment operational and functional, despite the pressure applied against them by the NATO aviation. As noted earlier, the missile units' technicians managed to repair a significant proportion of their equipment during the campaign and return it to the units. This was a clear sign of the quality of the RV i PVO's missile technical personnel.

4

NATO STRIKES ON THE RV i PVO INFRASTRUCTURE

Analysis of NATO and USAF bomber, fighter-bomber and strike aviation airstrikes on VJ units shows that targeting of ground forces remained a problem, especially taking into account bad weather, limitations in altitude, difficult terrain, masking and frequent movement of the VJ/MUP troops. Despite much of the information on the targets being dispatched in real time, BDA proved very difficult and did not show any sign of downsizing the VJ offensive. Weather conditions were a serious obstacle for successful targeting, even with improvements in the targeting devices that were used during Allied Force. The Serbian Air Defence proved to be a serious and unpredictable threat throughout campaign, even though it operated with obsolete systems produced in the 1970s or the early 1980s. Airstrikes did not actually limit the VJ/MUP operations against UCK guerrillas or force them into any kind of retreat from Kosovo.

As an example to show the level of airstrikes, it is instructive to look at the facts concerning strikes against RV i PVO positions, excluding other military or civilian targets. There were 512 strikes, with some 2,266 launches of some 21,410 projectiles, and around 4,000 tons of dropped ordnance. The largest targets were the air bases, which received a total of 219 strikes, while other targets most hit included air defence firing positions (120 strikes, 232 launches), radar positions (50 strikes, 98 launches) and command and communication sites (33 strikes, 70 launches). Abandoned positions and dummy firing positions, meanwhile, were targeted in 50 strikes with 270 launches.[1]

Attacks on RV i PVO Air Bases

The site which received the most attacks was Pristina Air Base (47 attacks/missions and 292 launched missiles or bombs), followed by those at Batajnica (38/380), Ponikve (38/210), Sjenica (23/132), Ladjevci (21/78), Niš (20/114), Sombor (18/90) and Podgorica (17/60).[2] Cruise missiles were not used against air bases without any permanent aviation presence: Sjenica and Ponikve, and the sports airfield near Leskovac, where transport aviation was relocated from Niš.

Destroyed hangars, positions of the Aviation Test Centre and Air Medical Institute at Batajnica Air Base. (VOC)

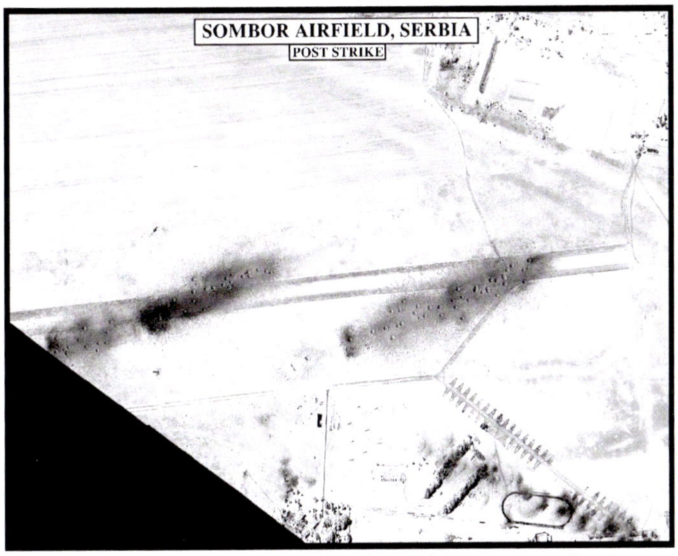

Aerial photograph showing carpet bombing of the runway at Sombor Air Base. This base was used for training of the RV i PVO conscripts and had housed no operational flying units since the early 1950s. No matter that it was not used for operational purposes, it still became a much-hit target for NATO airstrikes. (US Secretary of Defense)

During the first night of the operation, 24/25 March, all of the RV i PVO air bases except that at Niš were attacked, including the air base at Sombor which had no deployed aviation. On the following night (25/26 March), the airstrikes expanded to the air bases at Niš and Sjenica, where only a pair of MiG-21s were deployed from Pristina. During the first phase of OAF, airstrikes against RV i PVO air bases were nocturnal, usually in three timeframes – from 2000 hours–midnight, midnight–0300 hours and 0300–0500 hours. Later, daytime attacks were also launched (from 1000–1200 hours and 1200–1500 hours). The most heavily targeted air bases, those at Batajnica and Pristina, were targeted on a daily basis due to their importance as large fighter bases containing much vital infrastructure.[3]

The 83rd Fighter Regiment based at Pristina was targeted in 54 strikes on 26 days of the operation, while the 204th Fighter Regiment at Batajnica was targeted with 45 strikes on 23 days. Different ordnance was used in these attacks, from standard Mk-82/83/84 bombs to standoff AGM-130s and even usage of cruise missiles against Pristina Air Base at the very beginning of the operation. Pristina Air Base was frequently observed by the numerous UAVs that arrived from Macedonia prior to and after the strike packages. In the case of Batajnica, NATO occasionally used standoff guided missiles. In the beginning these were during the night and fired from distances of 20km and altitudes over 7,000 metres. Later during the day, standoff weapons were fired on targets at Batajnica from distances over 30km. At both these air bases, fighter aircraft discovered on the ramps were usually attacked with precision munitions, whereas runways were attacked with classic bombs of different weights, without special attention to accuracy.[4]

NATO strike packages attacked other RV i PVO air bases where further types of aviation (strike, trainers, helicopters) were based, including Ponikve, Sjenica, Niš, Ladjevci and Golubovci. NATO carried out a total of 226 airstrikes against aviation units on the ground at air bases. Various types of munition were used, from classic bombs to cluster and laser-guided GBUs and the latest guided standoff missiles. In the later stages of OAF, carpet bombing was used to cause further destruction at the air bases, mainly to the runways. All positions and spotted aircraft were targeted, but NATO noted that "personnel [were] not the object of the air attacks".

The strikes against the air bases were carried out in two- or four-ship formations, at the beginning of the operation only during the night, but later throughout the day no matter what the weather conditions. The usual altitudes for the attacks to be launched were between 3,000 and 5,000 metres, with the aircraft then diving and dropping their ordnance at 2,000 metres.

Among the 119 RV i PVO aircraft destroyed on the ground, 81 were at the time spread over the air bases and surrounding areas. There were 15 strikes on empty HAS (Hardened Aircraft Shelters) and six on dummy aircraft. The Rudnik underground shelter at Pristina Air Base received 17 airstrikes, but although the entrance was damaged, none of the aircraft of the 83rd Regiment which were inside suffered any damage. However, the aircraft of the 172nd Aviation Brigade that were parked inside the Zeta underground shelter at Golubovci Air Base were completely lost, with a total of 26 Galeb G-2s and G-4s burnt inside. No matter what munitions were used, the critical factor in these losses (or NATO successes) was that the ground crew had left the entrance doors open, with shrapnel hitting the first Galeb in the row inside and the subsequent blaze spreading to the second Galeb and then to all aircraft in the shelter.[5]

The HAS (or ABS, *armirano-betonska skloništa*) that the RV i PVO relied upon heavily as the means of protecting its combat aircraft proved to be completely useless during the first night of OAF. They were easy prey for various types of PGM launched by strike packages. Many of the aircraft or items of equipment that were parked inside the HAS were destroyed in the first few nights of the operation.[6]

RV i PVO personnel used several different means of improvised protection, including smoke screens provided by smoke bombs or through burning old tyres. A means of protection which showed better results was the constant moving of aircraft all over the air base

The destroyed entrance to the underground Rudnik shelter at Pristina Air Base. (M. Špica)

At the very beginning of the operation, NATO aviation assets attacked the earlier identified static positions of the air defence missile units, including barracks, radar and missile firing positions. The air attacks were synchronised with cruise missile attacks. For example, the firing positions of the 1st and 2nd Missile Battalion of the 250th Missile Brigade were simultaneously hit by cruise missiles and a strike package which used GBU-27 laser-guided bombs with bunker-busting capabilities. Cruise missiles were used against Missile Technical Battalions, which were important targets since they contained stores of Neva missiles, missile fuel, assembly tracks, overhaul and testing facilities and other missile support. Twelve attacks (three of them nocturnal) were made on the infrastructure and positions of the 250th Missile Brigade. In six cases, the attack was repeated, including, three times in 10 minutes. The barracks of the 1st Missile Technical Battalion at Sremčica were destroyed by a strike on the evening of 26 March. This devasted military facility later became a reserve target; despite already being destroyed, it was targeted another 26 times until the end of the operation.[8]

or using camouflage to blend them into the natural landscape. Much later, the surviving aircraft were dismantled and taken away from the air bases.[7]

Hunting the Missile Units

NATO managed to achieve air superiority in FRY airspace after a couple of days after claiming several RV i PVO MiG-29 fighters. Most NATO missions and targeting then switched to missile or radar air defence positions.

'Missile firing positions' (actually the location of individual SAM units) were targeted during most of the operations by the SEAD groups. The pattern of attack and neutralisation of a single missile (SAM-3/Neva) battalion used in the middle and later period of Allied Force was as follows. There could be four to six SEAD groups, with two or three of them at a distance of 20–25km and two or three some 10km behind them, each SEAD group about 4–6km apart. Groups would enter into the range of the missiles at a distance of some 15km, provoking the missile unit to turn on its radars. If the missile battalion turned on its guidance radar, the provoking groups would conduct a sharp 180-degree turn, while the other group would attack the missile battalion with HARM missiles, using the sideways gap in the illumination of the guidance radar. The groups which orbited in the second

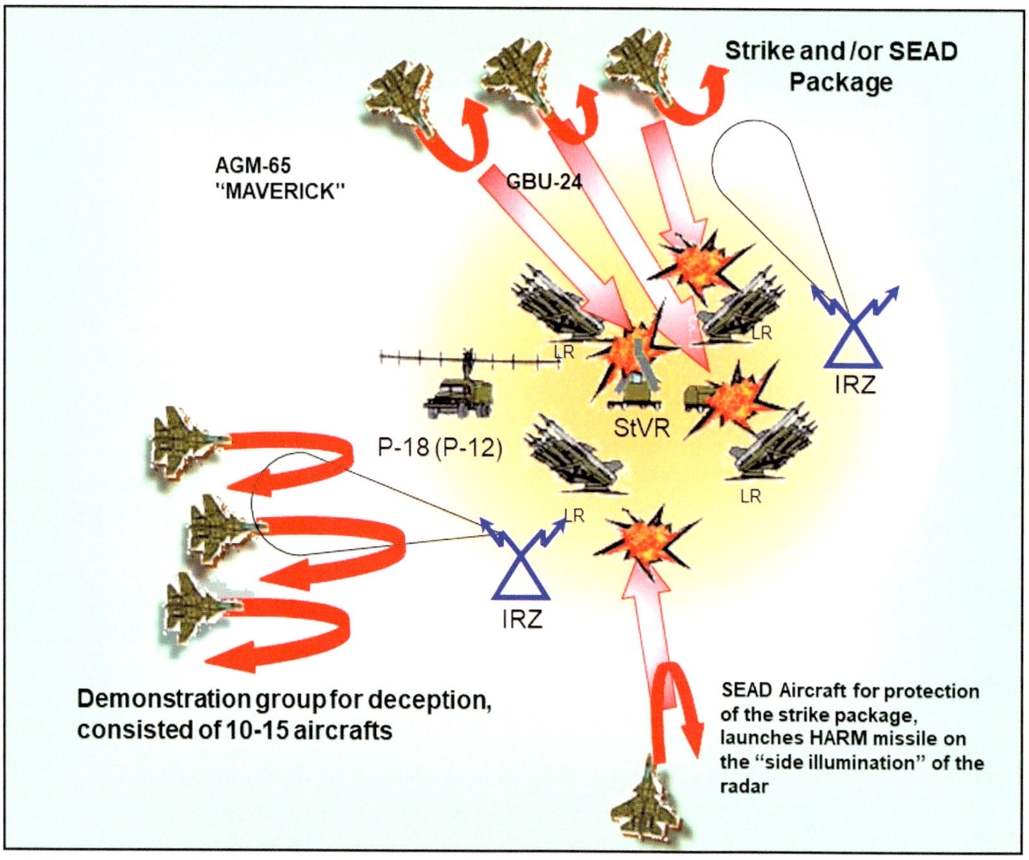

Diagram of an air attack against a Neva (SA-3) missile battalion.

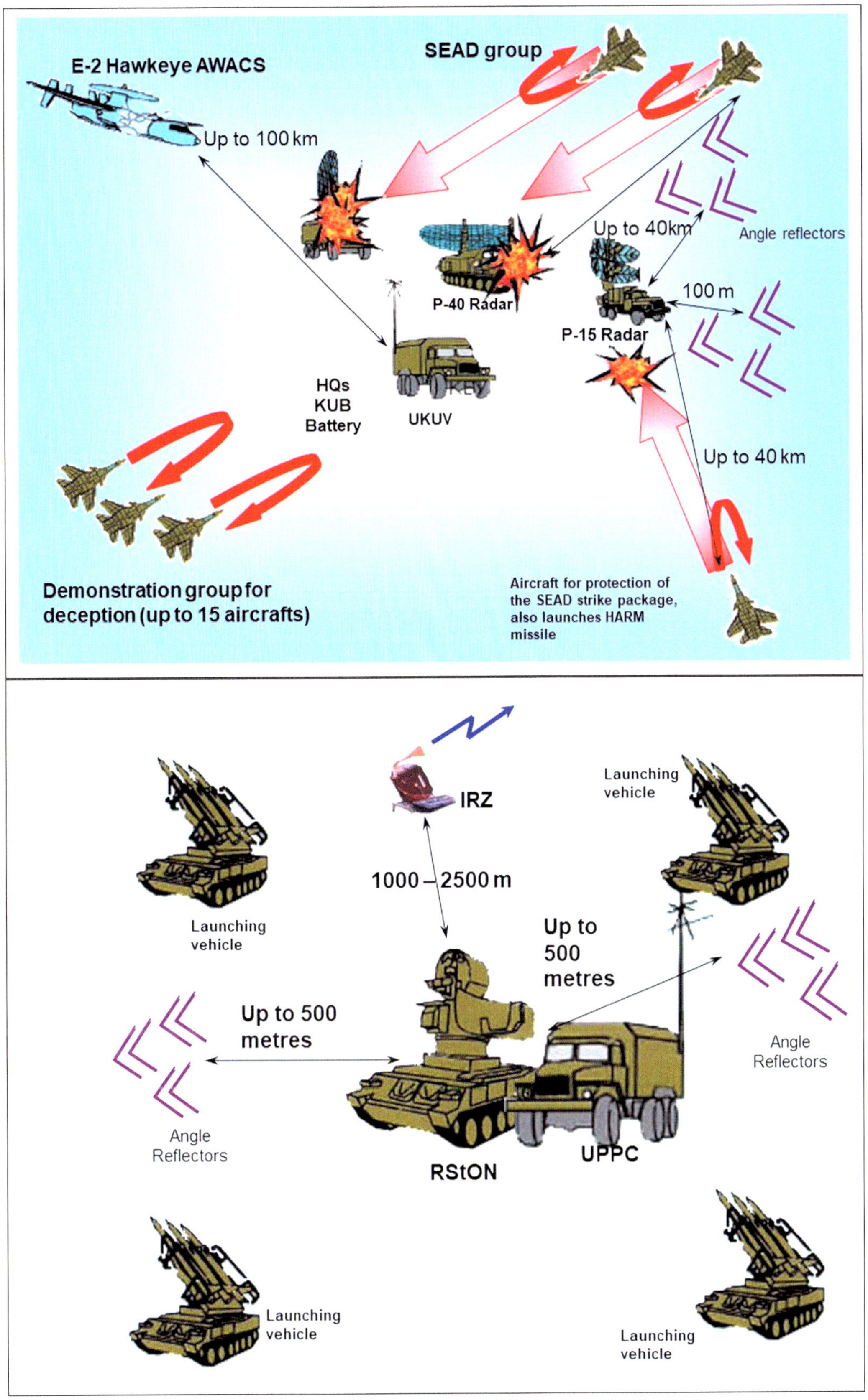

Diagram of an air attack against a KUB (SA-6) missile battery.

echelon, some 10km behind the first groups, would then attack the missile battalion position with standard ordnance to destroy the launching ramps, generators, supporting vehicles and anything else inside the perimeter. This was the DEAD phase: the destruction of enemy air defences, "involving pinpointing the exact location of such targets. The DEAD mission involves fighter-bombers attacking these targets, irrespective of them being active or not."[9]

HARM missiles were used against the 250th Missile Brigade on 14 occasions.[10] They were usually fired at the target acquisition/guidance radar (SNR-125, 'Low Blow', or as the Serbs called it, 'StVR') and in a single case against the P-15 (Flat Face) surveillance radar in the HQ battery. The firing distance was between 10 and 20km. Brigade reports assumed that more HARM missiles were fired upon the various imitators that were used to protect the missile units. The enormous speed of the HARM missiles led the brigade authorities to conclude that its "launching according to some indications was carried out autonomously and automatic without [the] pilot's preparation".[11]

Using experience gained from previous combat with NATO's SEAD and DEAD groups, the 250th Brigade HQ made several conclusions in mid-May, including that a small number of NATO aircraft entered into the 'zone of destruction' (Neva/SAM-3 effective range). Prior to entry into the Neva's effective range, the enemy jammed the surveillance radars with active noise jamming. The jamming stream could indicate the direction of the forthcoming attack. While entering into the Neva missile's range, NATO aviation carried out anti-missile manoeuvres, used passive ECM and jammed the radar screens and other instruments. If the battalion turned on the target acquisition radar, its positions would be soon discovered and there would be no more time to safely fire upon the attacking formations. The missile unit would also become a potential target in the next attack by the NATO aviation. The main focus of the SEAD groups was the surveillance radar, rather than the targeting radar. Daily DEAD attacks on the missile positions were carried out with LGBs belonging to several GBU types, such as the GBU-15 or GBU-24, and cluster bombs. Targets were the visible positions and facilities, which were attacked without any particular pattern and at different times. "Launching of the ordnance was mostly at distances which were larger than the range of the [SAM]

Inscriptions made by the ground crew of the 510th FS ('Buzzards Rule') on its F-16CG payload prior to a night mission over Serbia. (NAC)

A typical peacetime Neva firing position at Vrbica, destroyed in the air attacks on the first night of OAF on 24 March 1999. (250. rbr PVO)

missiles and by groups which approached 'covertly' in the area from which they fired or launched missiles."[12]

The 250th Missile Brigade deployed into action up to three missile battalions at most. Other units were not engaged due to the pressure of the NATO aviation, remaining 'silent' in their positions. The location of firing or radar positions was under constant NATO/USAF surveillance, using ELINT and the latest information obtained from SEAD groups that had attacked the brigade or from RC-135 platforms. The brigade lost nine of its personnel during the attacks.[13]

In the case of the other Neva missile unit, the 450th Missile Regiment, its experiences were similar, except that at the beginning of OAF its missile battalion positions were attacked by cruise missiles. This unit counted a total of 40 attacks: with 26 on its firing and radar positions, nine on dummy firing positions and four on objects. A total of 35 HARM missiles were identified as having been fired on its positions. Despite the more or less same SEAD strategy, the 450th Regiment noted that the DEAD strikes were carried out from much greater distances up to 45km, to avoid any possibility of being fired upon. It was estimated that the ordnance used were AGM-154 JSOWs. Nevertheless, the regiment suffered no casualties.[14]

Kub or SAM-6 self-propelled missile regiments were fiercely targeted. Since the days of Operation Deny Flight, and in particular since Captain Scott O'Grady was shot down by a Kub/SA-6 in 1995 over Bosnia, the USAF had been putting more emphasis on tactics that could make a difference in future conflicts.[15] The AN/ALE-50 towed decoys could be used as a measure against the Kub system.[16] During the first days of OAF, static positions of Kub regiments were attacked. Later during the operation, they were hunted in the wider terrain as Kub regiments were moving. In comparison to their unit strength, the Kub regiments suffered heavy losses, a total of 18 personnel.[17]

Captain Adam Meyers (22nd EFS) expressed the respect that was held for the Serb air defence skills:

> The Serbian air defence was sometimes good, sometimes not. Some like to say that the good SAM operators lived to the end of war, the bad fell out quickly and that they were generally smart. I don't know if that is true but sometimes they were rather tricky in deceptive tactics and the way they employed their radars… Sometimes the Serbs would be tricky and turn on their radar at the last second, before we would get a chance to see it and fire a missile. At that point you can turn nose to it and fire a HARM back, but it costs time and prevents your ability to defeat the missile or you have to start manoeuvring, so that the SAM misses you… They moved within 30 minutes after they had been fired because they fully understood we would find them if they didn't.[18]

Strikes on the Air Surveillance Brigade

The 126th Air Surveillance Brigade controlled all the surveillance (radar) assets of the RV i PVO. The brigade's units were attacked continuously, day and night, by strike aviation and cruise missiles in the early stages of the campaign. As was the case with missile units, at the beginning of Allied Force, NATO forces attacked the stationary positions of air surveillance units located on prominent heights and mountains such as Crni Rt, Kopaonik, Zlatibor, Stari Banovci, Kačarevo and Koviona. The initial attack was carried out with

Morning shed light on the Neva (SAM-3) firing position at Sibnica. (250.rbr PVO)

The Neva firing position at Bozdarevac, immediately after the attack on 2 May 1999. (250.rbr PVO)

cruise missiles at around 2000 hours, and eight hours later, in a follow-up mission, they were attacked simultaneously with bombs from strike packages and cruise missiles. During the following 15 days of OAF, most of the static positions of the 126th Brigade were attacked. In several cases, NATO strike packages overflew the deployed air surveillance units (4th Company/20th Battalion at Kitka and 1st Platoon/20th Battalion at Divoš) but did not attack them (or indeed identify them). In this phase, NATO/USAF carried out only observation and monitoring of the work of the RV i PVO air surveillance units.[19]

Over the following 30 days, NATO started to attack identified radar positions using HARM missiles and a classic assortment of bombs. The radar positions were usually identified a day or two prior to being attacked. Following such events, the 126th Brigade ordered that individual radar positions should only be used for up to 24 hours. The air surveillance units were ordered to start intensive movements to avoid being caught at an identified radar position, even when they had not been operating from them. The NATO aviation then changed their tactics: when a radar position was identified, SEAD groups would immediately fire HARM missiles or the strike packages would attack the radar position without delay. There were cases when a radar unit was attacked at one position, then NATO followed the unit's movement and attacked it again at a second position. Such was the case with the 3rd Radar Company, 31st AS Battalion, equipped with the Marconi S-605, at positions at Mount Bukovik.[20]

The experience of air surveillance, missile and other air defence units showed that the most versatile piece of kit for ECM jamming was the oldest

The camouflaged R-StON ('Straight Flush') radar of the 311th Self-Propelled Missile Regiment somewhere in Kosovo and Metohija during OAF. (250. rbr PVO)

Camouflage and masking were important for the survival of the Serbian Air Defence units. Timber and trenches provided effective protection against the HARM missiles, as seen here on a temporary firing position at Arnajevo. (250.rbr PVO)

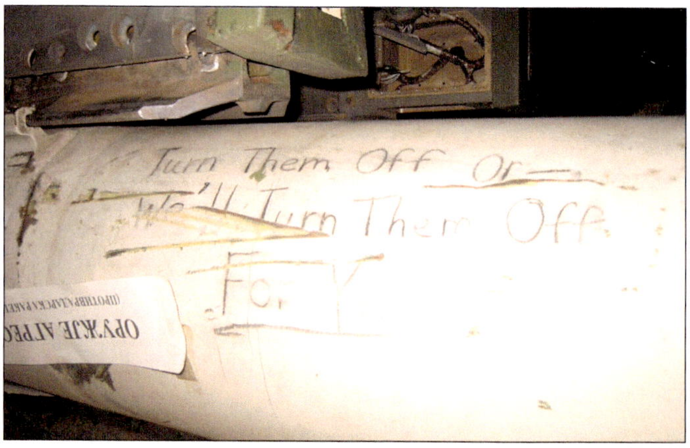

"Turn Them Off or We'll Turn Them Off" – a message on the AGM-88 HARM that hit a position of the 230th Self-propelled Air Defence Missile Regiment. The missile is kept almost intact in the barracks of the regiment at Niš. (B. Dimitrijević)

surveillance radar, the Soviet P-12. The most modern radars in RV i PVO use, the American AN/TPS63 and AN/TPS-70, were noted for their versatility. The British Marconi S-600 series of radars proved much less reliable and resistant than expected, mostly due to its characteristic high impulse power. The most vulnerable radars were the Soviet P-15s (Flat Face), which had a low level of performance, were easy to jam and were thus targeted and destroyed on several occasions. Seven of these radars, taken from ground forces by the 126th Air Surveillance Brigade as replacements for radars that were out of service, were damaged or destroyed.[21]

The Air Surveillance Brigade was attacked on 49 occasions at 57 different locations and in 55 different positions, which were mostly destroyed or badly damaged. Of these, there were a total of 15 attacks with cruise missiles, 98 with different GBUs and LGBs, 29 HARM missiles attacks and 13 with various AGMs on positions of the 126th Air Surveillance Brigade. CBUs (cluster bomb units) were used three times against positions at Kopaonik, Mokra Gora and most likely at Vidojevica. Several other static positions of the brigade were damaged in attacks on other units at Belgrade-Banjica barracks or at the air bases of Batajnica, Sombor, Niš and Podgorica.[22]

A typical P-15 (Flat Face) surveillance radar at a temporary position during the OAF campaign. (via R. Bosković)

Nothing much was left from this totally destroyed P-15 surveillance radar. (via R. Bosković)

Targeting the ELINT/SIGINT and Communications Centres

Because of their importance in communications-led warfare, the RV i PVO ELINT/SIGINT units were targeted from the beginning of Allied Force. The RV i PVO's 280th ELINT Centre (*280. centar elektronskog izvidjanja i ometanja*, or 280. cEIO) had its HQ at the '13 May' farm, on the right side of the Zemun–Batajnica road north of Belgrade. Its stations were based all over FRY territory. In the earliest moments of first night of OAF, the barracks at '13 May' were attacked. The ELINT position at Mount Mavrijan was destroyed, along with part of the equipment, while the Boske position at Mount Bukovac was luckily missed. NATO aviation managed to destroy other 280th Centre static positions at Kamenički vis on 28 March, Dobre Vode on 30 March, 'Ski centar' on 15 April and finally Boske at Mount Bukovac on 2 June. Despite the destruction of all static positions, the 280th Centre continued operating from reserve and improvised positions, providing invaluable information to the RV i PVO HQ.[23]

The VJ (RV i PVO) communications in general were also heavily targeted from the very beginning of the operation, because of the importance of communication among the units and HQs. Stationary communications systems were targeted right at the start of Allied Force, along with the ELINT and air surveillance positions.

Throughout the duration of the operation, of 21 stationary communication centres, a total of 18 were destroyed or heavily damaged. Only three remained intact. The communication centres were destroyed in the following pattern: the upper part was demolished, while the antennae system was destroyed on a significant scale. The personnel remained in their shelters near the positions and kept on working while the position remained operational.

Cruise missiles were used in the first strikes against the stationary communications centres. In most cases there were two attacks, with an interval of between 20 and 25 minutes. Some eight to 12 hours

An F-16CJ of the USAF's 52nd Fighter Wing during a mission on 31 March 1999. It is equipped with two AGM-88 HARM and four AMRAAM missiles, along with the HARM Targeting System/HTS-213 and AN/ALQ-131 ECM pod beneath the fuselage. (DoD)

A Soviet P-12 (Spoon Rest) at a radar position near Mladenovac. (B. Dimitrijević)

later, after recce missions and BDA were completed, the strikes were repeated with another salvo of two cruise missiles.

Between three and five days after OAF was launched, there was another wave of attacks, this time using LGBs and TV-guided missiles, mostly against the antennae which remained intact after the initial cruise missile attacks. This phase proved much more effective compared to the cruise missile attacks, and most of the stationary communication centres were damaged or destroyed.

In the following period, some eight to 15 days after OAF commenced, NATO aviation continued attacking the remaining stationary communication centres using LGB, TV-guided missiles and various bombs ranging from 500–2,500kg, the largest ones being used against the underground position at Straževica/Rakovica in southern Belgrade's suburbs. They targeted the positions and centres which remained in operation with the intention of destroying them completely. Launch distances were over 10km.

The airstrikes caused a "serious disturbance of the VJ [air surveillance] communication system" on three occasions when stationary communication centres of the RV i PVO were damaged or destroyed: at Straževica–Belgrade on 27 March, Mount Fruška Gora on 4 April and Mount Cer on 5 April.[24]

During the whole of Operation Allied Force, intensive ECM were conducted, from aviation that formed part of the strike packages, SEAD groups or specialised types (EC-130s, for example), UAVs and ground-based stations. The intensity of the ECM jamming varied from a single-degree-wide beam to the blockading of the whole radar screen. NATO ECM activities made radar-operating very difficult, and with the Soviet 'P' surveillance radars almost impossible. Active interference (noise, impulse or imitation) was conducted during and after combat missions. Passive interference (dipoles and, decoys) were also used during the course of the attacks.

In the early days of OAF, NATO carried out ECM with less intensity, but later in the operation its vigour and diversity were increased, significantly so after 18 April. A typical example was the arrival from Hungary of ECM platforms over Croatian airspace in the area of Zvornik (Republika Srpska/ BiH), which used active noise jamming. From 5 May, ECM started from Rumanian airspace with noise and impulse interference. It is interesting to note that ECM jamming from this region continued even some 15 days after the end of OAF.

Protection against ECM activities was limited to devices which were installed in particular radars by the manufacturer, but the radar operators found that they could continue to work despite the ECM jamming. Another means was to stop using the antennae and turn off the high voltage (AN/TPS-63). In most cases the false targets or other interferences remained on the screen after the radar was turned on again. Later, the targets on the screen were checked by visual observation stations which were monitoring the appearance of NATO aviation in the areas neighbouring the air surveillance or missile units. Most-resistant to ECM were the American AN/TPS-63 and AN/TPS-70 radars. The problem with the units equipped with US types of radars was that the communications were easily jammed. Experience showed that the highest resistance to ECM was shown by the oldest radar in RV i PVO service: the Soviet P-12 (Spoon Rest). Generally, the experience of the crews which used their radars properly and ingeniously improved their survivability on the battlefield.[25]

5
CONSEQUENCES OF THE AIR CAMPAIGN

Casualties in the Yugoslav/Serb Forces

As noted on many occasions, NATO forces did not have any casualties in combat during Operation Allied Force. On the contrary, Serbia/FRY suffered casualties among its troops as well as civilians, as did the Kosovar Albanians.

The Serbs did not reveal the total number of casualties its military suffered during the whole campaign. The first press release mentioning any casualties was on 25 March, when the figures given for the entire VJ were 10 killed, 38 wounded and one missing (MiG-29 pilot Major Arizanov, who was later returned to his unit). At the first press conference held by RV i PVO commander General Smiljanić on 29 March, it was revealed that there were seven killed and 17 wounded RV i PVO personnel.[1] Later during the campaign, censorship started to be seen and only individual cases were mentioned.

Only after Allied Force, in spring 2000, were complete statistics released for casualties of the VJ and MUP Srbije in the combat in Kosovo and during OAF, between February 1998 and June 1999. They revealed that there were 1,002 servicemen killed: 657 VJ and 345 MUP personnel, among them 581 VJ and 172 MUP fatalities during OAF. Additionally, there were 56 missing in action (31 VJ and 25 MUP), all of whom were later found to have been killed. The total toll for VJ/MUP forces thus reached 1,058. Interestingly, most of the casualties were caused by the Albanian guerrillas, with far fewer (249) being killed due to the effects of the NATO air campaign.[2]

Despite being taken out of Batajnica Air Base and moved to the nearby Belgrade–Novo Sad motorway, where it was camouflaged, this MiG-21bis, serial 17224, did not manage to survive an attack at 1320 hours on 11 May 1999. (204. lap)

The RV i PVO, however, suffered nearly all of its casualties from the NATO air campaign. Only two members of the 63rd Parachute Brigade were killed in clashes with UCK forces. There were 39 RV i PVO personnel killed in combat: 12 officers, nine NCOs, three contract soldiers, six regular conscripts and nine reservists. A further 110 were wounded: 19 officers, 24 NCOs, 11 contract soldiers, 44 reservists and two employed civilians.[3] Statistics showed that 85 percent of those killed and 63 percent of the wounded belonged to the Air Defence Corps. Of these, 54 percent of the fatalities and 38 percent of the wounded were serving with missile units.[4] The RV i PVO suffered the highest rate of fatalities among its commanding officers: one general (an assistant to the MoD), the commanders of the 204th Fighter Regiment and 241st FB Squadron, several commanders of missile batteries and others holding important roles within units.[5]

Losses of RV i PVO Equipment

During the campaign, both sides had a tendency to exaggerate with their estimations of their enemy's losses. In many cases NATO and Serbian claims were both as unrealistic. The authors will not enter deeply into debates on the scale of losses, which were plentiful for a couple of years after the campaign but will try to list figures that have been proven in the two decades following OAF.

Just as the VJ/RV i PVO could not tell what success its air attacks had on UCK guerrillas, the same was the case for NATO: battle damage assessment of strikes against VJ/RV i PVO forces, especially individual targets or weapons, remained a problem right until the end of the operation. Another problem was the massive difference between the categories 'damaged' and 'destroyed'. NATO had great difficulty with BDA throughout the campaign, and thus struggled to prove the success of Allied Force to the wider public. The end of the campaign and the withdrawal of VJ forces from Kosovo revealed that nearly all the 'facts' and figures released at the daily NATO press conferences were arbitrary.[6]

Initial estimations by the US DoD claimed that 120 tanks, 220 APCs and 450 artillery pieces were 'destroyed'. However, the withdrawal of the VJ/MUP forces from Kosovo in June 1999 cast great doubt on whether these figures were a correct estimation. A SHAPE (Supreme Headquarters Allied Powers Europe) estimation dated 11 September 1999, which gave lower figures, was still unrealistic – SHAPE claimed 93 tanks, 153 APCs and 389 artillery pieces. When it is understood that SHAPE was arguing with the USAF leadership during OAF over questions of the campaign's centre of gravity and the conducting of airstrikes, it is understandable that they supported the large numbers of destroyed VJ/MUP equipment as being a sign that they were right in their conduct of the operation.[7]

VJ generals revealed details about destroyed heavy equipment of their ground forces on two occasions. The commander of the Third

A destroyed Galeb G-4 of the Aviation Test Centre at Batajnica Air Base. (VOC)

Wreckage of the MiG-29 No. 18103, heavily damaged on the taxiway of Batajnica Air Base at 0034 hours on 22 April 1999. (204.lap)

Army, General Pavković, soon after the campaign, summarised the losses of his forces: 13 tanks (seven hit by NATO aviation), six APCs, eight artillery pieces, 19 AAA guns and a single radar.[8] Six months later, in December 1999, General Pantelić, Assistant for Logistics to the Chief of the General Staff, said: "Our total losses are 18 tanks, 10 APCs, 13 artillery pieces and others." Later figures for the Third Army mentioned the following losses: 13 tanks (seven to airstrikes), 12 APCs, 12 artillery pieces, 22 light AA guns, a single P-15 radar, two 120mm mortars, six engineering machines and 76 vehicles of various kinds. A further 11 tanks, 10 APCs and armoured cars, eight artillery pieces, three AA guns, eight engineering machines and 32 vehicles were damaged. Moreover, in Kosovo there remained another 14 combat vehicles, six other vehicles and five engineering machines in a usable condition.[9] Differences in the VJ numbers given were usually due to the fact that each HQ or unit counted its own losses, but not the assets (men and equipment) that were temporarily attached to its command, those which were detached to other units or those which were being overhauled.

In 2000, the US-led Allied Force Munitions Assessment Team toured Kosovo and analysed what remained of the destroyed heavy equipment there. They counted a total of 14 tanks, 18 APCs and 20 artillery pieces/mortars.[10] Those figures are almost identical to the ones that were released by VJ General Pavković, but far from those given by US and NATO officials during and after the campaign. We can conclude that the VJ ground forces actually suffered modest losses from the NATO airstrikes. The findings of the Assessment Team were published in an article in *Newsweek* by John Barry and Evan Thomas, who stressed that the team "spent weeks combing Kosovo by helicopter or by foot, [but] found evidence of just 58 successful strikes [out] of 744 'confirmed' strikes by NATO during the war".[11]

During 1999, there was ongoing 'bidding' over just what VJ/MUP equipment was destroyed in Kosovo. The Yugoslav RV i PVO, which was leading the battle against NATO forces, suffered much more serious losses than the VJ ground forces in Kosovo. It seems that destroyed radars or command vehicles were often counted and explained to the media as being tanks, APCs or artillery pieces. As General Joseph Ralston, vice-chairman of the US Joint Chiefs of Staff, commented in the aftermath of OAF: "The tank, which was [an] irrelevant item in the context of ethnic cleansing became a symbol of Serbian ground forces… How many tanks did you kill today? All of a sudden, this became the measure of merit although it had nothing to do with reality."[12] The Serbs had a similar tendency, increasing the number of claimed NATO aircraft and fuelling the image of the dissolution of NATO, which they said could be expected in a matter of days.

It is interesting to note that after OAF, neither NATO nor the USAF announced estimations of destroyed RV i PVO assets. According to a report made by General Smiljanić at the VJ General Staff collegium held on 2 July 1999, the RV i PVO lost a total of 151 aircraft, which he categorised as destroyed in the air or on the ground or damaged beyond repair. Smiljanić noted that there were "70 combat and 72 non-combat aircraft" in this figure.[13] RV i PVO statistics dated September 1999 stated that there were 156 irretrievably lost aircraft, while 20 more were estimated as still being possible to repair, giving a total of 176. A study by the VJ General Staff released the following month estimated 135 destroyed and 75 damaged aircraft, making a total of 210.[14] Later, this figure was clouded by the tendency for it to be downscaled by separating the types of aviation or introducing

The famous acrobatic pilot, Captain Ristić of the 252nd FB Squadron, poses with the wreckage of one of the J-22 Oraos destroyed at Ponikve Air Base. (M. Ristić)

A destroyed MiG-21bis of the 83rd Fighter Regiment at Pristina Air Base. (M. Špica)

the category of 'damaged'. Even General Smiljanić did so in his later book on the air war.[15] Such amended lists of destroyed RV i PVO aircraft included the following: 11 MiG-29s and a total of 43 lost MiG-21 fighter aircraft,[16] 43 strike aircraft (including 19 J-22/NJ-22 Oraos[17] and Galeb G-4s), 26 trainers (Galeb G-2s, G-4s and Utva 75s), seven transport aircraft (An-2s, An-26s and Jak-40s), 2 reconnaissance planes (MiG-21Ms) and 13 helicopters (Gazelles and Mi-8s, including three Mi-14PLs and two Ka-25PLs). The following number of aircraft were damaged: 28 fighters, 15 fighter-bombers, two reconnaissance planes, a single transport and four helicopters.[18]

The official facts and figures released by the RV i PVO and VJ differed from each other, no matter that they were treated as official. The reason for this is that the top brass wanted to minimise the high toll of destroyed equipment, in particular aircraft. Depending on the individual analysis, they counted separately totally destroyed aircraft and merely damaged ones.[19] Then they introduced the category 'possibility of repair', which in some cases turned out to be a correct estimation, but in many others not. Those aircraft which were not repaired were only taken out of the inventory years later. Another problem which complicated the exact matching of numbers of destroyed aircraft in different estimations is the fact that a number of them were at the 'Moma Stanojlović' Air Depot or the Utva factory waiting for repairs or overhaul. In official statistics, the RV i PVO did not count these (destroyed or damaged) aircraft since they were not with the RV i PVO at the moment of their destruction.

In the missile Air Defence units, at the end of the campaign there were seven Neva battalions and seven Kub batteries 'neutralised' or out of service.[20] In the Neva units, eight StVR (Low Blow) radars were destroyed, with six damaged (three repairable), while one launcher was destroyed and two damaged, of which one was repairable. Within the Kub units, five R-StON (Straight Flush) were destroyed, while four were damaged, all deemed to be possible to be repaired. Four surveillance radars were damaged, all being repaired. Four launching vehicles were destroyed, with three damaged with possibility of being repaired. Two L-70 40mm Bofors and five triple AA 20/3mm guns were destroyed.[21] Within the whole VJ (RV i PVO, ground forces and Jugoslav Navy), the following AA artillery pieces were destroyed: 16 M-75 20/1mm, 17 M-55 20/3mm, four BOV-3 (SP 20/3mm), a single SP 30/2mm 'Praga', a single ZSU 57/2 57mm and three Bofors L-70 40mm. Six M-55 20/3mm, four Bofors L-70 and a single BOV-3 gun were damaged.[22]

At the beginning of the conflict there were 17 radar units (nine companies and eight platoons). During OAF, 14 of them (82.3 percent) were neutralised/suppressed, including six damaged (four companies and two platoons). A total of 17 radars were destroyed, with 15 from the 126th Air Surveillance Brigade and the other two from the First Army. Eight radar units which were targeted (three companies and five platoons) suffered different levels of damage to a total of 19 of its radars. Three radar units (two companies and a single platoon) remained untargeted.

There were 90 vehicles destroyed and a further 56 damaged, but 50 percent of those vehicles were specialised for aviation and air force maintenance.

Despite the effective practice of moving spare materiel and ammunition out of storage areas, NATO airstrikes managed to wreck some 43 percent of RV i PVO stores in which they destroyed

TABLE 4: Radars of the 126th Air Surveillance Brigade lost in action[23]			
Unit	**Type**	**Serial No. or C/N**	**Location**
1 Coy, 20 Bn VOJIN	S-613	024	Pazova area
2 Coy, 20 Bn VOJIN	P-14 PRV-11	752115 112929	Kačarevo
3 Coy, 20 Bn VOJIN	AN/TPS-70	1001	Golijska Reka
4 Coy, 20 Bn VOJIN	AN/TPS-70	Kab 1003	Kitka
1 Plt, 20 Bn VOJIN	AN/TPS-63	A3B3	Vladimirci
1 Coy, 31 Bn VOJIN	S-1020 S-1017	007 035	Kopaonik
2 Coy, 31 Bn VOJIN	S-5016M S-5016S	011 014	Zlatibor
3 Coy, 31 Bn VOJIN	S-613 S-1017	023 027	Pazova area
4 Coy, 31 Bn VOJIN	S-5016M S-5016D	042 043	Pasjača
1 Plt, 31 Bn VOJIN	AN/TPS-63	A4B2	Maljen
1 Coy, 58 Bn VOJIN	S-5016D S-613 S-5013 S-1016 S-1017 P-15	029 003 023 009 026 M-4444/987640/	Crni Rt
1 Plt, 58 Bn VOJIN	S-5016M	006	Mokra Gora
Air Technical and Maintenance Bn	S-1016	010	Pazova area
1st Army	P-15	M-3034	Ulcinj
1st Army	P-15	K-1865	Paraćin

large quantities of munitions. The heaviest losses were at the Staničke Šume storage area at Pristina's 492nd Air Base. After the activities of the UCK, the storage, with some 370 tons of ordnance (AAMs, various guided and unguided AGMs, bombs and other munitions), was destroyed. The other storage of the 492nd Air Base which remained undispersed was a fuel store at Velika Slatina, which was also completely destroyed. The other cases included the stores of the 250th Missile Brigade with Neva missiles in Jakovo and Sremčica, where a total of 120 V-601P Neva missiles were destroyed. Some 30 percent of the RV i PVO quartermaster supplies were destroyed in stores at Ladjevci, as well as the materiel reserves of the 285th Air Base and 60th SP Missile Air Defence Regiment.[24] These losses occurred during the first few days of campaign. Later, the RV i PVO did an effective job in spreading around its logistics, reserves and anything else which could be destroyed inside the air bases.

Airstrikes on Infrastructure

From the first night of OAF, it was obvious that airstrikes were targeting the country's infrastructure. First it was the air force infrastructure, then military structures and materials in general, and in the later stages of the operation any civil infrastructure regarded as being used for military purposes. The list of targets from the initial night of 24 March showed that military infrastructure was targeted even though it had a questionable influence on events in Kosovo.

Most of the damage was caused to the RV i PVO infrastructure. Of the 1,406 different facilities, buildings and positions, a total of 958 (68 percent) were attacked, with 527 being destroyed and another 431 damaged but possibly repairable. However, closer analysis showed that actually 100 percent of the RV i PVO's hangars were destroyed and 74 percent of all concrete buildings, while runways were hit with a total of 454 projectiles.[25]

The highest HQs of the VJ were also attacked, including the General Staff and Federal Ministry of Defence in central Belgrade, the HQs of the First Army at Belgrade-Topčider and RV i PVO at Belgrade-Zemun, and the HQ of the Third Army in central Niš. Numerous barracks of the ground forces and air force throughout Serbia were also targeted, followed by the storage areas for military supplies and equipment.

Attacks were also launched against command and communication centres, coastal observation, air surveillance, and ELINT and SIGINT sites, mostly on prominent mountains in both Serbia and Montenegro, at Fruška Gora, Straževica-Belgrade, Avala, Cer, Divčibare, Maljen, Troglav, Kopaonik-Pančićev Vrh, Zlatibor, Izvor, Jastrebac, Goleš, Stari Trg, Butovački Breg, Jadovnik, Jastrebac, Lovćen, Obostnik, Luštica, Bar, Sutomore, Crni Rt and Ulcinj-Mavrijan.

Overhauling facilities were targeted at Air Depot 'Moma Stanojlović' at Batajnica and the Technical Overhauling Depot at Čačak, along with the following defence industry factories: Crvena Zastava at Kragujevac, 14. Oktobar at Kruševac, Sloboda at Čačak, Krušik at Valjevo, Utva at Pančevo, Milan Blagojevic at Lučani and Prva iskra at Baric.

Destruction of the RV i PVO infrastructure at Pristina Air Base. (M. Špica)

The headquarters of the Ministry of Interior in central Belgrade was set ablaze in April 1999. (M. Špica)

another heavily damaged. The telecommunications system was especially targeted: in 312 attacks, 115 sites were destroyed, from simple repeater sites to satellite stations and television towers.[26]

Historian Tim Ripley made the following comments about the NATO air campaign:

> The most controversial aspect of the Allied bombing campaign was the apparent inability of NATO to destroy large numbers of Yugoslav army main battle tanks, light armoured vehicles and artillery, inside of Kosovo. On the other hand, large fixed targets, such as bridges, communications sites and military barracks, were all hit [and] destroyed with great precision and little collateral damage, with most of the targeted bridges destroyed… The 'soft facilities' were all devastated by NATO bombs… Cruise missile attacks were clearly 'surgical' in their nature.[27]

Aviation and helicopter bases of the MUP Srbije at Belgrade International Airport and Lisičiji Jarak airfield north of Belgrade were also attacked.

Other targets included mainly civil infrastructure which had some link with the military, mostly communications, supply and information, or were locations of political importance. The oil refineries at Novi Sad and Pančevo were hit 19 times, along with 96 fuel storages and reservoirs and 14 petrol stations. The facilities and power network of the Elektroprivreda Srbije were hit on 17 occasions with graphite bombs and 102 times with standard ordnance. There were also nine attacks on gas facilities and 27 on water plants. No less than 179 attacks were made on the communication network, with 82 against bridges, 61 against roads and 22 against railways. Of eight bridges over the Danube, four were destroyed and

NATO Losses

When we compare the number of missions and the quantity of deployed assets, the losses suffered by NATO in Operation Allied Force were really only symbolic. Top USAF commanders General Jumper (USAFE) and General Leaf (31st AEW) expressed their satisfaction with these paltry losses, having run a complex air operation for 78 days and nights in a hostile environment under fire from Serb air defence units. Jumper said it was "incredibly good fortune … that NATO lost no aircrew".[28]

Throughout the campaign, the Serbians (the VJ, RV i PVO and media) claimed a two-digit number of NATO aircraft brought down. In many cases such claims were supported by supposed eyewitness accounts in which people spoke of what they had seen in the day or night sky. Others, however, alleged that "high state reasons" prevented the Serbs and the wider public from being informed about the exact number of downed NATO aircraft. One of the usual statements given was that aircraft simply exploded in mid-air or crashed in neighbouring countries. Even official RV i PVO documents claimed a high toll of NATO losses, such as one dated 22 April 1999, which alleged they amounted

Three US servicemen – Staff Sergeants Chris Stone and Andrew Ramirez and Specialist Steven Gonzales – were captured by VJ forces after crossing the Serbian–Macedonian border and entering deep into Serbian territory in their HMMWV vehicle. They and their escort are shown saluting the colours after their release in May 1999 on their return to Ramstein Air Base in Germany. (US DoD)

Aerial footage of the targets attacked in FR Yugoslavia during the Allied Force campaign (all images US Secretary of Defense)

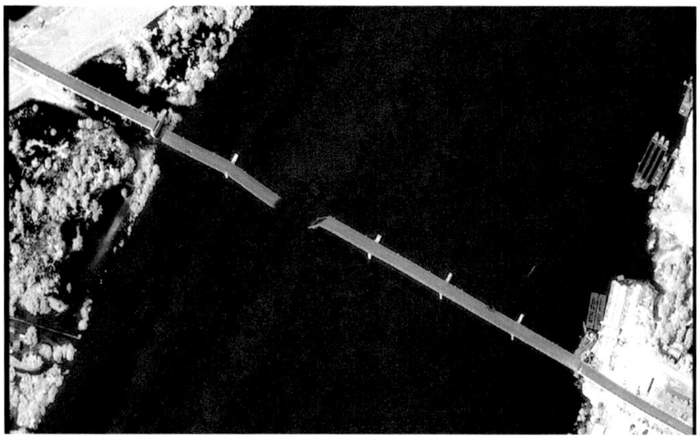
Ostruznica motorway bridge over the River Sava was cut with a direct hit.

Buildings of the Ministry of Defence and VJ General Staff in central Belgrade after being hit and badly damaged.

A post-strike image of the Third Army command post at Kuršumlija.

Pristina Air Base after the strikes. The entrances to the underground Rudnik shelter, where the 83rd Regiment kept its MiG-21s, are marked with white arrows.

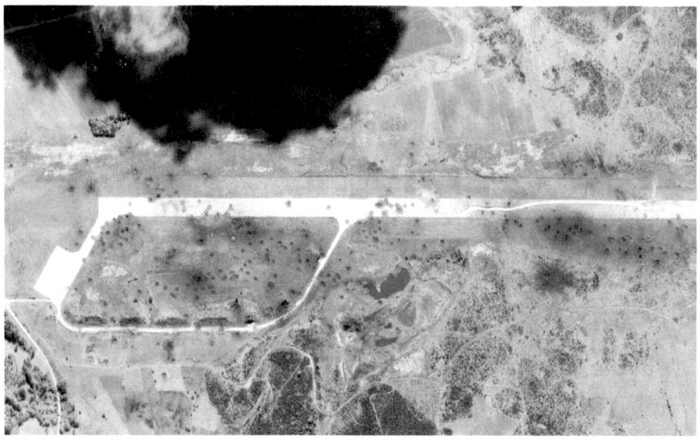
Dramatic aerial view of the taxiways and part of the runway at Ponikve Air Base after several airstrikes.

The barracks of the 60th SP Missile AD Regiment at Danilovgrad in Montenegro after an air strike.

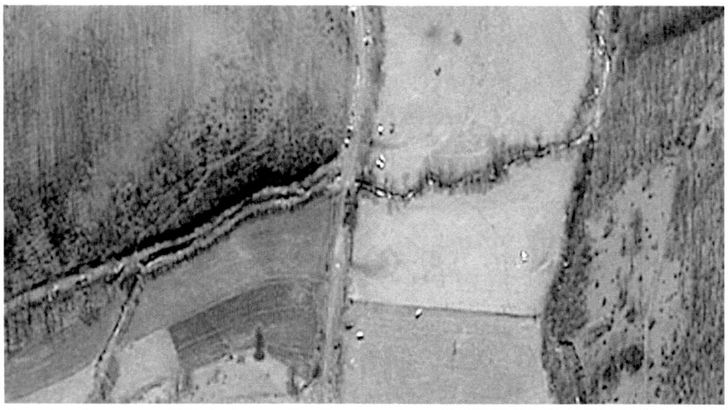
An attack on an IDP (internally displaced people, i.e. refugees) convoy in Kosovo.

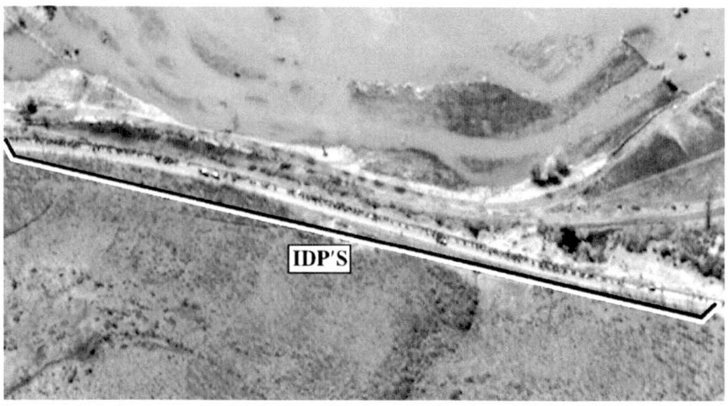

Internally displaced people near 'Dolevo' in Serbia. (The authors have identified this location as the village of Dolovo in central Kosovo.)

Table 5: NATO missions aborted

Date:	Type:	Landed at:	Reason:
25 March	F-15	Sarajevo	Engine 'flameout'
26 March	F-15E	Istrana	Emergency landing
4 April	F-16C, 31st FW	Sarajevo	Emergency landing (?), possibly confused with the next one on 5 April
5 April, 0250 hours	F-16	Sarajevo	Engine failure Confirmed by 280. cEIO[35]
10 April, 1330 hours	F-15C	Tuzla	Electronic system problems Confirmed by 280. cEIO
16 April	A-10, 81st EFS/40th EOG, serial: 81-0984/SP	Skoplje	Unknown reason
19 April	F-16A Royal Danish AF	Sarajevo	CAP mission; engine failure, confirmed and then denied by SFOR spokesman
19 April, 1240 hours	Two F-16Cs Turkish AF	Sarajevo	Unknown reason Confirmed by 280. cEIO
25 April	F-15, escorted by another F-15	Sarajevo	Hydraulic failure
30 April	F-117A Pilot Charlie Heinlein	Spangdahlem	Hit by SAM in the tail section
2 May	A-10, 81st EFS/40th EOG (belonging to the 23rd FG), serial: 81967/FT Pilot: Major Phil Haun	Skopski Petrovac	Hit by SAM in the engine cowling
3 May, between 1850 and 2145 hours	F-14D	Skopski Petrovac	Engine failure
11 May	A-10, 81st EFS/40th EOG Pilot: Captain Chris Short	Gioia del Colle	A-FAC mission; hit by 'mobile SAM', pilot returned safely
3 June, between 1150 and 1240 hours	Mirage 2000	Split	Lack of fuel
10 June, 1130 hours	F-16CJ	Skopski Petrovac	Unknown reasons
Exact day not known	Tornado, RAF Bruggen	Bruggen	Hit by SAM

to "40 enemy aircraft, six helicopters with dozens of killed soldiers and crew members, seven UAVs and over 160 cruise missiles".[29] A similar trend continued after the campaign was over, in the second half of 1999, with claims of "61 aircraft, seven helicopters, 30 UAVs and 338 cruise missiles", while the human "losses of the aggressor were not known".[30] Such exaggerations were given in an attempt to show the tremendous effort the VJ made in the defence of the country, to explain to the public that although NATO may have won the air campaign, they had only done so with severe losses. In other cases, high-level VJ commanders wanted to prove the effectiveness of the forces under their responsibility, and to draw the attention of the upper political echelons or even obtain promotion to a higher rank.

A claimed German Army CL-289 UAV at Pristina Air Base. (M. Špica)

But despite such propaganda efforts by the Serbs, the fact is that only two USAF aircraft

Preserved in the Yugoslav Air Force Museum at Belgrade International Airport are these RQ-1 Predator and French Crecerelle UAVs. (B. Dimitrijević)

A close-up shot of the claimed French SAGEM Crecerelle UAV that is preserved in the YAF Museum. It remained almost intact. (B. Dimitrijević)

were brought down during the course of the operation: an F-117A (82-0806) on 27 March and F-16CG (88-0550) on 2 May.[31] In both cases the pilots were soon discovered and rescued from Serbian territory.

The Americans also suffered non-combat losses, two involving AH-64 Apache helicopters. The first crashed on 26 April some 3km from Rinas Airport and the other about 75km from Tirana on 5 May, in which the crew, NCOs David Gibbs and Kevin Reichert, were killed. This was the only loss of life for NATO throughout OAF. A third loss involved an AV-8B belonging to the VMA-231 Squadron deployed with the 26th MEU on board USS *Kearsarge*, which crashed into the sea some 40km from Brindisi on 1 May. In this instance the pilot ejected safely.[32]

Three US soldiers (NCOs Chris Stone and Andrew Ramirez and Private Steven Gonzales) belonging to the 4th Regiment, 1st Infantry Division, were captured in their Humvee (HMMWV, High Mobility Multipurpose Wheeled Vehicle) when it became stuck on a huge stone in the Serb–Macedonian border area near the village of Mali Trnovac. They were released by their captors on 2 May.[33]

The authors have identified at least 16 cases of emergency landings or damage which forced NATO pilots to abandon their missions, caused by fire from Serb air defence units or other reasons. The only two aircraft with serious damage were both hit by SAM missiles, an F-117A on 30 April and an A-10 on 2 May (part of the latter's engine cowling falling into the hands of the VJ north of Gnjilane).[34] They are listed in Table 4 in chronological order.

The Serbian air defence managed to claim some 21 UAVs, which had at least six non-combat losses, making an important addition to NATO's losses. The UAVs lost included eight Hunters (five combat, three non-combat losses), three or four Predators (from the 11th and 15th Squadron, 57th Wing USAF), two Phoenix, five CL-289GEs (Serbians claimed seven), two CL-289FRs and three Crecerelles.[36] The first was lost on 7 April, the last on 30 May. There were also numerous cruise missiles and guided bombs that were claimed by the Serb light AA defence.

The fact that the UAVs operated below the established altitude limits for the combat aviation, along with their slow speed, meant that the number of UAVs lost should have been relatively high. Densely deployed Serb light AA artillery also should have brought down a large number of cruise missiles prior to them reaching their designated targets. Combating cruise missiles was predicted to be a major problem by the VJ planners prior to the air campaign. It turned out, however, that due to their low level of flight and low speed, and the noise they made, they were much easier prey for the light air defence units than anyone on the Serb side had expected. In many cases, the Serbs did not distinguish UAVs from cruise missiles, which were also believed to be small aircraft. This helps account for the differences among the numbers of total claims.

Generally speaking, the organisation of the missions during OAF, with whole systems backing the combat aviation at the spearhead, and strict respect of the rules of engagement – notably regarding

Kept in the barracks of the 3rd Missile Battalion/250th Air Defence Missile Brigade in Jakovo is one of the AGM-88 HARM missiles fired upon the unit. (B. Dimitrijević)

The chief of the YAF Museum, Lieutenant Colonel Stojanovic, inspects the cockpit of the claimed F-117A stealth fighter at the village of Budjanovci on the morning of 28 March 1999. What remained of this aircraft is now in the YAF Museum. (M.D. Ristić)

operational altitude, radio silence and constant pressure on the RV i PVO air defences – resulted in NATO forces suffering only minor losses for the number of deployed aircraft and missions carried out. Well-organised CSAR did not allow the Serbs to exploit the two aircraft brought down by capturing the pilots, as had happened in 1995 during the missions over Republika Srpska (Bosnia and Herzegovina). Both pilots who came down during OAF were rescued within a matter of hours in bold night CSAR missions into Serbian airspace. The USAF thereby demonstrated that it valued its combat pilots much more than their expensive airframes. This made the USAF/NATO pilots feel all the more secure during their combat missions.

However, the claiming of a stealth F-117A Nighthawk showed that the Serbian air defence remained a threat, as it had been in the Bosnian War. Many lessons learned from that earlier conflict were introduced into operational practice, but surprises still occurred. For example, even the oldest radars (Soviet P-12s) and outdated SAM systems (Neva) remained a threat to the most modern and advanced equipment, such as the F-117A. The loss of the stealth fighter on the fourth night of Allied Force proved to the NATO and US leadership that the Serbs had decided to make a fight of it. The claiming of the stealth fighter was a strong boost to the morale of the Serbian military and public, which almost mythologised the event. Nevertheless, the fleet of F-117 stealth fighters continued to attack targets in Serbia until the end of the campaign.

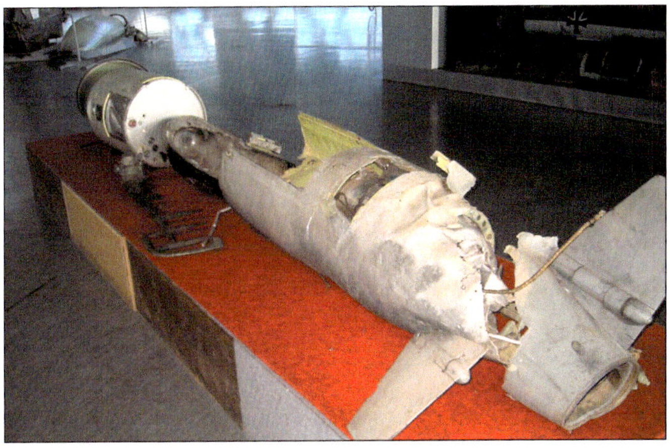

The remains of a BGM-109 Tomahawk cruise missile fired against Ladjevci Air Base on 24 March 1999. It is now kept in the YAF Museum. (B. Dimitrijević)

A US Army AH-64A Apache helicopter crashed into an Albanian hillside during training sorties on 26 April 1999. It was described as follows in the original photo caption: "On 3 May 1999, The Committee Against U.S. Intervention ran an exclusive set of pictures of the Apache AH-64A helicopter which went down." (www.cnn.com/US/9904/26/us.kosovo.military.02)

The lack of success of the US Army Apache helicopters was in total contrast to media announcements of their use, and even more so to the expectations of SACEUR General Clark, US Army senior officers and politicians. The loss of two Apaches in Albania prior to any combat involvement – one with two fatalities – made the whole Apache deployment a disaster. Unsuccessful use of the Apache helicopters was regarded by many officials as the most serious American mistake in the conducting of Operation Allied Force. As Adam J. Hebert, editor of *Air Force Magazine*, pointed out in 2009: "The US Army in 1999 was not configured or trained for expeditionary missions… Task Force Hawk was [an] anomaly."[37]

6
EXPERIENCES OF OPERATION ALLIED FORCE

Operation Allied Force – whether it be termed an aggression, air campaign, air war or even bombardment against the FR Yugoslavia – was not a classic military conflict, there being no direct ground clash of massive military forces. The war/campaign was carried out on three different levels, perhaps, as three separate 'wars'. The first was the direct clash between the Yugoslav/Serb forces and Albanian UCK guerrillas in Kosovo and Metohija province; the second was the air campaign (Allied Force) between NATO and Yugoslav forces throughout the FR Yugoslavia, later reduced to the territory of Serbia, excluding the attacks on Montenegro; and the third was in the sphere of politics, diplomacy and, even more so, the media, where it achieved the status of being perceived as almost the first 'virtual war'. Due to this 'trichotomy', the conflict was regarded by many as being 'asymmetric'.

NATO enlarged the air campaign from a limited one at the end of March to a full-scale operation by the beginning of June 1999, but did not employ ground forces. Actually, the UCK guerrillas represented a kind of NATO ground force, as it was the case with the Croats and Armija BiH in the latter stages of the war in Bosnia in the autumn of 1995. But as the UCK was only a guerrilla force, it was unable to achieve widespread success, even backed by US heavy bombers towards the end of the conflict. Together with the diplomatic efforts and ongoing negotiations, it all made for a complicated puzzle of a conflict in Kosovo, of which Operation Allied Force was only a part.

The regime in Belgrade responded to the NATO aerial assault with its own air defence operation, and by dispersing its own forces and assets, enlarging the media campaign, continuing its operations against the UCK in Kosovo province and using the MUP forces to expel the Albanian population there. But this was not done in an effort to 'ethnically cleanse' the province, as many contemporaries commented; arguably, it was instead Milošević's intention to spread the conflict into the wider region. The Albanian national and guerrilla movement continued to fight the VJ/MUP forces and to establish control over certain areas in Kosovo. Indeed, they responded very quickly to Milošević's tactics, and started to use the mass movement of the Kosovar population to show the international community how the Serbs were expelling the Albanians from their homes in effort to 'ethnically cleanse' the province.

Despite serious accusations by the international community's political leaders (particularly those of NATO countries) against the Milošević regime, the NATO air campaign was actually not launched to topple Milošević from power, nor to win over Milošević and the Serbs by using air power or to stop the alleged intentional 'ethnic cleansing' of Kosovo's Albanians. As had happened in Bosnia, a combination of air power and 'shuttle diplomacy' eventually led to the end of hostilities and a political solution. The only difference was the duration of the conflict. Most US State Department (and some NATO) political figures expected the air campaign would last for just a few days, after which all the parties would return to the negotiating table. But the stakes were raised after the start of campaign and the Serbian decision to fight back. Milošević actually needed a longer war to show to the Serbs that he did not just hand over the province of Kosovo, but only after a serious air/land conflict which was visible and caused suffering for nearly every Serb citizen. However, the outcome was the same; Operation Allied Force led to peace talks in June 1999 and the Kumanovo agreement which formally ended Serb governance in Kosovo and Metohija.

The Story from the Defenders' Side (Serbia/FR Yugoslavia)

The former Federal Republic of Yugoslavia was a medium-size or even one of the smaller European countries, being a part – or a rump – of Greater Yugoslavia, which consisted of Serbia and Montenegro, with the ratio of all resources on the scale of Serbia 95 percent and Montenegro 5 percent, except for the size of the

Black-greyish stealth B-2As with JDAM bombs were used to strike the most important targets in Belgrade and Novi Sad. This was their operational debut and their first use in combat. Here, the B-2A 'Spirit of Oklahoma' is seen after landing in 2001. (NAC)

The Serbian Air Defence, namely the missile units equipped with Neva (SA-3) missiles, achieved most of the success during encounters with NATO SEAD and strike packages. Here, a camouflaged Neva of a missile battalion is located in Zuce village, in the woods of the Avala Mountains. (B. Dimitrijević)

A team of USAF experts visited Serbia in September 2005 to exchange experiences with their RV i PVO counterparts. Here, two of the USAF officers visit a damaged Vranica HAS, especially built for MiG-29s at Batajnica Air Base. The aircraft in the rear is a MiG-29 serialed 18102. (B. Dimitrijević)

territory. It was under a UN embargo from June 1992. When the conflict in Kosovo province became widespread, the FRY did not have any ally in the international community, except perhaps for Greece. Moreover, it was completely surrounded by NATO countries or those which allowed NATO to operate freely from or over its territory and airspace.

The Vojska Jugoslavije (VJ) was actually the old small federal socialist Yugoslav People's Army (JNA) which remained in Serbia and Montenegro. Due to the UN embargo and lack of allies, it had not introduced any new armament or equipment, and relied on the pre-1991 JNA inventory. FRY President Slobodan Milošević was not actually a supporter of the VJ (neither of the JNA). He instead trusted the MUP Srbije forces: the Police and State Security, which developed their own paramilitary forces sufficient for the local ethnic warfare. The VJ was thus neglected throughout the 1990s. Neither the army nor the air force had a defined role, a complaint later made by many generals. Milošević's attitude led to the neglection of important defence issues, as was the case with the air defence. Moreover, the army top leadership believed that the air defence was a matter for the RV i PVO, while inside the RV i PVO, which was commanded by the "fighter mafia", air defence matters were felt to be the sole responsibility of the Air Defence Corps.

This standpoint among the highest FRY political and military authorities led to the neglect of the Air Defence resources in the pre-campaign period. More than half the missile units were classified as 'non-active' – serviceability of the MiG-29 fighters fell to just 44 percent in 1998, and there was a noticeable lack of conscripts.[1] Despite serious indications that NATO was about to launch an air campaign, most of the command personnel actually believed that it would be somehow avoided. This notion led to a delay in preparations and dispersion of resources.

The VJ (RV i PVO) estimations during their preparations in early 1999 ignored the following facts: that the initial strike would be a joint one with all types of strike/bomber aviation and cruise missiles; that Hungarian airspace would be used as it offered the shortest route for attacks from the beginning of OAF; and that the RV i PVO facilities in Montenegro would be targeted too. The VJ top brass believed that the airstrikes would be concentrated on Kosovo or south of the 44th parallel, and that a NATO ground invasion from Macedonia could be expected at an early stage.

During the air campaign, some decisions by the top brass caused serious damage to their forces. A handful of RV i PVO MiG-29 fighters, launched on the first night of OAF, showed themselves totally inferior to the NATO fighters, but a desperate wish to engage the enemy led to the almost complete annihilation of the MiG-29 fleet. NATO easily managed to establish full air superiority over the FRY airspace, only later being challenged by the RV i PVO SAMs. Other bad decisions included leaving the whole fleet of Galeb G-2/G-4 training aircraft at Golubovci Air Base in Montenegro, which were later completely destroyed; the taking out of a number of MiG-21s from the underground Rudnik position at Pristina Air Base with the intention to maintain QRA (quick reaction alert), which were also destroyed; the late decision to dismantle aircraft and move them to safety, away from the air bases; and leaving a large number of Neva missiles in stores, which were destroyed in the first nights of Allied Force.

Nevertheless, some positive decisions were also made: forbidding MiG-21 usage in air defence; dispersion of materiel resources and reserves prior to the launching of the air campaign; concentration of the operational centres of air surveillance and the Air Defence Corps in the underground Straževica position in a Belgrade suburb; the later introduction of visual observation stations and MANPADS in the defence of Belgrade; and work on the improvised 'RL' light missile system can be named.

The RV i PVO missile air defence units operated throughout the duration of OAF. They managed to claim two USAF airplanes and to damage several others with relatively the obsolete Neva (SA-3) missile system. They also claimed over two dozen UAVs and numerous cruise missiles using MANPADS and light AA artillery. In combat, the Serb MANPADS proved unsuccessful against the strike aviation which was used strictly according to the ROEs, but were lethal against the slow and low-flying UAVs, mostly over Kosovo and southern Serbia. The main success of the Serbian air defence units was their continuous presence and the use of every opportunity to open fire.[2]

By abandoning their peacetime positions, RV i PVO missile units managed to avoid destruction on the first night of OAF. Later, they developed tactics to avoid NATO strikes, including mobility, movement, manoeuvre, brief illumination, intentional passivity during the larger airstrikes and establishing ambushes. Such practice enabled it to survive the war with fewer casualties and to remain a threat to NATO aviation. Despite the low number of claimed NATO combat aircraft, most of the NATO/US leadership remarked

Two sides of the air war: (top) USAF pilots during preparation for a mission (NAC); (bottom) RV i PVO pilots in private premises near Ponikve Air Base. (252.lbae)

Serbian (VJ/MUP) ground forces in Kosovo, but elsewhere too, also developed numerous tactics to deal with and avoid the effects of the NATO airstrikes. They would operate scattered in small units, hiding their combat vehicles and artillery in settlements, near houses and in various civilian facilities. Depending on the activity of NATO aviation, they would move their assets or else leave them inactive to avoid traces of their tracks or the heat of their engines. Serbs camouflaged weaponry with branches and foliage, and while on the move, avoided detection by using bad weather or the night, civilian vehicles, lorries or coaches, and painted their vehicles in civilian colours or even blended in with refugee columns. They adapted their survival tactics on a daily basis. NATO strike aircraft which orbited over Kosovo only managed to attack them successfully when they made mistakes in their 'hide and seek' tactics, or when a sudden change of weather altered the scene on the ground and left VJ/MUP assets fully visible in the open. Many authors pointed out that VJ combat forces were never fully deployed, being kept back to deal with an eventual ground invasion.

The Yugoslav/Serbian defeat was caused by the interaction of many factors. Notably, Slobodan Milošević

on the Serbian air defences as being a "fully integrated, robust and lethal system". Perhaps the best praise for the Serbian air defences (especially the 250th Missile Brigade) was given by the pilots who flew in the SEAD missions, for they coped with them on a daily basis and had to deal with their tactics and threats.

A Dutch colonel from the CAOC in Vicenza stated in a post-operation interview that NATO had underestimated the ways in which the Serbs would use their air defence systems, remarking that they were innovative, used surveillance and tracking radars speedily and were mobile. CIA analyst David Isby remarked that the Yugoslav/Serbian Air Defence was not defeated, as had been the case with Iraqi air defences in the Gulf War of 1991. The commander of the US Sixth Fleet, Vice Admiral Daniel Murphy Jr, illustrated this point by saying: "We never neutralized the IADS. We weren't any safer on Day 78 than we were on Day 1." He continued that air doctrine required that the enemy air defence be neutralised "before taking on the targets that count. Well, if we had followed that doctrine, we would have pounded nothing but IADS for 78 days."[3]

failed to provoke a political dispute among the members of NATO. Furthermore, he did not manage to provoke a regional crisis by expelling thousands of ethnic Albanians out of Kosovo, and nor was he able to receive strong backing from Russia, still hanging on to a belief in the existence of a bipolar world. The widening of the air campaign, tremendous damage to the civilian infrastructure in Serbia proper, the possibility of a NATO ground attack from Macedonia and growing exhaustion among his troops deployed in Kosovo finally caused Milošević to surrender on 10 June 1999.[4]

Former Finnish president Marti Ahtisari, who negotiated with Milošević on behalf of the international community, allowed him two fictions for domestic usage: that NATO forces to be deployed in Kosovo should not be labelled as 'international' or even UN-controlled forces, and that Serbia/FR Yugoslavia would keep its territorial integrity, despite their defeat in the air war. This meant that Kosovo and Metohija remained under the sovereignty of Serbia.[5] These matters were backed by the UN Security Council Resolution 1244 which was issued at the time.

A 55th Fighter Squadron crew chief from Shaw Air Force Base, South Carolina, marshals an F-16CJ into its parking space on its return from Operation Allied Force on 30 June 1999. (NAC)

The first contingent of US Marines from the 26th Marine Expeditionary Unit, which would be deployed in Kosovo after 10 June 1999, loads on to a CH-53D Sea Stallion helicopter on the deck of USS *Kearsarge* on 8 June that year. (NAC)

When it became clear that limited airstrikes would be insufficient, the campaign was progressively increased in intensity.[6]

American analyst Anthony Cordesman said: "NATO did not execute a campaign that it had carefully planned before the fighting began, it improvised." He pointed out SACEUR General Wesley Clark's expectations that "there was a 40% chance that war would end within three days. Clark emphasised strikes on Serbian ground forces and the units involved in ethnic cleansing rather than expecting strategic bombing."[7]

Adam Hebert has said that OAF's "biggest weakness was that it took too long to gather steam",[8] while Ivo Daalader and Michael O'Hanlon claimed that Allied Force was almost a case study in "how not to wage a war" in its first weeks; NATO had not accumulated enough forces to be stronger than the Serb VJ/MUP, and due to political constraints it came close to losing its first real war. Daalader and O'Hanlon criticised NATO for launching the operation when unprepared for full combat, convinced that a short bombing campaign would be effective in bringing the crisis to a resolution.[9]

It seems that the harshest criticism of Operation Allied Force came from its key man, who was himself harshly criticised by many others: General Clark. In spite of the operation having an image of being a robust air campaign from the start, Clark noted in his book that it had many shortcomings. To begin with, he said the forces which took part in OAF were assembled at the last moment. A US aircraft carrier, which would inevitably form a major part of any air power campaign, arrived in only the second week of OAF. Furthermore, he said the engaged NATO forces did not understand the nature of the theatre and, even more, there were strong political constraints which limited the operation and produced strict ROEs. Clark stressed that OAF broke several strict military rules: that it should have a clear aim, unity of command and simplicity of operational plans, and that it should surprise the enemy and comprise offensive action. He added that while nominally the chain of command passed through "his channels", in practice the national chains of command were shaping and leading the operations, sometimes bypassing NATO altogether. Clark wrote

The Story from the Attackers' Side (NATO)

Operation Allied Force, like Operation Deliberate Force in 1995, was a further step away from the old Cold War role of NATO. OAF was a further promotion of the new NATO mission to react to a crisis and be a part of the crisis management in parts of Europe still not integrated into the Western Alliance.

As Air Chief Marshal Sir John Day, Deputy Chief of the British Defence Staff, pointed out on 7 March 2000:

> The Kosovo campaign was unusual in that it was the first time that NATO had been engaged in such a sustained offensive campaign. This brought the challenges of balancing the political and military aspirations of all 19 nations of NATO… The Kosovo air campaign was designed as a graduated campaign, to give Milošević the chance to change his mind about the ethnic repression of the Kosovo Albanians, once he realised that NATO was serious.

A pre-flight inspection for the 510th EFS at Aviano: a technician leans into the cockpit of an F-16CG on 2 April 1999. (NAC)

A US Navy F-14D Tomcat applies full afterburner as it prepares to launch from the flight deck of USS *Theodore Roosevelt* on the night of 7 April. This Tomcat belonged to the VA-41 'Black Aces' Squadron, which was attacking VJ targets in Kosovo. (NAC)

that the air campaign started with the intention to force the Serbs to return to the negotiating table with the Albanians, but soon expanded to other targets not related directly to Kosovo, and that after the NATO summit five conditions streamed the remainder of the campaign.[10]

Putting Clark's criticism to one side, Allied Force – which was regarded as a success by many politicians in the State Department and among NATO countries – was a new experience to NATO and in particular the US military. The operation, treated in the beginning as a minor regional contingency, brought many challenges for the USAF. After the end of the Cold War, the USAFE and other US forces in Europe were gradually and significantly downsized. OAF overstretched them much more than the Gulf War of 1991, when lots of Cold War assets were still available in Europe.

The ongoing conflict in 1999 brought the need for partial mobilisation of Air National Guard and Air Force Reserve personnel and units. Deployed USAF units were manned by personnel or entire units from CONUS which were not trained for overseas/expeditionary combat usage. Soon, while in theatre, a lack of spare parts became visible with certain CONUS-based airframes, such as the B-1 bomber. Thus, 'cannibalisation' was necessary for keeping the aircraft flying. Some units which arrived from CONUS brought additional aircraft for spare parts. The tanker fleet and small force of E-8 J-STARS were overstretched and constantly in the air. New and sophisticated pods such as the HTS-213 HARM Targeting System were almost all deployed for Allied Force, consequently leaving SEAD units back in America almost without any of these precious devices. Bad weather over the theatre and the natural features of the terrain also had a direct influence on the efficiency of the combat aviation. Experience showed that precision location of targets in the Balkans was a very demanding task. Expected to be the primary tool for such missions, the E-8 J-STARS showed many weaknesses in the discovery and location of ground targets.

Contrary to NATO/US political expectations, Operation Allied Force did not calm down the Kosovo crisis or stop the humanitarian catastrophe. Indeed, in several cases it just complicated matters. Despite the use of sophisticated targeting pods, PGMs and guidance from ABCCC or CAOC, there were a couple of occasions when columns of Albanian refugees were attacked, mistaken for VJ/MUP columns, resulting in many civilian casualties. These tragic events, labelled as 'collateral damage', influenced the introduction of strict ROEs in carrying out airstrikes. The strong desire to avoid further such cases of collateral damage produced caution and dilemmas among the politicians and dilemmas and anger among the pilots, who in all cases were eager to execute their missions successfully.

After clashing with a handful of RV i PVO MiG-29 fighters, NATO established air superiority over the theatre. There was no significant appearance by the Serbian fighters. The missile units of the air defence became the only credible challenge, as General Jumper, commander of USAFE, pointed out: "The activities of

The 78th EFS consisted of F-16CJs from several squadrons of the 20th Fighter Wing, based at Shaw AFB, and was deployed to the Balkan theatre to take part in SEAD missions against Serbian air defence units until the end of the campaign. (DoD)

Air refuelling was crucial for operations over the FR Yugoslavia during Operation Allied Force. A massive fleet of USAF, AFRES and ANG tankers, along with tankers of the European NATO allies, were constantly in the air during the campaign. Shown here is a KC-135 Stratotanker of the 121st ARW of the Ohio Air National Guard. (B. Dimitrijević)

Serbian air defence influenced the improvisation of new procedures and fast assessment of the targets." SEAD aviation became pivotal in combating the Serb air defences, but SEAD missions were by then totally different from those of the Gulf War in 1991 and Operation Deliberate Force in Bosnia in 1995. The Serbian air defence shortened their time of radiation and set up ambushes which were maintained for several days without illumination. They dispersed their units, used half of the regularly needed assets and created false firing positions. Such tactics were influential in the Serb air defence units remaining operational until the end of the campaign, despite being shaken by losses in equipment and personnel. Their activities revealed many SEAD shortcomings which were later the matter of debate in US military circles, including EA-6B Prowlers being used to support SEAD missions almost at the edge of their range.

After the bringing down of an F-117 stealth fighter, that night's lack of Prowler ECM coverage for the F-117 strike packages was not repeated again. It was later discovered that the F-117s lost some of their stealth features in certain parts of their flights, becoming visible to the oldest types of Soviet radars, such as the P-12. Another bitter experience was that stealth aircraft could be tracked by SIGINT reconnaissance through monitoring the communications of other crews along the path of the F-117s.[11] These experiences were influential in the type's early retirement.

The positive side of the claiming of both USAF aircraft over Serbia was the fast extraction of the pilots from enemy territory, preventing the Serbs from exploiting their capture in the media. Combat SAR were praised for their efforts during OAF, despite it taking a lot of effort to coordinate the whole operation; their actions proved that the whole USAF/NATO system stood behind the combat pilots when they crossed into enemy airspace.

The use of Precision Guided Missiles, which were employed earlier in Deliberate Force in September 1995, again became a perfect tool to influence the campaign. It was estimated that PGMs reduced collateral damage, making war less bloody and thus morally more acceptable. Fear of the use of these sophisticated munitions made the enemy more readily accept the political conditions imposed by US shuttle diplomats such as Richard Holbrooke. Several key US generals – among them Clark, Short, Jumper and Corley – became firm advocates of air power being used in managing conflicts. Air power thus became a tool of universal usage, euphoria for it ruling the US State Department and NATO after 1999.

A report by the US Department of Defense, submitted in front of Congress in 2000, focused on the following key experiences of the air war over FRY/Serbia:

- Parallel NATO and US chains of command complicated the successful outcome of the missions
- Technical differences and the technological advantage of the USAF over all other NATO air forces limited the optimal efficiency of OAF
- Planning and transport systems were burdened by a rising number of requests
- The huge burden placed on the SEAD aviation led to the need to discover a more effective way to suppress enemy air defences by co-ordinating current technologies
- Successful use of the latest generation of PGMs led to the enabling of further purchases of such munitions
- There was a need to develop models for the earlier involvement and usage of reserve forces
- Improvement was needed in the use of UAVs through mission planning, coordination and interaction with combat aviation and modernisation of existing types
- The experience of Task Force Hawk showed that there was a need to test such types of units without the usual support elements
- The humanitarian part of the air operation showed the importance of trained personnel and linguistic and engineering experts in such missions

Some of the shortcomings mentioned showed that the United States was hardly capable of successfully running two major wars in different parts of the world, as was accounted for in the current National Military Strategy.[12]

Operation Allied Force did not in the end prevent the ethnic cleansing of Albanians, which was one of the reasons why it was launched on 24 March 1999. It was seen to be impossible to prevent local conflicts without direct ground intervention. No restrictions or widening of ROEs could help in this direction until the arrival of

The Supreme Allied Commander in Europe, General Wesley Clark, was the key US and NATO figure who led Operation Allied Force. Despite Clark's difficulties in estimating just what the centre of gravity should be in Serbia, and numerous problems at the highest military and political levels, the operation was still regarded as a success. (NATO)

B Company, 7-159, based at Gibelstadt in Germany, prepares to carry out maintenance on a Blackhawk helicopter, deployed to Albania in support of Task Force Hawk. The unsuccessful deployment of Apache and other helicopters was in total contrast to media announcements of their usage and the expectations of the SACEUR, General Clark. (NAC)

ground forces. Nevertheless, the successful end of Allied Force and the expelling of the Yugoslav Army/Serb MUP forces from Kosovo province (despite some shortcomings) was confirmation for many in the US and NATO administrations that air power was the key for success when all political negotiations and diplomatic avenues had been exhausted. The advocates of air power would take the stand with such an approach to solve the crises in Afghanistan in 2001 and Iraq in 2003. This was mainly led by the expectation that the use of air power would solve any political problem and preserve the lives of US (and NATO) soldiers.

Serb Centre of Gravity?

Operation Allied Force demonstrated the difficulties in estimating just what NATO's centre of gravity was in Serbia. This issue was characteristic of the relationship between General Clark and General Short but was visible sometimes too to the pilots in the strike packages. Clark thought the main effort should be concentrated against the VJ forces in Kosovo and in supporting the Albanian population and preventing ethnic cleansing. On the contrary, Short, being a strike pilot himself, believed that the strikes on Belgrade and the FRY/Serb political and military leadership were crucial. In a now well-known exchange during one of the daily video teleconferences, Short expressed satisfaction that, at last, NATO warplanes were about to strike the Serbian special police headquarters in central Belgrade: "This is the jewel in the crown." Clark replied: "To me, the jewel in the crown is when those B-52s rumble across Kosovo." "You and I have known for weeks that we have different jewelers," said Short, prompting Clark to respond: "My jeweler outranks yours."[13]

Admiral Daniel J. Murphy Jr, Commander of the US Sixth Fleet and Striking and Support Forces, Southern Europe, commented that SACEUR General Clark had a perspective as commander of ground forces, which was why he engaged all his strength in chasing Serb forces in Kosovo. Clark did not have a competent air force general in his team to help with his decisions about the use of air power. On the contrary, General Short did not see the VJ's Third Army as a pivotal opponent, a standpoint supported by General Joseph Ralston, vice-chairman of the Joint Chiefs of Staff.[14] David C. Isby commented that Clark's opposition to the gradual escalation of control from Washington was one reason that his tour as SACEUR came to an early end after Kosovo. The subsequent appointment of Air Force General Joseph W. Ralston as SACEUR "was a head-line making event". He took over from Army General Clark, "who had fallen out of favor in the wake of OAF. It may be the answer to the question of the bigger role of the airmen as regional commanders."[15]

The problem of the primary focus of the campaign led to Operation Allied Force being run on two separate tracks, one using NATO forces against VJ/MUP units in Kosovo and southern Serbia, and the other north of the 44th parallel, around Belgrade, using only USAF assets. Nevertheless, it is likely that political limitations were more powerful than either Short's or Clark's standpoints. The politicians and their interests were stronger than the generals in this campaign, as General Clark testified in his memoirs.

CONCLUSION

The results of Operation Allied Force were extraordinary for both the United States and NATO. The operation was the first campaign in which the attacking side did not lose a single soldier from the direct action of the defenders. Even when the two aircraft were shot down, the pilots were successfully and quickly rescued. High standards had thus been set for the success of future operations.

However, the Chief of Staff of the USAF, General Michael Ryan, pointed in February 2000 that "it was as dangerous the first day of combat as the last day, because Allied airplanes had failed to tear down Yugoslavia's integrated air defence systems."[16] General Bruce Carlson, who held senior positions in the USAF HQ in Washington, also commented:

> The Serbs were much better prepared and trained to move their equipment, set it up quickly and respond more quickly to threats than the Iraqis. They were also much more flexible in netting it quickly, in using a maze of fiber optic cables, connections and cellular phones, everything to tie their air defence network together, including visual observations. They had a very good integrated air defence system in place when the Operation began… They may be crazy by Western standards of acceptable behaviour, but they are a worthwhile opponent. They are well trained, very innovative, tough and determined.[17]

Operation Allied Force highlighted the differences between the United Sates and the other NATO allies, not just in technology, but also in how the operation should be conducted. Most of the NATO allies had expected a short duration for the operation, as had been the case with Operation Deliberate Force in 1995. The Americans, however, soon changed this point of view, wishing to provide a decisive punch against Milošević and the Serbs. This soon led to a difference in the flow of intel information, which Americans were not eager to share with their European allies. The Europeans did not have assets such B-2s, F-117s or cruise missiles, so they started to create their own Air Tasking Orders, which existed alongside NATO ATOs. This sometimes caused confusion, with the forces in theatre operating upon two separate ATOs. Moreover, the Americans started to realise that sharing intel information with their allies would not benefit them, and to the contrary, details could be forwarded to the Serbs (as had happened with one French officer in 1998). They allowed Britons to take part in the intel loop, but almost nobody else. BDA was in many cases a strictly American possession, not shared with any others – 'NATO secret' started to be replaced with

British Defence Secretary George Robertson visited the RAF Harrier force at Gioia del Colle on 29 March. Here, he inspects one of the Harriers armed with Paveway PGMs. Mr Robertson told the pilots at Gioia del Colle Air Base that their actions were "awe-inspiring", risking their lives every night for a cause. (RAF)

US military meets US politics: General Jumper, Commander of USAFE, welcomes Secretary of Defense William Cohen at Ramstein Air Base in Germany on 8 April 1999 during Operation Allied Force. (NAC)

'US secret'. In American eyes, the USAF was conducting most of the fighting, while the Europeans were only asking questions and making comments while their contingents carried out secondary missions.

Within a year, it was the prevailing notion that June 1999 marked a real turning point in the history of warfare. As military historian John Keegan defined, and General Ryan repeated: "The capitulation of President Milošević proved that war can be won by air power alone."[18] Air Chief Marshal Sir John Day also pointed out: "This was the first time in history, that we used air power alone to achieve victory."[19]

The use of air power was a good choice to deal with President Milošević, who had already endured a similar experience with Operation Deliberate Force in Bosnia in 1995. Air power reduced the risk to NATO's own forces, while having a great effect on their opponents, and could be stopped at any given time to allow the diplomats to bring the situation to a conclusion. NATO's demands were a ceasefire and the withdrawal of VJ/MUP forces from Kosovo and Metohija province, the deployment of NATO-led international forces to maintain order in the province, the return of refugees and a political agreement regarding the future of Kosovo. A ground intervention and the expanding of the war to neighbouring countries did not happen, NATO did not suffer any combat casualties and the financial cost for the alliance was surprisingly low, as General Clark concluded.[20] The question of operational costs was commented upon by British historian Niall Ferguson a couple of years after the campaign: "Financially as well as strategically, the 1999 war represented a return to the era of low-cost gunboat diplomacy." Ferguson said that the lack of combat casualties for NATO meant "this was probably the safest army in history – safer, in fact, than some American high schools".[21]

General Clark wrote later that he had been conducting a limited war, with limited aims and limited financial resources. He pointed out that the West was not prepared for the limited campaign to escalate into a full-scale war, and marked this as one of the most obvious peculiarities of Operation Allied Force. Clark warned that no matter what efforts were made, this pattern would be repeated in the future.[22] The air campaigns in Afghanistan in 2001 and Iraq since 2003 have already proved to be dramatically different and more difficult situations.

NATO entered the war with FRY/Serbia preoccupied with the possibility of its own losses, and their negative influence on the ubiquitous media. Such media 'noise' if there should be eventual human losses to NATO forces could have ended the campaign in a moment. Niall Ferguson concluded: "What the war over Kosovo revealed – or, rather, what it confirmed – is that American power is not inhibited by the expense of military intervention, but the public aversion to the human cost… many Americans today seem unwilling to expend *any* American lives in foreign wars, no matter how noble the cause."[23]

Meanwhile, the Kosovo dispute still continues, more than 20 years after Operation Allied Force was launched to finish it.

BIBLIOGRAPHY

Archival Sources

Kabinet načelnika Generalštaba Vojske Jugoslavije [Cabinet of the Chief of the General Staff of Yugoslav Army].

Komanda RV i PVO [Air Force and Air Defence HQs] and annual histories of subordinated units: Vazduhoplovni korpus, Korpus PVO, 204. lovački avijacijski puk, 250. raketna brigada PVO, 98. lovačko-avijacijski puk, 230, 240. samohodni raketni puk PVO, 210. bataljon veze, 280 centar za EIO.

Muzej Jugoslovenskog ratnog vazduhoplovstva: fond jedinica RV i PVO [Yugoslav Air Force Museum, The RV i PVO Units Fond].

Unpublished Sources – Materials:

Davis, Charles H., *JDAM, The Kosovo Experience and DPAS*, The Boeing Company (presentation).

Đorđević, Slađan, *Iskustva iz borbenih dejstava RJ PVO malog dometa u agresiji NATO na Saveznu Republiku Jugoslaviju*, GŠ VJ, Sektor za ŠONID, ŠP škola (Beograd, 2000).

Draganić, Jovica, *Potrebne snage za odvraćanje u PVO*, stručni rad, ŠNO (1999).

Iskustva iz borbenih dejstava Vojske Jugoslavije u suprotstavljanju agresiji NATO na SR Jugoslaviju, za strategijski nivo (monografija), GŠ VJ; Sektor za ŠONID, ŠNO; VT-Str. Pov (Beograd, oktobar 1999).

Iskustva iz borbenih dejstava Vojske Jugoslavije u suprotstavljanju agresiji NATO na SR Jugoslaviju (sintetička studija), GŠ VJ; Sektor za ŠONID, Institut za ratnu veštinu; VT-SP (Beograd, 1999).

Iskustva iz borbenih dejstava osnovnih zdruzeno-taktičkih jedinica Vojske Jugoslavije u suprotstavljanju agresiji NATO na SR Jugoslaviju, GŠ VJ; Sektor za ŠONID, Vojna akademija; VT-SP (Beograd, 1999).

Iskustva iz borbenih dejstava osnovnih taktičkih jedinica Vojske Jugoslavije u suprotstavljanju agresiji NATO na SR Jugoslaviju, GŠ VJ; Sektor za ŠONID, Vojna akademija; VT-SP (Beograd, oktobar 1999).

Materijali sa razmene iskustva o operaciji AF 1999 (Zemun/Ramstein, 2005).

Milinković, Milan, *Operativni zahtevi za dogradnju i modernizaciju lovačke avijacije*, Stručni rad, VA, ŠNO, GŠU 45. klasa (Beograd, 2002).

Ristić, Slađan, *Organizacija i funkcionisanje veza sistema VOJ u VJ, u uslovima narušenog sistema veza VJ*, diplomski rad Sektor za ŠONID, Generalštabna škola VJ, smer RV i PVO (Beograd, 2000).

Todorov, Staniša, *Iskustva iz učešća 450. rp PVO u suprotstavljanju NATO operaciji „Milosrdni anđeo" 1999. godine*, ST-INT seminarski rad VA ŠNO, KŠU (Beograd, 2007).

Published Sources – Materials:

Agresija NATO pakta na Saveznu Republiku Jugoslaviju (Belgrade, Bezbednost, ratno izdanje 2–3, 1999).

Amnesty International, *NATO/Federal Republic of Yugoslavia 'collateral damage' or unlawful killings? Violations of the Laws of War by NATO during Operation Allied Force* (June 2000).

Bolkcom, Christoper, *Military Suppression of Enemy Air Defenses (SEAD): Assessing Future Needs*, CRS Report for Congress.

Combined Prepared Statement of General Wesley Clark, USA, Admiral James Ellis, Jr., USN, and Lieutenant General Michael Short, USAF, Of the United States European Command Before the Senate Armed Services Committee (21 October 1999).

Electronic Warfare, Comprehensive Strategy Needed for Suppressing Enemy Air Defenses, US General Accounting Office, Report to Congressional Requesters (January 2001).

European Contributions to Operation Allied Force, Implications from Transatlantic Cooperation, Project Air Force (RAND, 2001).

Hardy, Scott A., LCDR, USN, US Air Force, *The Search For Air Dominance: Stealth Versus SEAD*, A Research Report Submitted to the Faculty in Partial Fulfillment of the Graduation Requirements (Maxwell Air Force Base, Alabama, April 2006).

Kometer, Michael W., Lt Col, USAF, *Command in Air War: Centralized vs. Decentralized Control of Combat Airpower*, Submitted to the Engineering Systems Division in partial fulfillment of the requirements for the degree of Doctor of Philosophy in Technology, Management, and Policy (Massachusetts Institute of Technology, May 2005).

Kosovo Air Operations, Army Resolving Lessons Learned Regarding the Apache Helicopter, Report to the Chairman, Committee on Armed Services, House of Representatives, US General Accounting Office (May 2001).

Kosovo Air Operations, Report to the Chairman, Committee on Armed Services, House of Representatives, US General Accounting Office (May 2001).

Kosovo and Macedonia, US and Allied Military Operations, CRS Issue Brief for Congress, updated 8 July 2003 (Steve Bowman, Foreign Affairs, Defense and Trade Division).

Kosovo, One Year on, Achivement and Challenge (Lord Robertson of Port Ellen, Sec. Gen. of NATO).

Kosovo: Operation Allied Force, House of Commons, Research paper 99/48 (29 April 1999).

Kosovo: U.S. Naval Lessons Learned During Operation Allied Force, March–June 1999: Statement of Vice Admiral Daniel J. Murphy, Jr, Commander, U.S. Sixth Fleet and Striking and Support Forces, Southern Europe. Statement of Brigadier General Robert M. Flanagan, Deputy Commander, II Marine Expeditionary Force. Statement of Vice Admiral James F. Amerault, Deputy Chief of Naval Operations (Logistics).

Military Aircraft, Information on Air Force Aerial Refuelling Tankers, Testimony Before the Subcommittee on Protection Forces, Committee on Armed Services, House of Representatives, US General Accounting Office (June 2003).

Nardulli, Bruce R., Perry, Walter L., Pirnie, Bruce, Gordon IV, John & McGinn, John G., *Disjointed War Military Operations in Kosovo 1999*, Prepared for the United States Army, Approved for public release; distribution unlimited (RAND Arroyo Center, 2002).

Nicolls, Boone, MSgt, USAF (ret.), *Airman's Guide*, 6th Edition (Stackpole Books, 2004).

Parker, Brandon D., Major, US Air Force, *Caught in a Jam: the US Air Force's Electronic Attack Conundrum*, Research Report Submitted to the Faculty in Partial Fulfillment of the Graduation Requirements (Maxwell Air Force Base, Alabama, April 2008).

Leaf, Brigadier General Daniel P., press conference, NATO HQ, Brussels (19 April 1999).

Prepared Statement of General Henry H. Shelton to the Senate Armed Services Committee Hearing on Operations in Kosovo (20 July 1999).

Stone, Troy R., *The Air War Over Serbia: Denial, Punishment, Or Balance of Interest*, Thesis presented to the Faculty of the School of Advanced Airpower Studies (Airpower Studies, Air University, Maxwell Air Force Base, Alabama, June 2001).

The Reader's Guide to the NATO Summit in Washington (23–25 April 1999).

Report to Congress, Kosovo/Allied Force After-action Report, Unclassified (31 January 2000).

Statement of General John P. Jumper, Commander, United States Air Forces in Europe.

Magazines:

Aeromagazin, Air Action, Air Force, Air Forces Monthly, Airmen, Combat Aircraft, Jets, Odbrana, Royal Air Force Yearbook (2000–2001), *Službeni vojni list, Soldier of Fortune, United States Air Force Yearbook* (1999–2002), *Vojska, World Air Power Journal.*

Web Pages:

US DoD, USAF, USAFE and its units: 31st, 48th, 52nd, 86th and 100th Wing.

US Air Forces in Europe, New Service (March–July 1999), www.usafe.af.mil/news/news99.

Articles:

'Allied Force Debrief, Interviews and photos by Eric Hehs', *Code One Magazine* (October 1999).

Cooper, A. Scott, 'Air Power and the Coersive Use of Force', *The Washington Quarterly* (Autumn 2001), pp.81–93.

Cordesman, Anthony H. (Arleigh A. Burke Chair in Strategy), 'The Effectiveness of the NATO Strategic Air and Missile Campaign in Kosovo', *A Working Paper Revised* (August 2000).

Cordesman, Anthony H. (Arleigh A. Burke Chair in Strategy), 'The Lessons and Non-Lessons of the Air and Missile Campaign in Kosovo', Revised (August 2000).

Devries, Donald C., 'Reserve Intelligence Support for Operation Allied Force', *JFQ* (Spring 2000), pp.81–87.

Dimitrijević, Bojan, 'Rat NATO-a protiv Srbije 1999. godine: vojni aspekti posledice', *Nova srpska politička misao, posebno izdanje Srbija i NATO (I), Srpski diskurs rata* (Belgrade, 2000), pp.161–174.

Dimitrijević, Bojan, 'Vazdušne operacije NATO u Jugoslaviji i posledice', *Istorija 20. veka* (Belgrade, January 2000), pp.109–120.

Gazzini, Tarcisio, 'NATO Coercive Military Activities in the Yugoslav Crisis', *European Journal of International Law*, Volume 12, Issue 3, 1 (June 2001), pp.391–436.

Gordon IV, John, Nardull, Bruce & Perry, Walter L., 'The Operational Challenges of Task Force Hawk', *JFQ*, Autumn/Winter (2001–02), pp.52–57.

Jumper, P. John', 'General, Rapidly Deploying Aerospace Power, Lessons from Allied Force', *Aerospace Power Journal* (Winter 1999).

Lambeth, Dr Benjamin S., 'Kosovo and the Continuing SEAD Challenge', *Aerospace Power Journal* (Summer 2002).

'Mission ready: Canada's role in the Kosovo Air campaign', *Canadian Military Journal* (Spring 2000), pp.55–61.

Ochmanek, David A., 'What Operation Allied Force Can Teach Us About Capabilities Needed for Future Military Operations', RAND.

Richter, Andrew, 'Lessons From the Revolution: What Recent US Military Operations Reveal About the Revolution in Military Affairs and Future Combat', *Journal of Military and Strategic Studies*, Vol. 7, Issue 3, Spring (2005).

Schatz, Lt Col Rowayne A., 'USAF Theater Airlift Lessons from Kosovo', *Air & Space Power Journal*, Chronicles Online (2000).

Solana, Javier, 'NATO's Success in Kosovo', *Foreign Affairs* (November/December 1999), pp.114–121.

Tirpak, John A., DTIC, 'Dealing with Air Defenses the Balkan War pointed up how short the force is for electronic combat', *Early Bird, Air Force Magazine* (November 1999).

LITERATURE (MONOGRAPHS, MEMOIRS):

Agresija NATO, uzroci, karakter i posledice krize na Kosovu i Metohiji (Belgrade: Klub generala i admirala Vojske Srbije, 2008).

Ahtisari, Marti, *Misija u Beogradu* (Belgrade: Filip Višnjić, 2001).

Aničić, Đorđe S., *Smena (ratni dnevnik)* (Belgrade: Agrotop Marketing, 2009).

Crickmore, Paul, *Lockheed F-117 Nighthawk Stealth Fighter*, Air Vanguard 16 (London: Osprey Publishing Ltd, 2014).

della Croce, Roberto, *Priča jednog borbenog pilota* (Novi Sad: Stylos Art, 2013).

Daalader Ivo H. & O'Hanlon, Michael E., *Winning Ugly, NATO's War to Save Kosovo* (Washington DC: Brookings Institution Pres, 2000).

Dimitrijević, Bojan, *Kurjaci sa ušća, istorijat 252. lovačkobombarderske eskadrile* (Beograd: ISI, 2004).

Dimitrijević, Bojan & Draganić, Jovica, *250. raketna brigada PVO* (Beograd: VIZ, 2007).

Dimitrijević, Bojan & Draganić, Jovica, *Vazdušni rat nad Srbijom* (Belgrade: ISI, 2010).

Drendel, Lou, *Bone, B-1 Lancer in action*, Aircraft number 179 (Carrollton, Texas: Squadron/Signal Publications, 2002).

Đošan, Miloš, *Generalov kosmetski put* (Beograd: autorsko izdanje, 2004).

Haave, Christopher E. (Col USAF) & Haun, Phil M. (Lt Col USAF), *A-10s over Kosovo, The Victory of Airpower over a Fielded Army as Told by the Airmen Who Fought in Operation Allied Force* (Maxwell Air Force Base, Alabama: Air University Press, 2003).

Henriksen, Dag, *Operation Allied Force, A Product of Military Theory or Political Pragmatism?, An Examination of the Role of Air Power in handling the Kosovo Crisis 1999–99*, PhD Dissertation (University of Glasgow: December 2005).

Junaci Slobodnog neba (Belgrade: Komanda RV i PVO, June 2000).

Klark, Vesli K., *Moderno ratovanje, Bosna, Kosovo i budućnost oružane borbe* (Belgrade: Samizdat, 2003).

The Kosovo News and Propaganda War, edited by Peter Goff (Wien: International Press Instituten, September 1999).

Kraljevske lisice 1977–2002, povodom 25 godina 450.raketnog puka protivvazdušne odbrane (Belgrade: VINC, 2002).

Lamb, Michael W. Sr, Lt Col, USAF, *Operation Allied Force, Golden Nuggets for Future Campaigns*, Air War College Maxwell Paper No. 27 (Maxwell Air Force Base, Alabama: August 2002).

Larsen, Wayne A., *Serbian information operations during Operation Allied Force*, Research Report (Maxwell AFB: Air Command and Staff College, Air University, April 2000).

McKinney, Maj. Mike & Ryan, Mike, *Chariots of the Damned, Helicopter Special Operations from Vietnam to Kosovo* (New York: St Martin's Paperbacks, 2003).

Micevski, Milan & Dimitrijević, Bojan, *83. lovački avijacijski puk* (Niš: Galakisijanis, 2016).

Olulć, Saša, Antić, Goran & Dimitrijević, Bojan, *204. lovački avijacijski puk* (Belgrade: VINC, 2005).

Radić, Aleksandar, *Orao, pogled iz jugoslovenskog ugla* (Belgrade: Medija centar, 2012).

Smiljanić, Spasoje, *Agresija NATO, RV i PVO u odbrani otadžbine* (Belgrade: autorsko izdanje, 2009).

Vojska Jugoslavije u odbrambenom ratu 1999. godine, volume I (Belgrade: Klub generala i admirala Srbije, 2019).

NOTES

Chapter 1

1 Andrew Richter, 'Lessons From the Revolution: What Recent US Military Operations Reveal About the Revolution in Military Affairs and Future Combat', *Journal of Military and Strategic Studies*, Vol. 7, Issue 3, Spring (2005); *Report to Congress, Kosovo/Allied Force After-action Report*, Unclassified (31 January 2000), pp.7–8.

2 *Report to Congress*, pp.7–8.

3 Vesli K. Klark, *Moderno ratovanje, Bosna, Kosovo i budućnost oružane borbe* (Beograd: Samizdat, 2003), p.457.

4 Under the new arrangement, the Commander-in-Chief, US Air Forces in Europe, and the Commander-in-Chief, US Naval Forces, Europe, were removed from the chain of operational control, and the Commanders, 16th Air Force and Sixth Fleet, became joint task force commanders reporting directly to the US Commander-in-Chief, Europe. *Report to Congress*, pp.16–17.

5 *Report to Congress*, p.45; Gert Kromhout, 'Allied Force – Planning NATO Attacks', *Air Forces Monthly* (December 1999), p.51; Cordesman, Anthony H. (Arleigh A. Burke Chair in Strategy), *The Lessons and Non-Lessons of the Air and Missile Campaign in Kosovo*, Revised (August 2000), pp.258–259.

6 Kromhout, 'Allied Force – Planning NATO Attacks', p.51.

7 Kromhout, 'Allied Force – Planning NATO Attacks', p.51.

8 Wing Commander Andrew Brookes, 'European Lessons', *Air Forces Monthly* (June 2000), p.29.

9 Jim Hedge, 'Chinese Embassy Bombing', *Air Forces Monthly* (May 2000), pp,31–34.

10 US Air Force Academy: General (ret) John Jumper Talks Operation Allied Force at USAFA – YouTube <https://www.youtube.com/watch?v=1hpkE_FClYY&t=287>

11 Christopher E. Haave (Col, USAF) & Phil M. Haun (Lt Col, USAF), *A-10s over Kosovo, The Victory of Airpower over a Fielded Army as Told by the Airmen Who Fought in Operation Allied Force* (Maxwell Air Force Base, Alabama: Air University Press, 2003), pp.86–96.

12 Haave & Haun, *A-10s over Kosovo*, pp.71, 77–86; Archer, Bob, 'Spangdahlem Force', *USAF Yearbook* (2000), p.46.

13 Haave & Haun, *A-10s over Kosovo*, pp.72–74 ; Archer, 'Spangdahlem Force', p.46.

14 Adam J. Hebert, 'The Balkan Air War,' *Air Force Magazine* (March 2009), p.45.

15 Amnesty International, *NATO/Federal Republic of Yugoslavia 'collateral damage' or unlawful killings? Violations of the Laws of War by NATO during Operation Allied Force* (June 2000).

16 Klark, *Moderno ratovanje*, p.478.

17 Cordesman, *The Lessons and Non-Lessons*, p.94.

18 Kromhout, 'Allied Force – Planning NATO Attacks', pp.50–54.

19 Ben Dunnell, 'Allied Force', USAF Yearbook (1999), p.13; Kromhout, 'Allied Force – Planning NATO Attacks', p.54.

20 'After Kosovo', RAF Yearbook (2000), pp.40–42.

21 'After Kosovo', pp.40–42.

22 *European Contributions to Operation Allied Force, Implications from Transatlantic Cooperation*, Project Air Force, (RAND, 2001), pp.28–29; Isby, David C., 'Allied Force – US Lessons', *Air Forces Monthly* (May 2000), p.27.

23 *Iskustva iz borbenih dejstava osnovnih združeno-taktičkih jedinica Vojske Jugoslavije u suprotstavljanju agresiji NATO na SR Jugoslaviju*, GŠ VJ; Sektor za ŠONID, Vojna akademija; VT-SP (Beograd, 1999), p.33.

24 *The Reader's Guide to the NATO Summit in Washington*, 23–25 April 1999.

25 Cordesman, *The Lessons and Non-Lessons*, p.44.

26 'The RAF's Year 1999', *RAF Yearbook* (2000), p.86; *European Contributions to Operation Allied Force*, pp.22–23.

27 Tim Ripley, 'UK's Precision Bombing', *Air Force Magazine* (October 2000), p.26; 'The RAF's Year 1999', p.86.

28 Brookes, 'European Lessons', pp.24–29.

29 Jean-Louis Prome, 'Allied Force – French Operations', *Air Forces Monthly* (December 1999), pp.29–35; *European Contributions to Operation Allied Force*, pp.18–21.

30 *European Contributions to Operation Allied Force*, pp.21–22.

31 Dr Riccardo Niccoli, 'Improving the Tornado, Italian Style', *Air Forces Monthly* (April 2001), p.64.

32 Henri Pierre Grolleau, 'Hornet Mission the CF-18 in action', *Combat Aircraft*, Vol. 2, No. 11, pp.870–877; Randy Jolly, 'Balkan Debrief No. 1', *Combat Aircraft*, Vol. 2., No 8 (2000), pp.644–45. This author quotes different facts: 18 CF-188s logged 522 combat missions and accumulated 1,873 hours of flying time.

33 Kromhout, 'Allied Force – Planning NATO Attacks', pp.50–54; *European Contributions to Operation Allied Force*, p.22.

34 Jolly, 'Balkan Debrief No. 1', pp.644–645.

35 For more details, see: *European Contributions to Operation Allied Force.*

36 Isby, 'Allied Force – US Lessons', p.27.

37 *Iskustva iz borbenih dejstava osnovnih združeno-taktičkih jedinica*, pp.181–189.

38 Komanda RV i PVO (K-da RV i PVO): 'Analiza borbenih dejstava 1999: Analiza rada oragana KRV i PVO, "Komandovanje". General Smiljanić left his personal account on the OAF: General Spasoje Smiljanić, *Agresija NATO, RV i PVO u odbrani otadžbine* (Belgrade: II autorsko izdanje, 2009).

39 Cordesman, *The Lessons and Non-Lessons*, p.37.

40 *Iskustva iz borbenih dejstava osnovnih združeno-taktičkih jedinica*, p.38; Report on combat activities during 1999 of the 280th ELINT

Centre (report is still confidential; this is descriptive tittle). Further as: 'Report 280th ELINT Centre'.

41 Radić Aleksandar & Micevski Milan, 'NATO u agresiji na SR Jugoslaviju', *Novi Glasnik,* Belgrade (February 1999).

Chapter 2

1 Cordesman, *The Lessons and Non-Lessons,* p.41.

2 Jamie Hunter & Richard Collens, 'Invisible Spirits', *USAF Yearbook* (2000), pp.6–9; Peter Grier, 'The JDAM revolution', *Air Force Magazine* (September 2006), pp.60–63.

3 Ross Simpson, *Stealth Down* (Charleston, South California: Narwahl Press, 2002), pp.9–11.

4 *Iskustva iz borbenih dejstava osnovnih združeno-taktičkih jedinica,* p.40.

5 *Vojska – ratno izdanje,* broj 363–364, 3.5.1999.

6 *Vojska Jugoslavije u odbrambenom ratu 1999. godine*, volume II (Beograd: Klub generala i admirala Srbije, 2019), p.419.

7 *Iskustva iz borbenih dejstava osnovnih združeno-taktičkih jedinica,* p.35.

8 'Report 280th ELINT Centre'.

9 *Iskustva iz borbenih dejstava osnovnih združeno-taktičkih jedinica,* p.35.

10 'Report 280th ELINT Centre'.

11 Dylan Eklund, 'Liberty Warriors', *USAF Yearbook* (2000), pp.40–43.

12 Prome, 'Allied Force – French Operations', pp.29–35.

13 Niccoli, 'Improving the Tornado, Italian Style', p.64.

14 'Report 280th ELINT Centre'.

15 *Iskustva iz borbenih dejstava osnovnih združeno-taktičkih jedinica,* pp.33–34.

16 Dylan Eklund, 'Liberty Warriors', *USAF Yearbook* (2000), pp.40–43.

17 'Report 280th ELINT Centre'.

18 Haave & Haun, *A-10s over Kosovo,* pp.29–31.

19 Bob Archer, 'Spangdahlem Force', *USAF Yearbook* (2000), p.46.

20 Carrier Air Wing 8 consisted of: 24 F/A-18Cs (VFA-15 and 87), 22 F-14s (VF-14 and 41), four EA-6Bs (VAQ-141), four E-2Cs (VAW-124), eight S-3Bs (VS-24), seven SH/HH-60s (HS-3) and two C-2As (Det 1/VRC-40). Tom Kaminski, 'Where are the Carriers?', *Combat Aircraft,* Vol. 2, No. 8 (2000), p.664; Cordesman, *The Lessons and Non-Lessons,* p.31.

21 Tony Holmes, 'Bombcats on the Prowl', *Combat Aircraft*, Vol. 6, No. 6, p.40.

22 'Kosovo Naval Lessons Learned During Operation Allied Force', March–June 1999, Statement of Vice Admiral Daniel J. Murphy Jr, US Navy, Commander, US Sixth Fleet, and Striking and Support Forces, Southern Europe, at: <www.history.navy.mil/research/library/online-reading-room/title-list-alphabetically/k/kosovo-naval-lessons-learned-during-operation-allied-force.html#murphy>

23 Cordesman, *The Lessons and Non-Lessons,* p.245.

24 Dylan Eklund, 'To Seek and Strike… RAF Bruggen', *RAF Yearbook* (2000), p.24.

25 Cordesman, *The Lessons and Non-Lessons,* p.43.

26 Prome, 'Allied Force – French Operations', pp.29–35; Chistophe Gasztych & Benjamin Vinot Prefontaine, 'Mirage F-1CT', *Air Forces Monthly* (February 2004), p.62

27 Cordesman, *The Lessons and Non-Lessons,* p.30; Henri-Pierre Grolleau, 'Farewell Foch', *Combat Aircraft*, Vol. 3, No. 2, p.152; Prome, 'Allied Force – French Operations', pp.29–35.

28 Cordesman, *The Lessons and Non-Lessons,* p.43.

29 Prome, 'Allied Force – French Operations', pp.29–35.

30 *Iskustva iz borbenih dejstava osnovnih združeno-taktičkih jedinica,* p.36; *Report to Congress,* p.89.

31 Haave & Haun, *A-10s over Kosovo,* pp.11–14.

32 'Report 280th ELINT Centre'.

33 Peter Grier, 'The JDAM revolution', *Air Force Magazine* (September 2006), pp.60–63.

34 Cordesman, *The Lessons and Non-Lessons,* p.46.

35 Lou Drendel, *Bone, B-1 Lancer in action*, Aircraft number 179 (Carrollton Texas: Squadron/signal publications, 2002). pp.32–37; Dunnell, 'Allied Force', p.13.

36 *Iskustva iz borbenih dejstava osnovnih združeno-taktičkih jedinica,* pp.37–38.

37 *Report to Congress,* p.97.

38 Dylan Eklund, 'Fairford at War', *USAF Yearbook* (2000), pp.10–13; Cordesman, *The Lessons and Non-Lessons,* p.318; Drendel, *B-1 Lancer in action,* pp.32–37.

39 Eklund, 'Fairford at War', pp.10–13; Mark Farmer, 'Roving Sands', *Combat Aircraft*, Vol. 3, No. 3, p.214; Cordesman, *The Lessons and Non-Lessons,* p.263.

40 *Iskustva iz borbenih dejstava osnovnih združeno-taktičkih jedinica,* pp.37–38.

41 Eklund, 'Fairford at War', pp.10–13.

42 Tim Ripley, 'Allied Force: Battle damage in Kosovo', *Air Forces Monthly* (January 2000), p.31.

43 Cordesman, *The Lessons and Non-Lessons,* p.248.

44 Eklund, 'Fairford at War', pp.10–13.

45 Dunnell, 'Allied Force', p.12; Grier, 'The JDAM revolution', pp.60–63.

46 Depending on the author, the number of JDAMs dropped vary between 651 and 656. It is the same with a number of sorties: 45 or 49. Cordesman, *The Lessons and Non-Lessons,* p.38; Jamie Hunter & Richard Collens, 'Invisible Spirits', *USAF Yearbook* (2000), pp.6–9. Mark Ayton, 'Ten Years of American Spirit', *Air Forces Monthly* (February 2004), p.25; Grier, 'The JDAM revolution', pp.60–63.

47 Brad Elward, 'The Stealth Bomber at War, Allied Force Strike Missions of the B-2A Spirit', *Combat Aircraft*, Vol. 2, No. 11, pp.870–877.

48 Minutes from expert talks between RV i PVO and USAFE, Zemun, September 2005: Expose of Colonel Vujic, commanding officer of the 280th ELINT Centre during OAF.

49 Grier, 'The JDAM revolution', pp.60–63. This author states that "after action reports showed that 98 percent of the 652 JDAM s used in the campaign hit their targets".

50 John A. Tirpak, 'With the Stealth in Balkans', *Air Force Magazine* (October 1999), p.22.

51 Elward, 'The Stealth Bomber at War', pp.870–877.

52 Elward, 'The Stealth Bomber at War', pp.870–877.

53 Minutes from expert talks: Expose of Colonel Vujic.

54 Slaviša Golubović, *Pad noćnog sokola* (Belgrade: MC Odbrana, 2016), pp.271–301.

55 *Military Supression of Enemy Air Defenses (SEAD): Assessing Future Needs*, Christopher Bolkcom, CRS Report for Congress.

56 Brookes, 'European Lessons', p.27.

57 *Iskustva iz borbenih dejstava*, p.209.

58 Gert Kromhout, 'Viper Weasels in action', *Air Forces Monthly* (August 2000), pp.22–26.

59 Tim Ripley, 'Viper Weasels', *USAF Yearbook* (2000), pp.15–16.

60 Rick Burgess, 'Prowling the New Century', *Air Forces Monthly* (September 2001), pp.46–47.

61 'Report 280th ELINT Centre'.

62 'Kosovo Naval Lessons Learned During Operation Allied Force', March–June 1999, Statement of Brigadier General Robert M. Flanagan, Deputy Commanding General II MEF (Marine Expeditionary Force), US Marine Corps, at: <www.history.navy.mil/research/library/online-reading-room/title-list-alphabetically/k/kosovo-naval-lessons-learned-during-operation-allied-force.html#murphy>. Flanagan claimed that EA-6B Prowlers had logged 464 combat missions.
63 Jolly, 'Balkan Debrief No. 1', p.645.
64 'Kosovo Naval Lessons Learned During Operation Allied Force' (Flanagan).
65 *European Contributions to Operation Allied Force,* pp.32–33.
66 Niccoli, 'Improving the Tornado, Italian Style', p.64.
67 Eklund, 'To Seek and Strike… RAF Bruggen', p.24.
68 Jon Lake, 'Weapons for Weasels', *Air Forces Monthly* (April 2001), p.73.
69 *Iskustva iz borbenih dejstava,* p.209.
70 Rajica Bošković, *Nebo na dlanu – Vek Vazdušnog osmatranja, javljanja i navodjenja* (Beograd: autorsko izdanje, 2017), p.556.
71 *Iskustva iz borbenih dejstava,* p.210.
72 Ripley, 'Viper Weasels', pp.15–16.
73 Ripley, 'Viper Weasels', pp.15–16.
74 'Report 280th ELINT Centre'.
75 'Report 280th ELINT Centre'.
76 David C. Isby, 'EC-130s At War', *Air Forces Monthly* (November 2003), pp.32–33.
77 *Iskustva iz borbenih dejstava osnovnih združeno-taktičkih jedinica,* p.40.
78 *Iskustva iz borbenih dejstava osnovnih združeno-taktičkih jedinica,* p.38; 'Report 280th ELINT Centre'.
79 Prome, 'Allied Force – French Operations', pp.29–35.
80 'The RAF's Year 1999', p.86.
81 'Reconnaissance in Force', *Air Force Magazine* (December 2004), pp.38–45.
82 'Kosovo Naval Lessons Learned During Operation Allied Force'.
83 Prome, 'Allied Force – French Operations', pp.29–35.
84 'Report 280th ELINT Centre'.
85 *Iskustva iz borbenih dejstava osnovnih združeno-taktičkih jedinica,* p.39; 'Report 280th ELINT Centre'.
86 Ken Worthington, 'Electronic Eavesdroppers', *USAF Yearbook 2001,* pp.26–28.
87 'Report 280th ELINT Centre'; *Iskustva iz borbenih dejstava osnovnih združeno-taktičkih jedinica,* p.39.
88 'Report 280th ELINT Centre'.
89 Henri Pierre Grolleau, 'French SIGINT Revelations', *Air Forces Monthly* (March 2002), pp.60–61; Prome, 'Allied Force – French Operations', pp.29–35.
90 Gert Kromhout, 'AWACS assist', *Air Forces Monthly* (March 2002), pp.62–64.
91 Dylan Eklund, 'Fighter Control', *RAF Yearbook* (2001), pp.70–71.
92 'Report 280th ELINT Centre'.
93 *Iskustva iz borbenih dejstava osnovnih združeno-taktičkih jedinica,* pp.34–35.
94 'Report 280th ELINT Centre'.
95 Kromhout, 'AWACS assist', p.64.
96 Archer, 'Spangdahlem Force', p.45.
97 'Report 280th ELINT Centre'.
98 'Report 280th ELINT Centre'.
99 'Report 280th ELINT Centre'.
100 'Report 280th ELINT Centre'.
101 Jean-Louis Prome, 'Horizon – French J-STARS', *Air Forces Monthly* (June 2000), pp.70–73; Prome, 'Allied Force – French Operations', pp.29–35.
102 *Report to Congress,* pp.56–57; *Iskustva iz borbenih dejstava osnovnih združeno-taktičkih jedinica,* p.39.
103 Tim Ripley, 'UAVs over Kosovo', *Air Force Magazine* (September 2000), pp.57–60.
104 Cordesman, *The Lessons and Non-Lessons,* p.322.
105 Ripley, 'UAVs over Kosovo', pp.57–60.
106 Ripley, 'UAVs over Kosovo', pp.57–60.
107 *Iskustva iz borbenih dejstava osnovnih združeno-taktičkih jedinica,* p.39; 'Report 280th ELINT Centre', pp.57–60.
108 *European Contributions to Operation Allied Force,* p.21.
109 'Report 280th ELINT Centre'.
110 The Commander of the 16th AF, Lt General Michael Short, had learned from a conversation with his son, an A-10 pilot, that although Predator operators could see targets the UAV was reconnoitring, there was no effective way to direct strikes to the targets. What typically resulted was a cumbersome and inefficient conversation as the Predator operators attempted to 'talk' the fighter pilots to the targets. Walter J. Boyne, 'How the Predator Grew Teeth', *Air Force Magazine* (March 2009), p.43.
111 Boyne, 'How the Predator Grew Teeth', pp.43–44.
112 Cordesman, *The Lessons and Non-Lessons,* p.323.
113 Brookes, 'European Lessons', p.27.
114 Ripley, 'UAVs over Kosovo', p.59.
115 Tim Ripley, 'Kosovo Tanker Mission', *USAF Yearbook* (2000), pp.37–38; 'Report 280th ELINT Centre'.
116 Ripley, 'Kosovo Tanker Mission', pp.37–38
117 Derek Bower, 'Brize Norton – RAF "Superbase"', *RAF Yearbook* (2000), p.70. Squadron Leader Stuart Mitchell of No. 216 Squadron was decorated with the Distinguished Flying Cross (DFC), thus being the first member of the tanker fleet to be decorated with such a high decoration.
118 *Iskustva iz borbenih dejstava osnovnih združeno-taktičkih jedinica,* p.38; 'Report 280th ELINT Centre'.
119 *Iskustva iz borbenih dejstava osnovnih združeno-taktičkih jedinica,* p.38; 'Report 280th ELINT Centre'.
120 General John P. Jumper, 'Rapidly Deploying Aerospace Power, Lessons from Allied Force', *Aerospace Power Journal* (Winter 1999), pp.4–10.
121 'Report 280th ELINT Centre'.
122 *Report to Congress,* pp.39–40; Peter R. March, 'Globemaster lifts the RAF', *RAF Yearbook* (2000), p.8; Mark Nicholls, 'Strategic success story', *Air Forces Monthly* (January 2000), p.60.
123 'The RAF's Year 1999', p.86.
124 Tim Ripley, 'Kosovo CSAR success', *USAF Yearbook* (2001), pp.44–46; 'Report 280th ELINT Centre'.
125 Minutes from expert talks: Expose of Colonel Vujic.

Chapter 3

1 Komanda RV i PVO: 'Analiza borbenih dejstava 1999: Avijacija'; Smiljanić, *Agresija NATO, RV i PVO,* p.366, table 18.
2 Bojan Dimitrijević & Milan Micevski, '*Silver Birds over the Estuary', The MiG-21 in Yugoslav and Serbian Air Force Service, 1962–2019* (Warwick, England: Helion, 2020); *Iskustva iz borbenih dejstava Vojske Jugoslavije u suprotstavljanju agresiji NATO na SR Jugoslaviju* (sintetička studija), GŠ VJ; Sektor za ŠONID, Institut za ratnu veštinu; VT-SP (Beograd: 1999), p.206.
3 *Iskustva iz borbenih dejstava,* p.206; Bojan Dimitrijević, *Kurjaci sa ušća, istorijat 252. lovačkobombarderske eskadrile* (Beograd: ISI,

2004), p.71; Aleksandar Radić, *Orao, pogled iz jugoslovenskog ugla* (Belgrade: Medija centar, 2012), pp.229–235.

4 Komanda RV i PVO: 'Analiza borbenih dejstava 1999: Avijacija; *Iskustva iz borbenih dejstava*', p.206.

5 Smiljanić, *Agresija NATO, RV i PVO*, pp.320–321.

6 Komanda RV i PVO: 'Analiza borbenih dejstava 1999: ARJ PVO'; Smiljanić, *Agresija NATO, RV i PVO*, pp.341–343.

7 Smiljanić, *Agresija NATO, RV i PVO*, pp.342–343.

8 *Iskustva iz borbenih dejstava*, p.217. Those statistics (General Staff, VJ) did not count the launchings from the earlier RL system that was used by the 252nd FB Squadron, and those belonging to the Pristinski Corps in Kosovo.

9 *Vojska Jugoslavije u odbrambenom ratu 1999. godine*, p.553; Komanda RV i PVO (K-da RV i PVO): 'Analiza borbenih dejstava 1999: ARJ PVO'; *Iskustva iz borbenih dejstava*, p.217.

10 Slaviša Golubović, *Pad noćnog sokola*, pp.201–204.

11 Working material for Komanda RV i PVO Analiza borbenih dejstava session: 'Borbena dejstva ARJ I PVO'.

12 *Iskustva iz borbenih dejstava*, p.213; *Iskustva iz borbenih dejstava osnovnih združeno-taktičkih jedinica*, pp.111–113.

13 Đošan Miloš, *Generalov kosmetski put* (Beograd: autorsko izdanje, 2004).

14 Komanda RV i PVO: 'Analiza borbenih dejstava 1999: VT i Tsl', *Iskustva iz borbenih dejstava osnovnih združeno-taktičkih jedinica*, p.104.

15 Dimitrijević, *Kurjaci sa ušća*, pp.75–76.

16 Komanda 250.rbr PVO, 24.05.1999. 'Komandiru odeljenja RL-4M, borbeno naredjenje Op.br.206'; Smiljanić, *Agresija NATO, RV i PVO*, pp.306–308.

17 *Iskustva iz borbenih dejstava osnovnih združeno-taktičkih jedinica*, p.104; Smiljanić, *Agresija NATO, RV i PVO*, p.308; Đorđević Slađan, *Iskustva iz borbenih dejstava RJ PVO malog dometa u agresiji NATO na Saveznu Republiku Jugoslaviju*, GŠ VJ, Sektor za ŠONID, ŠP škola (Beograd: 2000).

18 Komanda RV i PVO: 'Analiza borbenih dejstava 1999: Analiza rada VOJ'; Bošković, *Nebo na dlanu*, pp.517–527.

19 Komanda RV i PVO: 'Analiza borbenih dejstava 1999: VOJIN'.

20 Bošković, *Nebo na dlanu*, pp.528–536.

21 *Iskustva iz borbenih dejstava Vojske Jugoslavije u suprotstavljanju agresiji NATO na SR Jugoslaviju* (sintetička studija), GŠ VJ; Sektor za ŠONID, Institut za ratnu veštinu; VT-SP Beograd 1999; Bošković, *Nebo na dlanu*, pp.537–583.

22 Bošković, *Nebo na dlanu*, pp.586–588.

23 Bošković, *Nebo na dlanu*, p.590.

24 Smiljanić, *Agresija NATO, RV i PVO*, pp.396–397.

25 Oluić Saša, Antić Goran, Dimitrijević Bojan, *204. lovački avijacijski puk*, (Belgrade: VINC, 2005), p.115.

26 'Report 280th ELINT Centre'.

27 'Report 280th ELINT Centre'; Komanda RV i PVO: 'Analiza borbenih dejstava 1999: Ostali rodovi, EI I PED'.

28 'Report 280th ELINT Centre'.

29 Minutes from expert talks; Expose of Colonel Vujic; *Vojska Jugoslavije u odbrambenom ratu 1999. godine*, p.565.

30 Isby, 'Allied Force – US Lessons', pp.27–28.

31 Cordesman, *The Lessons and Non-Lessons*, p.294.

32 *Iskustva iz borbenih dejstava*, pp.220–221; Komanda RV i PVO: 'Analiza borbenih dejstava 1999: ARJ PVO'.

33 Stanković.

34 *Iskustva iz borbenih dejstava osnovnih združeno-taktičkih jedinica*, pp.33–34.

35 *Iskustva iz borbenih dejstava osnovnih združeno-taktičkih jedinica*, p.82.

36 Komanda 250. rbr PVO, Pov.br. 03/139-674, 25.04.1999. and telegram: Komanda RV i PVO pov.br. 40-2/8929-2, 22.04.1999; KOMANDA 250.rbr PVO, Str.Pov.br.03/139-1589-1, 02.06.1999. godine 'Uputstvo za borbenu upotrebu IRZ i pasivnih reflektora, dostavlja'.

37 Written statement of Colonel Dragan Stanković, acting commander of the 250th Missile Brigade, to authors (Belgrade: 2009).

38 Written statement of Colonel Stanković; Komanda RV i PVO: 'Analiza borbenih dejstava 1999: ARJ PVO'.

39 K-da RV i PVO: 'Analiza borbene gotovosti RV i PVO za 1998. Godinu'.

40 Komanda RV i PVO: 'Analiza borbenih dejstava 1999'.

41 K-da RV i PVO: 'Analiza borbene gotovosti RV i PVO za 1998. godinu'; Smiljanić, *Agresija NATO, RV i PVO*, pp.282–283.

42 Komanda RV i PVO: 'Analiza borbenih dejstava 1999'.

43 Smiljanić, *Agresija NATO, RV i PVO*, pp.284–286.

44 Smiljanić, *Agresija NATO, RV i PVO*, pp.377–378.

45 Smiljanić, *Agresija NATO, RV i PVO*, pp.377–378.

46 Smiljanić, *Agresija NATO, RV i PVO*, pp.379–381.

47 Smiljanić, *Agresija NATO, RV i PVO*, pp.381–382.

Chapter 4

1 Komanda RV i PVO: 'Analiza borbenih dejstava 1999: OIP: Dejstva vazduhoplovnih snaga NATO po SRJ i snagama i objektima RV I PVO'.

2 Some other RV i PVO statistics counted a total of 15,023 different projectiles being dropped, including 3,425 classic bombs, 70 cluster bombs, 48 cruise missiles and 11,550 other projectiles and munitions.

3 *Iskustva iz borbenih dejstava osnovnih združeno-taktičkih jedinica*, p.81.

4 *Iskustva iz borbenih dejstava osnovnih združeno-taktičkih jedinica*, p.79; Oluić, Antić & Dimitrijević, *204. lovački avijacijski puk*, pp.116–119; Milan Micevski & Bojan Dimitrijević, *83. lovački avijacijski puk* (Niš: Galakisijanis, 2016), pp.147–149.

5 *Iskustva iz borbenih dejstava*, p.207; *Iskustva iz borbenih dejstava osnovnih združeno-taktičkih jedinica*, pp.80–88.

6 *Vojska Jugoslavije u odbrambenom ratu 1999. godine*, p.574.

7 *Iskustva iz borbenih dejstava osnovnih združeno-taktičkih jedinica*, pp.81–82.

8 Bojan Dimitrijević & Jovica Draganić, *250. raketna brigada PVO* (Belgrade: Vojnoizdavački zavod, 2007), pp.94–95.

9 Archer, 'Spangdahlem Force', pp.44–46.

10 Komanda RV i PVO (K-da RV i PVO): 'Analiza borbenih dejstava 1999: ARJ PVO'.

11 Dimitrijević & Draganić, *250. raketna brigada PVO*, pp.97–98, 110.

12 Dimitrijević & Draganić, *250. raketna brigada PVO*, pp.97–98, 110.

13 Dimitrijević & Draganić, *250. raketna brigada PVO*, pp.167–194.

14 *Kraljevske lisice 1977–2002, povodom 25 godina 450.raketnog puka protivvazdušne odbrane*, (Belgrade: VINC, 2002); Todorov Staniša, *Iskustva iz učešća 450. rp PVO u suprotstavljanju NATO operaciji 'Milosrdni anđeo' 1999. godine*, ST-INT, seminarski rad VA ŠNO, KŠU, Beograd 2007.

15 Kromhout, 'Viper Weasels in action', p.26.

16 Slaviša Golubović, *Pad noćnog sokola*, p.201.

17 Dimitrijević & Draganić, *250. raketna brigada PVO*, pp.167–194.

18 Kromhout, 'Viper Weasels in action', pp.25–26.
19 Bošković, *Nebo na dlanu*, pp.537–582.
20 Bošković, *Nebo na dlanu*, pp.537–582.
21 *Iskustva iz borbenih dejstava*, p.220.
22 Bošković, *Nebo na dlanu*, p.590.
23 Komanda RV i PVO: 'Analiza borbenih dejstava 1999: Ostali rodovi, EI I PED'; 'Report 280th ELINT Centre'.
24 Komanda RV i PVO: 'Analiza borbenih dejstava 1999: An.Veza. rat1'.; Slađan, Ristić *Organizacija i funkcionisanje veza sistema VOJ u VJ, u uslovima narušenog sistema veza VJ*, diplomski rad Sektor za ŠONID, Generalštabna škola VJ, smer RV i PVO, Beograd 2000.
25 *Iskustva iz borbenih dejstava*, p.220.

Chapter 5

1 *Vojska – ratno izdanje*, broj 348, 30.3.1999.
2 *Junaci otadzbine* (Beograd: Spomen-knjiga, June 2000); Smiljanić, *Agresija NATO, RV i PVO*, p.251. *Vojska Jugoslavije u odbrambenom ratu 1999. godine*, volume 2, pp.291, 530–531, 632.
3 Kabinet načelnika Generalštaba Vojske Jugoslavije (KNGŠ VJ), 'Kolegijum, Sednice kolegijuma Načelnika Generalštaba Vojske Jugoslavije, 02. 07. 1999'. (report by General Smiljanić), p.19.
4 Material: 'Analiza borbenih dejstava ARJ PVO'.
5 Komanda RV i PVO: 'Analiza borbenih dejstava 1999: Org. Mob, Gubici u ljudstvu'; *Vojska Jugoslavije u odbrambenom ratu 1999. godine*, pp.572–573.
6 Cordesman suggested this conclusion: "The effectiveness of the NATO air attacks on Serbian forces in the field must be judged in terms of impact in strengthening the credibility of the KLA (and prospective NATO ground option), and not simply in terms of how much of the Serbian land force was destroyed and whether this halted ethnic cleansing." Cordesman, *The Lessons and Non-Lessons*, p.236.
7 Ripley, 'Allied Force: Battle damage in Kosovo', p.29.
8 *Vojska, ratno izdanje*, broj 381–382, 14.6.1999.
9 *Vojska Jugoslavije u odbrambenom ratu 1999. godine*, p.502.
10 Cordesman, *The Lessons and Non-Lessons*, p.147.
11 Cordesman, *The Lessons and Non-Lessons*, p.147; Stephen P. Aubin, 'Newsweek and 14 tanks', *Air Forces Magazine* (July 2000).
12 Cordesman, *The Lessons and Non-Lessons*, p.303.
13 KNGŠ VJ (report by General Smiljanić), p.19.
14 *Iskustva iz borbenih dejstava Vojske Jugoslavije u suprotstavljanju agresiji NATO na SR Jugoslaviju, za strategijski nivo* (monografija), GŠ VJ, Sektor za ŠONID, ŠNO, Beograd oktobar 1999.
15 In Smiljanić's detailed study on air war (also the General Staff), the general tried to be precise. He claimed 127 (or 107) destroyed aircraft (119 (or 99) on the ground and eight in the air) and 50 damaged aircraft (one in the air), which makes a total of 177 (or 157). The first figure was published in General Smiljanić's book (Smiljanić, *Agresija NATO, RV i PVO*, pp.437–438); the second in the synthesis *Vojska Jugoslavije u odbrambenom ratu 1999. godine*, p.573, which he also wrote. In the period when he wrote the analyses (2000–?), there were 17 aircraft (out of 50) that were returned to service after repairs. Smiljanić counted 151 (140) aircraft as irretrievably lost, or 41.09 percent of the total number.
16 Dimitrijević & Micevski, 'Silver birds': the author's research counted 43 lost MiG-21s from an initial 72. Among them 32 were destroyed (23 bis, six UMs and three Ms) and 11 damaged but remained unserviceable (eight bis and three UM)s. A total of 29 MiG-21s were used in the period after OAF: 20 bis, six UMs, two Rs and a single M.
17 Radić counted a total of 19 destroyed Oraos (16 J-22s and 3 NJ-22 two-seaters): at Ponikve (seven), Batajnica (five), Ladjevci (three), Moma Stanojlović Air Depot (two), in combat mission (one) and damaged beyond repair (one). Radić, *Orao*, pp.293–303.
18 *Iskustva iz borbenih dejstava osnovnih združeno-taktičkih jedinica*, pp.84, 89, 92. This study noted the following numbers of destroyed aircraft: nine J-22 Oraos, three NJ-22 Oraos, two N-62T/Galeb G-4s, two V-53/UTVA-75s, six N-62/Galeb G-4s, 11 N-62S/Galeb G-4s, 17 N-60/Galeb G-2s, one H-42/Gazelle SA-341, two HP-43/ Kamov Ka-25PLs, three HP-44/MI-14PLs (a total of 56), plus six HT-40/Mi-8s that belonged to the 119th Helicopter Regiment. *Vojska Jugoslavije u odbrambenom ratu 1999. godine*, volume I (Klub generala I admirala Srbije, Beograd 2019). p.581; Komanda RV i PVO (K-da RV i PVO): 'Analiza borbenih dejstava 1999: PoOb, Ibid, VT I Tsl'.
19 *Iskustva iz borbenih dejstava Vojske Jugoslavije u suprotstavljanju agresiji NATO na SR Jugoslaviju, za strategijski nivo* (monografija), ČŠ VJ, Sektor za ŠONID, (ŠNO, Belgrade, October 1999).
20 KNGŠ VJ (report by General Smiljanić), p.19.
21 Komanda RV i PVO (K-da RV i PVO): 'Analiza borbenih dejstava 1999: ARJ PVO, Ibid, VT i Tsl. *Vojska Jugoslavije u odbrambenom ratu 1999. godine*, p.587, table 9. The other facts counted the following losses in air defence units: Radars: P-15 (three destroyed/ two damaged), P-18 (one/one), P-12 (three/two), R-StON or 1S91M2 (five/10), PRV-16 (none/two), 1RL-128D-1 (none/four), guidance cab Dvina (none/one). Cabs: UNV-M (nine/four), UNK-M (three/seven), RKU-N (five/six), and other commanding and guidance equipment: PRM (one/one), UV-600 (none/one), UPPC (none/two) and UKUV (one/none). Generators (10/six), vehicles (33/seven). Self-propelled launching vehicle Kub (three/ four), Launching ramp Neva (one/none). Missiles Neva (122/five) and Kub (nine/none). Light AA Artilery: L-70 Bofors (three/four) and PAT 20/3 (six/none).
22 *Iskustva iz borbenih dejstava*, p.219.
23 *Vojska Jugoslavije u odbrambenom ratu 1999. godine*, pp.573–574; Komanda RV i PVO (K-da RV i PVO): 'Analiza borbenih dejstava 1999: VOJIN'.
24 *Vojska Jugoslavije u odbrambenom ratu 1999. godine*, pp.541–542; Smiljanić, *Agresija NATO, RV i PVO*, pp.442–443
25 *Vojska Jugoslavije u odbrambenom ratu 1999. godine*, p.574; KNGŠ VJ (report by General Smiljanić), p.19. Smiljanić stated that there were 510 objects destroyed or damaged beyond repair.
26 For details see: *Agresija NATO pakta na Saveznu Republiku Jugoslaviju* (Belgrade: Bezbednost, ratno izdanje 2–3, 1999); Smiljanić, *Agresija NATO, RV i PVO*, pp.213–250.
27 Ripley, 'Allied Force: Battle damage in Kosovo', pp.30–31.
28 Isby, 'Allied Force – US Lessons', p.25.
29 Akt Komande RV I PVO int.br.25/8899-2, 22.04.1999.
30 *Iskustva iz borbenih dejstava Vojske Jugoslavije u suprotstavljanju agresiji NATO na SR Jugoslaviju* (sintetička studija).
31 A detailed account on the Serb side including the testimonies of each member of the 3rd Battalion and F-117 pilot Lt Colonel Delko in: Golubović, *Pad noćnog sokola*; Paul F. Crickmore, *Lockheed F-117 Nighthawk Stealth Fighter*, Air Vanguard 16 (London: Osprey Publishing Ltd, 2014), p.57.
32 Cordesman, *The Lessons and Non-Lessons*, p.48.
33 *Vojska – ratno izdanje*, broj 365, 6.5.1999.
34 In recent years, among the crews of the 3rd Battalion, 250th Missile Brigade, and part of the wider public, a tale was launched of claiming the B-2A at 0012 hours on 20 May 1999. Golubović, *Pad noćnog sokola*, pp.272–302.

35 'Report 280th ELINT Centre'.
36 Ripley, 'UAVs over Kosovo', p.59; *Iskustva iz borbenih dejstava osnovnih združeno-taktičkih jedinica*, p.104.
37 *Report to Congress*, pp.75–77; Hebert, 'The Balkan Air War', p.45.

Chapter 6 and Conclusion

1 *Vojska Jugoslavije u odbrambenom ratu 1999. godine*, vol. I, p.528.
2 *Iskustva iz borbenih dejstava*, pp.211–214.
3 Isby, 'Allied Force – US Lessons', p.26; *Kosovo Naval Lessons* (Murphy, Jr).
4 Cordesman, *The Lessons and Non-Lessons*, p.26
5 Marti Ahtisari, *Misija u Beogradu* (Beograd: Filip Visnjic, 2001); *Vojska – ratno izdanje*, broj 381–382, 14.6.1999. pp.2–3.
6 'After Kosovo', pp.40–42.
7 Cordesman, *The Lessons and Non-Lessons*, p.18.
8 Hebert, 'The Balkan Air War', p.46.
9 Ivo H. Daalader & Michael E. O'Hanlon, *Winning Ugly: NATO's War to Save Kosovo* (Brookings Institute Press, 2000).
10 Klark, *Moderno ratovanje*, pp.452–461.
11 Golubović, *Pad noćnog sokola*, pp.40–195.
12 Cordesman, *The Lessons and Non-Lessons*.
13 Cooper A. Scott, 'Air Power and the Coersive Use of Force', *The Washington Quarterly* (Autumn 2001), pp.81–93.
14 Jim Hedge, 'Chinese Embassy Bombing', *Air Forces Monthly* (May 2000), pp.31–34.
15 Isby, 'Allied Force – US Lessons', p.26; Rebecca Grant, 'Why Arimen Don't Command', *Air Force Magazine* (September 2008), p.48.
16 Simpson, *Stealth Down*, pp.228, 245.
17 Simpson, *Stealth Down*, p.229.
18 'Introduction', *USAF Yearbook* (2000), p.5.
19 'After Kosovo', pp.40–42.
20 Klark, *Moderno ratovanje*, pp.451, 472.
21 Niall Ferguson, *The Cash Nexus, Money and Power in the Modern World* (London: Penguin Books, 2002). pp.412–413.
22 Klark, *Moderno ratovanje*, pp.494–495.
23 Ferguson, *The Cash Nexus*, pp.412–413.

ABOUT THE AUTHORS

Bojan Dimitrijevic is a historian working as Deputy Director of the Institute for Contemporary History, in Belgrade, Serbia. Educated at the Universities of Belgrade and Novi Sad, CEU Budapest and the University of Bradford, he was the custodian of the Yugoslav Aviation Museum before, in 2003-2009, serving as advisor to the Minister to the Serbian MoD, the Minister of Foreign Affairs and to the President of Serbia, and as Assistant to the Minister of Defence. He has extensively researched the military history of the former Yugoslavia and the Balkans in the Second World War, the Cold War, and various conflicts since, and has published over 50 books and 100 scientific articles in Serbia and abroad.

Lieutenant-General Jovica Draganić (ret.) was educated at the Air Force Technical Military High School, Air Force Technical Military Academy (1984), Command-Staff Academy (1996) and National Defence School (1999), and also graduated at Belgrade Electro-technical Faculty, Belgrade University (1990). He served in the 250th Air Defence Missile Brigade for over two decades, in nearly all commanding positions from platoon to brigade commander. Between 2005 and 2017 he served on senior posts within the Serbian Armed Forces as: Chief of Staff of the Air Force and Air Defence HQ, Chief of Training/Doctrine Department of General-staff (J-7), Director of the Defence Inspectorate and as Deputy Chief of Staff Serbian Armed Forces. During Operation Allied Force, he commanded the 4th Missile Battalion of the 250th Air Defence Missile Brigade.